JAPAN 1908

JAPAN 1908

The Adventure of Fourteen-Year-Old Clarence James Gamble

クラレンス
ジェームス
ギャンブル
十四歳の冒険

**Edited
by
Frances Miriam Reed**

**Special Assistance
from
Tsutae Hamada Novick**

Japan 1908: the adventure of fourteen-year-old Clarence James Gamble.

Copyright © 2014 Frances Miriam Reed.

All rights reserved. This book or any portion thereof may not be reproduced or used in any manner whatsoever without the express written permission of the publisher, except for the use of brief quotations in a book review or other non-commercial purposes permitted by copyright law.

Japan 1908, the book, is based on "A Daily Journal" written by Clarence James Gamble and one-hundred-twenty photographs taken by Clarence James Gamble and Sidney David Gamble during the ten weeks the Gamble family toured Japan in 1908. The "Daily Journal" and the one-hundred-twenty photographs are published herein with permission of The Schlesinger Library, Radcliffe Institute, Harvard University.

Published in the United States: Miriam Reed Productions.

Fourteen-year-old Clarence James Gamble, his parents, and his seventeen-year-old brother Sidney David Gamble spent ten weeks in Japan in 1908. One-hundred-twenty photographs taken by the brothers are reproduced in this volume, along with a journal by Clarence detailing their travels. Clarence James Gamble was an international philanthropist, who promoted women's health and contraception and founded Pathfinder International, a global non-profit organization that provides maternal health care and education for women.

This book is printed on acid-free paper.

Printed and bound in China.

Reed, Frances Miriam, Editor.
    Japan 1908: The adventure of fourteen-year-old
    Clarence James Gamble. / Clarence James Gamble,
    1894-1966; Tsutae Hamada Novick, Special Assistance.

Gamble, Clarence James, 1894-1966 -- Diaries; Gamble, Clarence James, 1894-1966 -- Travel -- Japan; Gamble family; Gamble, Clarence James, 1894-1966; Gamble family; Travel; Japan -- Description and travel; Japan -- Pictorial works; Japan; Diaries; Pictorial works.

Parallel title in Japanese.
Creation Date: 2014
Format: xxxix, 120 pages: illustrations (chiefly color), maps, 29 cm.
Language: English
Hard Cover ISBN: 978-0-578-13303-4; ISBN: 0578133032
Soft Cover   ISBN-13: 978-1499118131
              ISBN-10: 1499118139
OCLC Number: 903540223

For permissions and special orders,
speaking engagements, and displays, contact
miriam@miriamreed.com.

TABLE OF CONTENTS

Frontispiece: Introduction

Map: Gamble Orient Tour 1908

Introduction	i
Endnotes "Introduction"	xxx
To the Reader "Introduction"	xxx
The Gamble Family in Japan 1908: Background for the Itinerary	xxxi
To the Reader "A Daily Journal 1908"	xxxiii
The Gamble Family in Japan 1908 Itinerary	xxxiv
"My Trip to the Orient: A Daily Journal 1908" by Clarence James Gamble	
April 10 to May 8	1
June 18 to July 31	59
Japan April 2012 Afterword	89
Appendices	
Clarence's Writing Schedule	100
Annual Rainfall in Japan	101
Biographical Notes "Introduction"	102
Line Notes "A Daily Journal"	104
Historic Time Line	105
Selected Bibliography	106
Sources and Credits	108
Index	111
Photos by Category	116
Acknowledgements	117
Contributors	119

To 伝 *Tsutae San*
　七転び八起き

Seven times down;
Eight times up.

INTRODUCTION

五月雨や大河を前に家二軒　松尾　芭蕉

富士一つうづみ残して若葉かな　与謝　蕪村

さまざまの事思出す桜かな　松尾　芭蕉

**David & Mary
Sidney & Clarence
GAMBLE
ORIENT TOUR
1908**

The Japan Visit
April 10 to May 8
June 18 to July 31

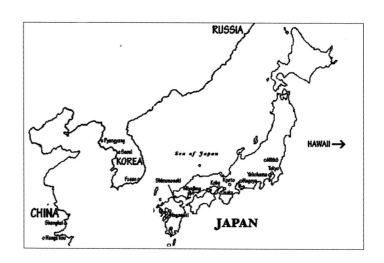

1908 ITINERARY

3/10 San Francisco	4/19 京都 Kyoto	5/9 CHINA	7/14 霧降 Kirifuri
S.S. "Siberia"	4/24 彦根 Hikone	5/29 KOREA	7/17 中禅寺 Chūzenji
3/16 HAWAII	4/25 京都 Kyoto	6/18 宮島 Miyajima	7/18 日光 Nikkō
3/30 S.S. "Manchuria"	4/29 奈良 Nara	6/22 京都 Kyoto	7/21 伊香保 Ikaho
4/10 横浜 Yokohama	4/25 京都 Kyoto	6/24 横浜 Yokohama	7/23 軽井沢 Karuizawa
4/13 東京 Tokyo	5/2 大阪 Osaka	6/27 東京 Tokyo	7/25 浅間 Asama
4/13 横浜 Yokohama	5/3 神戸 Kobe	7/3 宮ノ下 Miyanoshita	7/27 東京 Tokyo
4/15 名古屋 Nagoya	5/5 S.S. "Mongolia"	7/8 大地獄 Ōjigoku	7/27 横浜 Yokohama
4/17 京都 Kyoto	5/6 下関 Shimonoseki	7/8 湯本 Yumoto	7/28 鎌倉 Kamakura
4/18 保津川 Hozu Gawa	5/7 長崎 Nagasaki	7/9 箱根 Hakone	7/29 横浜 Yokohama
		7/11 日光 Nikkō	7/31 S.S. "Manchuria"

INTRODUCTION

To the Reader: *It should be noted that, in 1908, the terms "Jap" and "coolie" were consonant with the speech of the day and not then considered deliberate racial slurs.*

With a birthday in January, Clarence James Gamble was just fourteen years old in March of 1908, when he, his seventeen-year-old brother, Sidney, and his parents, David and Mary Gamble, left Cincinnati, Ohio, for a brief stay in Pasadena, California, and a lengthy tour of the Orient. Clarence's family was a fortunate one. His father, David Berry Gamble, was the seventh child of James Gamble, who with William Procter founded the now global Procter & Gamble company. David had retired from daily participation in P&G in 1895; he enjoyed his family, and he enjoyed travel. Now, in the year 1908, after two weeks in Hawaii, he and Mary and his two younger sons would be on their way to China, Korea, and most particularly, a ten-week tour of Japan. Son Clarence had been appointed amanuensis for the trip, and we know much about the Gambles' time in Japan because Clarence's Journal describes many of the daily events. The entries that comprise his Journal, now held by the Schlesinger Library in Cambridge, Massachusetts, offer a fairly detailed account of the shrines, temples, museums, castles, hotels, shops, and individuals that were seen by the Gambles, as recorded by a fourteen-year-old with a keen intelligence and a wry sense of humor:

David Berry Gamble 1906

> Later, we went to another large temple on the side of a steep hill. Judging by the shops at the entrance, one might think that it was erected to the patron god of porcelain and china.
>
> At the entrance, there was a sign that informed us in large capitals that 'VISITORS ARE REQUESTED NOT TO ACCOMPANY DOG IN GARDEN.' As we didn't have any dog to accompany, we managed to get in all right.

Clarence was everything you might expect of a fourteen-year-old boy. Fortunately for us, he also kept a brief diary for the several months of 1908 preceding the Asia trip, beginning those entries on the first of January. And so we know that at the end of his Christmas vacation, he played in the hay loft on the barn roof with Fred and one afternoon saw Kellar the Magician with Father. He took his Christmas money and bought "ball bearing steel rollar rollar [*sic*] skates" and skated every morning and afternoon—at least until the Monday he had to return to the "grind of school" (he was in the ninth grade of Cincinnati University School) and the "horrid Mr. Dahl." After that, he skated every afternoon, except when it was raining and he couldn't and until he lost two nuts from the skates and then a ball bearing. For his birthday on the tenth of January, he received a bag for his collars, stationery, and what must have pleased him more, a ratchet screw driver and a pair of tin shears from Father and a telephone receiver from Sidney. Clarence was building a "wireless" telephone and learning about induction coils. He "fixed up way to shock people with only one wire. Caught Aunt M[innie], Father, Mother, Uncle C[ochran] etc." The next Saturday, he "Took induction coil to Freds PM and had lots of fun shocking people." When Clarence was not skating or shocking people, he was taking photographs and developing his own film in Sidney's new tank developer, which "works very well." He went ice skating when it got cold and with Fred made fudge, which turned out "very sticky." When his exams came up at the end of January (he was taking German, Latin, Geometry, History, and English), he did "a whole lot of studying." One day he "studied about 3 hours (! ! !)." The studying paid off; he did well in his examinations, and when it came time for him to document the family trip in Asia, he wrote dutifully, sometimes with enthusiasm, taking into consideration, however, that he would be most specific about those things most appealing to a fourteen-year-old boy and would note them accordingly:

> The goldfish are trained, as we find all well-bred Japanese goldfish should be, to come when you clap and eat bread when you choose to throw it to them.

Once returned to Pasadena, Clarence trained the goldfish in the pond at his new home to do the same. He also liked pigeons, and when feeding those he finds in Japan on the sacred island of Miyajima, he

Mary Huggins Gamble
1924

describes with obvious relish having eleven birds on his hand, on his arm, and on the tiny feeding tray he is holding. Later in his life, he would have his own flock of pigeons and enter them in homing contests.

Only slightly familiar with Japanese history, Clarence fails to identify all of the sites that the family visits, and some names are missing from this fourteen-year-old's Journal entries: In Nagoya, "Sidney, the guide, and I went to a large temple"; in Kyoto, "Our next visit was to a large temple"; and "Later we went to another large temple on the side of a steep hill." At the same time, Clarence was curious about Japanese customs and writes perceptively of the lives around him. He observes the many children in the streets:

> Japanese children seemed to be everywhere, sometimes almost blocking the road from side to side. Most of the girls carried babies on their backs.

an observation that uncannily foreshadows his life's work, work that four decades later would return him to Japan.

In 1920, Clarence graduates from Harvard Medical School with his M.D. degree. He meets Margaret Sanger, who was to found Planned Parenthood, and his personal plans for pure medical research take a very practical turn. With his inherited wealth, he begins his search for a dependable contraceptive and funds the opening of maternal health clinics in fourteen states of the United States. In the 1950s, Clarence again has an interest in Japan. In close collaboration with Dr. Yoshio Koya, then Director of the National Institute of Public Health, Clarence supports public health research for a Japan that has become concerned over its high rate of abortions. His largess leads to Japan's government-sponsored maternal health clinics for Japanese women. In 1957, Clarence founds The Pathfinder Fund, a non-profit corporation dedicated to supporting reproductive health services wherever needed throughout the world. Today, The Fund, now Pathfinder International, continues to work to that end, fulfilling the vision of its founder.

That the Asia tour had a formative influence on the lives of both Clarence and his brother Sidney is clear. As might be expected from this conscientious family, Sidney David Gamble, too, was an excellent student. In March of 1908, Sidney, having completed a year at

Clarence James & Sidney David Gamble
1902

Introduction iii

The Thatcher School in Ojai, California, was looking forward in the coming fall to attending Princeton University.[1] The Presbyterian founders of Princeton actively supported missionary work in China, as did Sidney's parents. At Princeton, Sidney learned of and then became part of the Princeton University Center and of the Y.M.C.A. in Beijing. The empirical study of China became his life's work. He went on to document the changing face of China in the 1920s and 30s with sociological studies, the first ever made of China, and supported his findings, now classics in the field of Sinology, with his photographs. Presently archived at Duke University, the more than 5,000 black-and-white photographs stand as an unparalleled exhibit of the changing face of China prior to the communist revolution of 1949.

i

As young men, Clarence and Sidney were both enthusiastic photographers, embracing a technology that had been but recently developed. In 1888, George Eastman introduced the Kodak camera with roll film, roll film replacing the cumbersome glass plates that had been the standard. Shortly thereafter, Eastman made it possible to load a camera without being in a darkroom; next, he offered a simplified process for developing film. In 1900, Eastman put the Brownie camera on sale for one dollar, a roll of film for fifteen cents. Photography was an affordable, unexplored art and on the cutting edge of the turn into the twentieth century.

When Sidney was twelve, which would have been in 1902, he is said to have won a camera as first prize in a contest. That would have been two years after George Eastman introduced the Brownie for sale at one dollar, a likely contest prize for a twelve-year-old. Whatever the source of his first camera, Sidney became fascinated with photography—a fascination that stayed with him throughout his life—and, soon enough, younger brother Clarence followed suit. Just before sailing from San Francisco, Clarence had bought a new camera. During their Asia trip, Sidney and Clarence were always thinking about photography and cameras, and Clarence in his Journal is constantly reiterating his, and surely Sidney's, "wish very much for a bright day and our cameras." Unfortunately, the weather did not always favor the photographers.

Sidney David Gamble
1910

The "buckets of rain," for which Tokyo and much of Japan are famous, fell often during the Gambles' time in Japan. Clarence would write,

> 6/29 Regular Tokyo weather, or at least our idea of it.
> 7/1 Still we have Tokyo weather....It does seem as though it would never stop raining.

Bright days did come. Not only did Clarence and Sidney take many, many photographs of Japan—far more than the one hundred and twenty herein—but they were developing their own film. "Before supper we developed three dozen films and left them to wash until afterwards. When we returned, we found that the maid had turned on the hot water...and there was nothing left of the photos. Just imagine our feelings!" laments Clarence. The loss did not discourage the photographers. "Our cameras worked hard all morning," writes Clarence, "for everything seems so new and strange."

ii

The enthusiasm for do-it-yourself photography coincided with the emergence of Japan as a nation on a par with the great nations of the West. When Commodore Perry first reached Edo Bay in 1853, Paixhans shell guns at the ready, Japan was a feudal backwater, with long-swordsmen, archers, musketeers with smoothbores, spearmen with pikes standing guard on the Japan shore.[2] Fifty-one years later, after Japan's successful defeat of China in the Sino-Japanese War (1894-95), Japan was considered of such importance that William Howard Taft, then Secretary of War, led a diplomatic team, which included forty-two Congressmen, on a three-month tour of Asia to encourage negotiating an end to the Russo-Japanese War begun in 1904. President Theodore Roosevelt then invited all parties to his home at Oyster Bay and oversaw negotiations that ended the War in September 1905.

The Japanese transition from feudal to industrial had been extraordinary. Galvanized by the sight of a China for years under the domination of Great Britain, Japan determined to have no such fate for itself. Once in control in 1868, the Meiji government immediately moved to turn a backward Japan into a modern society fit to compete with the best of the West.

The first action of the Meiji was to invite into tightly closed, impenetrable Japan foreigners of all

President Theodore Roosevelt
circa 1905

stripe to serve as teachers and consultants who would instruct the Japanese in the ways of the progressive West. Experts in their respective fields, such as civil engineer Richard Henry Brunton from Edinburgh; zoologist Edward Sylvester Morse of Salem, Massachusetts; plant chemist Oscar Loew of Bavaria; physicist and electrical engineer William Edward Ayrton from England poured into Japan. The foreigners, well paid for their trouble, taught the Japanese to modernize and industrialize and through their residencies enabled a proud Japan to stand on the same footing as the advanced Western nations.

This invited group, *o-yatoi-gaikokujin*, or "hired foreigners," along with diplomats and nationals representing their governments, set up bustling communities in the ports allowed by the Harris Treaty of 1858, especially in the port of Yokohama, which became the main point of entry for European and American travellers. Shortly came merchants, eager to tap the untapped Japanese market, and missionaries, concerned for the lost heathen souls, building hospitals, schools, and Christian churches. With Japan now available as a strategic refueling stop for the U.S. garrison in the Philippines and the massive British navy on the high seas, a sizeable group of Western naval and military personnel were regularly in and out of the treaty ports. Their stories and strange souvenirs trickled back to the West to entice yet another group of hairy barbarians, travellers who could afford to travel for the novelty and adventure, such as Charles Longfellow, wealthy son of renowned poet Henry Wadsworth Longfellow. "Charlie" Longfellow arrived a year before the publication in 1872 of Jules Vern's *Around the World in Eighty Days,* the book that set up a template for the globe-trotters, whose trotting created for Japan a new industry: Tourism.

With the opening of the Suez Canal and completion of the transcontinental railway in America in 1869, the far-away land of Japan became more accessible to the West. By the late 1870s, Japan could be reached by regular steamship service weekly or twice-weekly. The influx of merchants and globe-trotters reaffirmed the Meiji determination to modernize. Soon enough, railways, improved and up-to-date, made travel feasible within Japan, and Japanese hotels, shops, and

Charles ("Charlie") Longfellow
circa 1872

restaurants began offering Western-style accommodations, these improved accommodations bringing yet more Westerners and tourists into Japan. Throughout the 1880s and 90s, those who had the money to do so or who hoped to make the money—or an impression—by having done so came to Japan in growing numbers.

Among the travellers, and unknown to Clarence at the time, were the parents of Clarence's future wife, Sarah Bradley, whom he would marry in 1924. The photo below is that of Richards Merry and Amy Aldis Bradley, the parents of Sarah, Amy in a *jinrikisha* and Richards standing beside her, on their honeymoon trip to Japan in 1892. On the ship sailing to Japan with Amy and Richards were the Rudyard Kiplings, friends and briefly their neighbors in Brattleboro, Vermont, where the Kiplings lived for a short time before returning permanently to England. A trip to Japan was the thing to do.

A quick look at the many memoirs, recollections, impressions, diaries, and journals, whose topic was Japan, published in American books, newspapers, and magazines in the last decades of the nineteenth century would suggest that, in fact, everyone who went to Japan (with the exception of Richards Merry and Amy Aldis Bradley) wrote and usually published an account of the experience: Rudyard Kipling and other famous authors, brave women, early feminists, diplomat's wives, grandmothers, businessmen's daughters, a boy of eleven, seamen, scientists, Congregational ministers, capitalists, missionaries, astronomers, artists, successful merchants, wealthy tourists, and not-so-wealthy tourists.

Richards Merry & Amy Aldis Bradley 1892

Travel writings had always been popular; those about Japan were seized upon by a public eager to learn more, more, more about Japan. The audacity of Perry had, for Americans, been especially newsworthy, appealing to national pride and natural curiosity. The first travel-to-Japan book to be published after the "Opening" by Perry in 1853 was *A Visit to India, China and Japan* by the very well-known Bayard Taylor, who had accompanied Perry (much to his annoyance) on the initial voyage and whose account of the trip appeared in 1855, well before Perry's official document was even completed

Introduction vii

in December 1857. With good sales of Taylor's *Visit*, publishers had reason to believe in the public's interest in Japan.

Horace Greeley, as editor of the New York *Tribune*, was well aware of that interest. Greeley commandeered Taylor's friend Francis Hall to serve as Japan correspondent for the *Tribune*, the most influential newspaper of the time, and Hall's thoughtful and balanced monthly dispatches from 1859 through 1866 were front-page news, even during the years of the Civil War. Shortly, other professional writers were writing about Japan and being published, such as Isabella Bird, whose *Unbeaten Tracks in Japan* appeared in 1878, exciting more would-be Japan travellers.

The many writings, professional and otherwise, along with shared but unpublished personal family letters from Japan, unwittingly gave strong support to what in today's terms would be considered an ongoing massive public relations campaign by Japan to market itself as the idyllic tourist destination. Fortunately for the new Japan tourist industry, America was in the firm grip of the "Japan Craze." This Craze was heightened in 1871 with the arrival in America of the Iwakura Mission led by Prince Iwakura Tomomi, a leading figure in the Japanese government, who is pictured seated in the center of the photo on this page. The Mission comprised a group of government ministers and their staff, forty-eight in all, along with sixty students, among them Tsuda Umeko, who later returned to Japan to found the girls' school that became Tsuda College and whom the Gambles meet in Tokyo on June 29, and Kaneko Kentarō, whom the Gambles did not meet but who had an influence on Teddy Roosevelt's decision to negotiate the end of the Russo-Japanese War. The Iwakura Mission came to study Western industrialization and its culture and was to tour the West for only a few months but instead stayed on for two years. And for two years, the Mission members' every move evoked curiosity and

岩倉使節団
Iwakura Mission
1872

generated newspaper and magazine articles. Similarly did the elaborate Japanese exhibits at the international expositions, the world's fairs so popular with the general public until the beginning of World War I, earn for Japan, Japanese wares, and Japanese fine and applied arts notice and adulation.

After creating a sensation with the exhibit at the *Weltausstellung* in Vienna in 1873, Japan spared no expense, three years later, in reconstructing, on the grounds of the U.S. Centennial International Exposition in Philadelphia, a Japanese garden complete with tea house, an official residence for sixty persons, and a typical Japanese bazaar. This microcosm of Japan drew awe-struck crowds, the Japanese hosts in traditional dress guiding visitors past displays of porcelain, bronzes, cloisonné, ivories, silk screens—extraordinary art that communicated "eloquently for itself."[3]

In 1893, an equally elaborate display at the World's Columbian Exhibition in Chicago drew Frank Lloyd Wright, who was said to have visited the Japanese display repeatedly, along with Charles and Henry Greene, whom in 1907 the Gambles would choose as architects for their winter home, now known as The Gamble House, in Pasadena, California.[4] The Japanese exposition exhibits, along with museum shows, opened American sensibilities to a new style of art, one totally unfamiliar to the West. This new aesthetic was soon impinging on the design of everything from the utilitarian—wallpaper, dishes, furniture, fabric (whose cheap imitations were quickly to flood the Western marketplace)—to architecture and the most refined arts, sparking all things Japanese as an ever more topical subject for discussion and the land of Japan as an even more enticing destination for armchair and actual tourists. Yet in the early days after the Perry "Opening," Japan forbade foreigners entry into its interior and contact with its people. For fourteen long months, Townsend Harris, America's First Consul General to Japan, was deadlocked in Shimoda, waiting for permission to travel to Edo (later called Tokyo) to

The Gamble House
Pasadena
California
1908

present the letter to the *Shogun* that would initiate negotiations and open Japanese ports to Western ships and trade. In the finally agreed-upon Harris Treaty, the designated treaty ports, Yokohama, Kobe, Nagasaki, Niigata, and Hakodate, and the Open Cities of Tokyo and Osaka were encircled by a twenty-five-mile radius beyond which foreigners were not permitted. Within the open ports and cities, foreigners were viewed with the greatest suspicion. Francis Hall, the New York *Tribune* correspondent, complained often of the insolent public officials who inspected bags and personal belongings at every checkpoint and who had spies observing his most insignificant interaction with any Japanese national. For a time, Japan remained much as it had for centuries, essentially closed to foreign intercourse and foreign prying eyes.

Enter the commercial photographer, his studio located in bustling Yokohama, who traveled into the interior of Japan, camera in hand, to bring back photos of temples, shrines, and landscapes that lay beyond the twenty-five-mile radius, a land unsullied by factories or filth, an idyllic land wherein dwelt quaint Japanese in quaint costume. Thus was created the genre of the *Yokohama shashin*, the Yokohama photographs. Works of art in their own right, carefully posed, artfully staged, these photos fall into two general categories, landscapes and people, and had a vested interest in portraying a Japan that was fast disappearing, their typical subject matter peasant-workers with century-old tools, white-faced *geisha* with perfectly arranged *obi*, samurai carrying the two swords outlawed in 1876, heavily tattooed men. These unique hand-tinted photos gave concrete evidence of an exotic Japan. For almost three decades, the outpouring of these anachronistic *Yokohama shashin* secured worldwide for Japan its romantic image.

The commercial studios of these Yokohama photographers, so often located on the Bund, the wide street facing the Yokohama waterfront, were for newly arrived Western tourists their immediate destination, where outfitted in traditional Japanese garments, their photos were taken, just as Clarence is seen on page 21 in the Journal text and Charles Longfellow on page vi here above. Along with these personalized costumed portraits, the studios were selling

江南 信國
T. Enami
農夫とその妻
NŌFU TO SONOTSUMA
Farmer & his Wife
1895

the *Yokohama shashin* in sets of fifty or a hundred to be pasted by the purchaser or the studio into albums with expensive covers of lacquer or woven silk, the photos and albums then carried back to America as gifts and souvenirs, where they were admired and finally given the place of honor on the parlor bric-a-brac shelf.

Yokohama shashin were for sale everywhere, in the photographers' studios in all the treaty ports, in the curio shops, and purchased by just about everyone who came to or stayed in Japan—the military, the temporary residents, the merchants and missionaries, the visiting dignitaries. These photos were sold worldwide, in America at Sears Roebuck and Montgomery Ward, in art galleries, and wherever an enterprising shopkeeper intended to turn a profit. They were put onto glass slides for use in the "magic lantern," or stereopticon, and always the *Yokohama shashin* kept before the eyes of the viewer this intriguing view of a strange and mysterious land.

As the 1870s became the 80s, a more self-confident Japan became accustomed to the white intruders. Special permits became available, allowing tourists to travel beyond the twenty-five-mile radius. When Eastman simplified the camera in 1888, more tourists started taking their own pictures. In 1899, the twenty-five-mile radius was officially abandoned. By that time, the commercial photographers were developing and hand-tinting, not their own, but the foreigners' photos, such as the hundred and twenty photos of Clarence and Sidney, seen in this book alongside Clarence's Journal entries.

By 1900, studio income was no longer dependent on the sale of *Yokohama shashin* and pricey albums with lacquer covers, but on the sale of new cameras and photography equipment and photography supplies bought up by the globe-trotting tourist.

iii

When the Gambles reached Japan in 1908, they found new modern trains and Western-style hotels, *jinrikisha* and century-old festivals and processions. Top Hats and Bustles, the dress of choice by the emperor and his court, alongside cotton kimono and clogs. Curio shops, outdoor market stalls, and street peddlers, electric

日本漆
NIHON URUSHI
Lacquer
Album Cover
A. Farsari & Co.
1890

Introduction xi

lights and trolley cars and large smoke-emitting factories. They found things "that seemed quite un-Japanese."

Tokyo and Yokohama were becoming highly westernized, and the more savvy traveler recognized that modern industrialism was the pulse of the nation, that great factories were replacing the independent shops of the artisan, as Japan aggressively sought Western markets and tourist dollars. And yet the image of an untouched Japan with an exotic pre-industrial lifestyle—the images presented by the *Yokohama shashin*—permeated the American consciousness, and Japan, by virtue of its focused self-promotion, remained a most desired destination for the American tourist as well as for the Gambles.

iv

"The Jap, commercially, is always and everywhere a tricky little wretch," was the assessment of Edward Stager Wright, a seasoned traveller, who set out his personal advice on the subject in his book *Westward 'round the World*, published in 1908, the year of the Gambles' visit to Japan. Wright was emphatic: "Every tourist who comes to Japan is legitimate prey for the natives," and Wright reminds the would-be Japan tourist what awaits him after he has hired his government-licensed guide:

> Even the best of the guides will use the man who employs him. You know before many days [sic] travel that he is getting commissions from hotels, shop-keepers, and railways, but if he grafts gently, it is best not to quarrel; nothing is gained in the end. If the foreigner dispenses with a guide, the man he does business with takes the extra himself. It is a case of charging the foreigner an average of about forty per cent more than the native or resident European or American.

Basil Hall Chamberlain points out what the Wright's foreigner ignores:

> It is but fair that the the foreigners should pay more than natives, both for accommodation and for jinrikishas. They usually weigh more, they almost always want to travel more quickly, they give infinitely more trouble at an inn with their

江南 信國
T. Enami
籾殻取り
MOMIGARATORI
Winnowing Grain
circa 1895

demands for fresh water in the bath, the occupation of a portion of the kitchen to cook their European food, and a dozen other such requirements.

A word about Chamberlain, the foremost interpreter of Japanese culture for the West during the Meiji era (1868-1912). Basil Hall Chamberlain co-wrote with W.B. Mason the third edition of the Japanese Murray guidebook first published in 1894, entitled *A Handbook for Travellers in Japan,* and the revised editions published through 1912.[5] Murray of London was a prestigious publishing firm founded in 1768, which began publishing its guide books for travellers in 1836, hence, references by Wright and others to "your Murray." The Murray guidebooks, which covered every part of the globe, were famous for details that facilitated the tourist's travels: Itineraries; timetables; descriptions of buildings and notable sights; dates of cultural events and festivals; foldout maps of individual regions; descriptions of the culture, geography, food, and government; along with advice on what to avoid, what to pack, and a list of useful phrases. No traveller of the late nineteenth and early twentieth century would be without his Murray and the advice it contained. With no other real option, the chances that the Gambles used the 1907 edition of *A Handbook* are almost assured, so popular was it at the time.

Inserted after the front and before the back covers of the 1907 edition are advertisements of many of the hotels and shops mentioned in Clarence's Journal. Some of these advertisements and some of the maps, along with excerpts from Chamberlain's comments, have been set alongside Clarence's Journal entries, where they further explicate Clarence's writing.

Basil Hall Chamberlain
circa 1888

v

Murray *Handbook* in hand, the world traveller prepared for his travel with serious packing. In his diary, Clarence writes of the process: On the first of February, "Got the trunk about half packed," and two days later, "Packing like the ____. Got time for lunch. Finally got everything in trunk."

The globe-trotting tourist did not, could not, travel lightly. Custom, propriety, and necessity required an assortment of garments suitable for every occasion and for every climate. The eldest of David and Mary's three children, Cecil Huggins Gamble, twenty-five years old in 1908 and readying for his marriage in the coming fall, had renounced world travel forever after a family jaunt through Europe in 1902, when, as a young scout, he had been required to handle all the family luggage for the entire trip.

In the Orient, notes Wright, "You will find people dressing extremely well." He points out that proper clothes are an imperative: steamships and railways offer a generous luggage allowance; therefore, inappropriate dress is inexcusable:

> For two people, two large steamer trunks, one dress-trunk and hat-trunk, or hat box, are the least number possible. One large suit case, a hand-bag, one hold-all for steamer rugs and pillows, and a canvas laundry bag with lock are all necessary.

Included by Mr. Wright in his book is the advice of Mrs. Wright on what is important for the ladies to bring, especially when travelling by steamship:

> Three cloth suits will be useful, two are necessary. One for travelling and general wear should be of smooth mixed cloth and warm enough for winter weather; the other also for travelling, should be of lighter weight material, mohair or voile.

> A white serge, broadcloth or mohair coat and skirt, with lace and chiffon waists, two white linen suits, two natural colored linen suits, with a half-dozen white shirtwaists and three lingerie blouses, will all be comfortable to have. Pique skirts are desirable, as they do not wrinkle and show every mark of the steamer chair. A silk jumper dress with jacket and a black net or lace gown will always prove useful.

> Three dinner gowns to wear on steamer will be needed while crossing the Pacific. They should be high neck, but with transparent collar and yoke to be comfortable and if of crepe, silk, or other unmussable material will cause less annoyance than if made of linen and other distinctively summer materials. One handsome decollete gown is needed for formal dinners & balls.

> Several sorts of wraps are needed...a long fur or fur-lined coat, a long ulster, and a coat to wear with light dresses....I found an evening coat of silk, lace, and chiffon useful as well.

Advertisement
Pacific Mail Steamship Company
1906

Mrs. Wright goes on to recommend the proper hats, the necessity of an assortment of veils, and shoes with rubber heels. While the Gambles were not involved with the social set that required Mary to wear a "handsome decollete gown," the Gambles were always well-dressed. Mary carried a small parasol while in Japan and wore a stylish hat with roses on it. Her clothes were of great interest to the Japanese, and at Hozu, Clarence counts "six women in a line behind Mother, taking in her dress."

We know from their photos that the Gambles were always attired in the current fashion. And we know from Clarence's 1908 diary that, on reaching Chicago on February 4, he went shopping and purchased "3 suits shorts bathing suit etc."—this after finally getting "everything in trunk" the day before. The next day he "went d[own] t[own] + tried on suits." Once in Pasadena, having arrived there on February 8, Clarence shopped for shoes on the twentieth and "4 prs of shoes" on March 3. No wonder that when the Gambles left Pasadena for San Francisco on March 7, Clarence was "busy packing all morning."

vi

On March 8, the Gambles reached "Frisco" and booked into the St. Francis Hotel. On March 9, Clarence "made parachute and dropped from 11th story,"and on March 10,

> The Great day arrived. Finished trunks at 9. We arrived at steamer at 11 - sailed at 1. Golden gate interesting. Our rooms G, H + I. Read - studied a little. Great to be actually off. Meals are fine. Quite a number of Chinese gamblers on board.

Once returned to the States, Clarence at some point edited and typed up the first four weeks of his handwritten Journal entries.[6] The typed Journal entry for March 10, drawn in part from his handwritten diary entry of the same date, is worth our quoting here, for in his edited version he captures nicely the excitement surrounding a steamship departure in the early 1900s:

St. Francis Hotel
Union Square
San Francisco
California
1902

> TUESDAY MARCH 10. The great day of our departure has actually arrived. Our trunks, stuffed to the bursting point, were off before our late breakfast, and soon after we started with our dress-suit cases and hand trunk, commonly known as wrist bag.
>
> At the steamer we found Aunt Fannie and Mrs. Wherry. Our staterooms seemed to be filled with flowers, and our baggage was in evidence everywhere. Promptly at one o'clock, after lots of hot-air, "all-ashores," and farewells, our great steamer the Siberia left the dock and, swinging around, headed for the golden gate and the Orient.

Clarence's typed entry of March 11 explains the identity of the "Chinese gamblers" mentioned in March 10 entry quoted above:

> WEDNESDAY MARCH 11. The crew was given a fire and boat drill this afternoon. At the first whistle, all the Chinamen came hurrying on deck to get the hoses out. They had the water running from eighteen nozzles in about two minutes. Then turning off the water, they swung the boats out and lowered them to the rail and then all lined up to wait for the big siren to give the signal of dismissal.

Wright further explains the "Chinese gamblers" on board:

> The first glimpse of the Orient is caught at San Francisco. While the officers of the ship are white, the crew and stewards are Chinese, who do their work cheerfully and well and in the intervals of labor gamble earnestly on the steerage deck or smoke opium in the den provided for them, at the stern of the ship.

Page One
My Trip to the Orient.
**A Daily Journal
1908**

On board the S.S. *Siberia*, Clarence watches the "gamblers" and the Chinese "passengers" in steerage playing a game with dominos much like ours and Chinese chess. As the saying is that they do everything backwards in China, so instead of playing on the squares of the chess board, they [play] on the places where the lines cross. The afternoon was taken up with developing films.

And so passes Clarence's time at sea. Just as at home and in Pasadena while waiting to leave for the Orient, he is busy with his own interests (except for the skating, of course): taking photos and developing film almost daily, people-watching and people-talking —he practices French with Mrs. Stone's French maid and later German, which "seems right hard." He plays shuffleboard, except when he is too stiff from the former day's activity and, perhaps what is not so usual for a fourteen-year-old free of regulated school hours, he is studying. Many of the entries written during the days in Pasadena mention reading and studying: "Studied all morning"; "Finished Caleb West. Got new book." On board the S.S. *Siberia*, he is reading "Caesar's travels" and he finishes Dickens' *Old Curiosity Shop*. "Read all morning" and "Studied read etc." along with "Developed film" are a constant among his diary entries.

vii

Arriving at Honolulu Harbor on March 16, Clarence and his family spent the next two weeks in Hawaii. Clarence had little time for reading now, but he was, as usual, busy with his camera. He went swimming almost every day—making good use of his new swimming trunks—and was thrilled with his ride in a surfboat: "Indescribable" and "Exhilarating." With Sid and his parents, he saw the sights: Diamond Head, the aquarium ("not as large as the one in Naples," remarks Clarence, the world traveler, recalling his 1902 visit to Europe), the Hawaii museum, Iolani Palace, a carnation farm, Kings' mausoleum, Mount Tantulus, a sugar planter's experiment station, a Chinese jewelry store, the fish and vegetable market: "Got a breadfruit....Tried the bfruit. Not very good."

He also enjoyed experiences that accorded with his parents' wealth and position: breakfast ("some of the finest papaya we've eaten") with Governor Walter Francis Frear, third territorial governor of Hawaii; a horseback ride with Sidney up Diamond Head on Governor Frear's horses; dinner with the eminent Cookes of Castle & Cooke, after which he sees goldfish trained to come "when you clapped."[7]

David and Mary were probably more enthusiastic about dinner with the Loves, where they met the Rt. Rev. Doremus Scudder of the Hawaiian Evangelical Association and Hawaiian Board of Missions, who took them to visit the Palama Settlement, a model of successful community support services.[8] Their days in Hawaii set the pattern for those to follow throughout the Orient trip and during their time in Japan: sightseeing, shopping, visiting schools and

Clarence James Gamble
1911

missions, meeting individuals of standing in the community, and engaging with the missionaries, many of whose minds were some of the keenest and who as a group were most attuned to the new social awareness and raising of social consciousness that defined the Progressive Era in America.

viii

On Monday, March 30, the Gambles left Hawaii for the eleven-day voyage from Honolulu to Yokohama. Once on the Japanese ship S.S. *Manchuria*, the Gambles missed the comforts of the S.S. *Siberia*, which when launched in 1901 was the finest and most luxurious ship to sail the Pacific, no expense having been spared for its appointments. The S.S. *Manchuria*, leased and operated as well by the Pacific Mail Company, was a larger and newer ship, having been launched in 1903. In 1905, the S.S. *Manchuria* had been chosen to carry Secretary of War William Howard Taft and his Congressional team on the three-month Asia tour that prepared for negotiating the end to the Russo-Japanese War. Yet although Clarence found the staterooms better in the S.S. *Manchuria*, he complained that, on it, "rolling and vibration are much more noticeable."

According to Wright, vessels of the Pacific Mail Steamship Company had the reputation for "bumptious" captains and indifferent food but better appointments, while the Japanese ships with their English officers catered to tourist whims with every courtesy. Clarence found the *Manchuria* captain "bumptious":

> Our seats at table are next to the captain, and he is a queer queer character. His main principle of conversation seems to be contradiction, and [he] has a very good opinion of his share of the world's knowledge.

Pacific Mail Steamship Company
S.S. *Mongolia*
1903-1915
Gambles' ship to China

Except for the lost day of the third of April, the day when the Gambles crossed the international date line, the sailing was uneventful, until on the ninth, when, one day away from Japan, came stormy weather. Clarence describes the scene on board the S.S. *Manchuria* during the storm:

> The boat tipped from the great wind pressure until it was impossible to walk through the hall without touching one side or the other, and we seemed to be rolling in all directions at once....Only about half the people got to supper, and most of them didn't stay long.

David and Mary had an especial interest in Japan; the ten weeks allotted for their stay in Japan attest to that. While they were travelling in Asia, their winter residence, now known as The Gamble House and a National Historic Landmark, was being built in Pasadena, California, by architects Greene & Greene. The architect brothers, Charles Sumner and Henry Mather Greene, were at the forefront of the American Arts and Crafts Movement. They became interested in the Japanese decorative arts, and as their work matured, they became known for incorporating into their output elements of Japanese design.

The Gambles' home in Avondale, Cincinnati, was a typical Late-Victorian structure; the much different Pasadena house would require much different appointments, ideally those of an Asian character. Both David and Mary had a great appreciation of art, this particularly true of Mary, whose mother, Mary Frances Smith, had been an artist and painter and had shared her passion for art with daughter Mary. Shopping in Japan would allow David and Mary to discover the most desirable *objets d'art* to complement their new, very contemporary house, a work of art in itself.

Clarence, judging by his diary entries and Journal comments, also had an especial interest in Japan. Unlike his parents, he would never maintain a lifelong enthusiasm for architecture and fine art, much to the dismay of his wife Sarah. When Sarah wanted an original oil, Clarence was surprised that she would not be just as happy with a well-done copy. His architectural concerns dealt with construction of the pigeon loft and his landscaping concerns with flooding the tennis courts in winter for the children's ice skating. Music was important to Clarence.

Gamble Avondale Residence
Cincinnati
Ohio
1898

At Princeton, he learned to play the piccolo and bass viol for the Princeton orchestra; later he serenaded his growing family with the flute. And always, he enjoyed listening to music.

Because the subject of Japan was so topical and because all the Gambles had met Japanese nationals at the Cincinnati Missionary Training School, Clarence, along with his parents, appears to have been particularly interested in seeing Japan, alluding to the Japanese books "we" read and what "we" expected in Japan. The diary that Clarence began on January 1, 1908, makes no mention of China or Korea, but it does of Japan. On January 21, Clarence writes of being invited to dinner at Kindergarten Hall at the Training School, where the family had "quite a time with the Japanese women."⁹ Then on February 2, their last Sunday in Cincinnati before the family left for Asia, Clarence goes, as usual, to "S[unday]S[chool] + church. Everybody saying good-bye. Seventeen callers in the afternoon. Had quite a talk with Japanese women from the Training School." In late February, the Gambles by then in Pasadena, Clarence writes that he saw a lantern show on Japan, but still no mention of China or Korea.

The lantern show surely featured the most popular tourist sites of Japan: Kiyomizudera in Kyoto, Tokugawa tombs in Nikkō, the great Buddha of Kamakura. The Gambles would see much more than the usual tourist sights—the temples, shrines, castles, museums—during their ten weeks in Japan—for as important as was the sightseeing and shopping to David and Mary, above all, they were in Asia to see for themselves the work of the Christian schools and missions that they were helping to finance.

x

From the beginning of their marriage, David and Mary Gamble had proven themselves generous supporters of the Presbyterian Church and particularly of the foreign missions. David was a member of the Presbyterian Board of Missions and Mary the energetic, organizing hostess of regular fundraising events. In their Avondale home outside of Cincinnati, they regularly

Mary Palmer Gorbold
circa 1925

entertained missionaries on leave and delegations of evangelists, which included the most important Christian Protestant leaders, such as G. Sherwood Eddy, international evangelist and lifelong worker for the Y.M.C.A. and John Mott, founder of the important International Student Volunteer Movement for Foreign Missions and a Nobel Peace Prize recipient. Dinner was served without wine; conversations were concerned with how best to educate and how to spread the Gospel. As David and Mary were making their plans to travel in 1908, from their many friends and contacts in the field they were receiving personal invitations to visit in China, Korea, and Japan the schools and missions that their philanthropy was supporting,

According to Chamberlain, Protestant missionaries began work in Japan in 1859, and by 1907 a network of stations covered the empire with some forty-four societies, "chiefly American and English." The Westerners came to "spread the Gospel to whatever parts of the heathen and anti-Christian world the Providence of God might enable the Society to extend its evangelical exertions," exertions exemplified in the lives of Raymond and Mary Gorbold, Presbyterian missionaries working in Kyoto in 1908.

In Kyoto, the Gorbolds welcomed the Gambles warmly, showing them every hospitality, introducing them to others in the field, taking them to secular and sacred sites of interest. Mary Palmer Gorbold, born in 1866, came to Japan as a missionary in 1892 and earned a Master's Degree in 1897. She and Raymond Gorbold were married in 1905, shortly after he arrived in Kyoto, and they labored together until his death from heart failure.

So insistent had Raymond Gorbold been on becoming a missionary that, when his first appointment to the field in 1902 was abruptly withdrawn on the basis of his heart condition, he came to Japan on his own and taught in a government school. The Presbyterian Board of Missions were so impressed with his resolve that in 1905 they reappointed him. After his death in 1915, Mary Gorbold continued as evangelist and teacher in Japan until 1934, when she retired and returned to the United States. She died in 1952 and was buried with her husband.

Mary Gorbold's years of teaching girls and women would have been of particular interest to Mary Gamble, just as had been her visits in Hawaii to the Archbishop's Girls School and to the St. Elizabeth's School for Girls funded by Mrs.

Raymond Gorbold
circa 1910

Procter of Procter & Gamble. The Presbyterians, in addition to their evangelical work, operated schools that educated both boys and girls, the education of girls personally touching Mary Gamble, whose own pursuit of an education had been much thwarted by her health problems. Out of this interest, in Kyoto, the Gambles visit Dōshisha University, and in Tokyo, Tsuda Women's Institute, both institutions among the first in Japan to offer education to girls.

xi

Clarence arrived in Japan with his earnest, liberal-minded, education-loving parents, committed and devoted to a Christian way of life and comfortable with their position in life. With a father of infinite amiability and a strong feminist for a mother (unusual in 1908), Clarence was blessed with parents who encouraged his curiosity and his involvement with new experiences. Clarence was quick to learn all he could about Japan, and he had no trouble moving within its culture, quickly picking up basic phrases and how to count in Japanese. He came to Japan, as we know, having done some preparation, and it set him up for some surprises. As Clarence explains,

> We went to sleep last night in a storm and woke up this morning in a calm and sunny harbor. We felt rather cool and when we looked out to get the first glimpse of Japan, we saw a line of low snow-covered hills....The storm of yesterday passed through here and left about four inches of snow....The air was very cold and the piles of snow on the side of the street did not seem very suggestive of Japan as we had expected to find her.

Grand Hotel
横浜 Yokohama
circa 1907

The Gambles settled into the Grand Hotel in rooms whose temperature was 58 degrees. The next day, Clarence found that the vaunted cherry blossoms "were not as pink as we had expected":

> From some of the books on Japan, one might be led to believe that the whole landscape was covered with cherry blossoms and the sky given a peculiar glow on their account, but as we found out, they are to be seen only in parks or gardens where they have been specially cultivated.

xxii Introduction

Later, on their train ride to Nagoya, the Gambles "passed large factories that seemed quite un-Japanese to us." E.S. Wright, quoted above from his *Westward 'round the World,* noticed as much: "Great cotton mills, silk mills, and metal-working places are springing up every where [*sic*]."

When, however, the Gambles had disembarked from the S.S. *Manchuria, jinrikisha,* man-powered cars, virtually the emblem of old Japan, were there to take them to the Grand Hotel. "It certainly seems very queer and unnatural to ride...with a man running in front to pull you," writes Clarence. It was and is only *gaikokujin,* foreigners, who use the term "rikisha," as Clarence does throughout most of his Journal; the Japanese always include the *jin,* which translates *man,* and say "jinrikisha." E S. Wright, with his reference to the "little men" pulling the carriages articulates that mixture of curiosity and condescension with which the Western foreigner often regarded the Japanese:

> These little carriages are drawn by men in blue blouses and naked legs, who do not weigh over a hundred and ten or fifteen pounds, but they will pull twice or three time their weight and make as good time as the average horse, for the magnificent sum of thirty sen an hour. These little men with their carriages whisked us up to the Grand Hotel, which we found organized after the American type with good beds, hot and cold running water baths, fire and acceptable food.

At the Grand Hotel, the Gambles were immediately fitted for suits (although Clarence had just purchased several suits in the States). Wright explains,

> The Chinese [tailors] are the best outfitters, they will measure a man for white clothes, as many suits as he likes, and turn them over to him in twenty-four or at most forty-eight hours. They will copy exactly some well-beloved suit which will be as well-fitted as if the new clothes had been made by a favorite tailor at home.

Because the Gambles were following the usual tourist routes and activities, young Clarence writes of many of the same things as does the well-travelled Wright. When the Gambles begin shopping, they immediately discovered that the Japanese, as Clarence writes, "have a sliding scale of prices varying according to the customer and one is seldom expected to pay the first price that is asked." With this

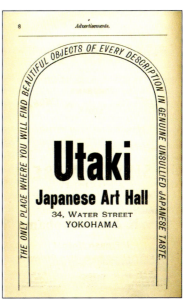

Advertisement
A Handbook for Travellers
1907

Wright concurs: "Prepare to bargain for everything. There is no such thing as a one price store in Japan."

The Gambles' fourth day in Japan was spent in the rain in Tokyo, "the Japanese city of magnificent distances...we spent more than half our time getting around the city," writes Clarence. Wright elaborates: "Tokyo is enormous and unbeautiful...The climate is gloomy and in the autumn, rain falls in buckets, sometimes for days at a time." But Tokyo was a necessary stop where the Gambles would secure from American Ambassador O'Brien their permits to visit the exceptional sights of Japan. As Wright advises,

> Before leaving Tokio [sic], it is well to get government permission to visit the Emperor's palace in Kioto, the old fortress and palace of the Shogun, and the entrancing Imperial Garden, which lies by itself in the suburbs. This permission can be procured through your Ambassador and it is absolutely necessary if you desire to visit these three places, which are as well worth seeing as anything in Japan.

As important as the sightseeing was the shopping, and during his shopping, Clarence soon found tawdry merchandise:

> The little china stores where I stopped were queer in their arrangements but in their stock were not very different from some of the cheap stores in our country.

Wright finds the same inferior merchandise:

The Hundred Steps
横浜 Yokohama
circa 1900

6031. "The Hundred Steps," Yokohama, Japan. These steps form a connecting link between Yokohama and "The Bluff," (the European residential part of Japan)

> The Japanese artist and artisan no longer work for arts {sic} sake regardless of time or price. What they cannot sell at a profit, they will no longer create, so the great stores are filled with a mass of stuff, much of which is cheap and gaudy.

And while Wright makes no comparable comment, Clarence shows himself the astute shopper:

> With the Japs, as with us, the name of the artist and the age of the picture seem to count for more than anything else in determining the price of the picture.

xii

After four days in Yokohama, after combing the curio shops and climbing The Hundred Steps to the Bluff where the foreigners lived, and the suits having been made overnight, the

Gambles took the train to Nagoya to see Nagoya Castle and Atsuta Shrine, then went on to Kyoto, that most traditional of Japanese cities. They settled into the Kyoto Hotel for two weeks, spending time with the Gorbolds, combining sightseeing and shopping with school visits and missionary gatherings, exploring Kyoto and its surrounding areas. On one not untypical day (apparently the Gambles never got tired), they visited the Emperor's City Palace in the morning, then went by *jinrikisha* to a Christian kindergarten, and in the afternoon watched the procession of the *Oiran*. The day before, they were driven in carts (not cars) to the outskirts of Kyoto to view the Imperial Garden as allowed by their permits, whereupon Clarence spotted an uncharacteristic Japanese bureaucratic error and pointed out,

> The country through which we passed was beautiful....
> but the climax was reached when Mr. and Mrs. Gamble
> and their two daughters entered the [Imperial] gardens.

Wright, who had no daughters, wrote, "The Imperial Garden is, perhaps, the most beautiful thing in Japan."

On May 1, the Gambles left Kyoto for Osaka, "a dirty and smoky city of rough streets and long distances," where a missionary acquaintance walked them through a cotton spinning factory:

> Three thousand girls were sleeping in two twelve-hour shifts in a three-by-six-foot space, twelve girls to the room, for ten to thirty cents a day, less four cents for board and lodging....How would it seem to live on seven cents a day in the U.S.?

asks Clarence. Wright also comments on child labor in Japan:

> Commercial interest is forcing the women and children of today... to the cotton factories and sugar mills. These are equipped with the very best American and English machinery, warranted to make the very best and cheapest product, while also grinding the life out of the human workers, mostly children.

Continuing on to Kobe, the Gambles met Annie Howe and visited Glory Kindergarten, then boarded the S.S. *Mongolia* in preparation for the trip to China, passing through the Shimonoseki Straits, then

江南 信國
T. Enami
Future Factory Workers
circa 1898

Introduction xxv

stopping in Nagasaki, where they saw coal being loaded and purchased the tortoise shell items for which Nagasaki was known. The next two and a half weeks were spent in China, in Shanghai and Hanzhou; the following three weeks in Korea, in Seoul and Pusan.

On June 18, the Gambles were back in Japan for a final six weeks, first enjoying four days on the magical island of Miyajima, where letters from home awaited them. Returning to Kyoto to spend a day with the Gorbolds, they then traveled on to Yokohama and Tokyo, where Clarence found the salesmen extremely aggressive.

After Tokyo, David and Mary were sufficiently worn out to stop at the famous Fujiya Hotel in Miyanoshita, Hakone, for a week of doing little, while Clarence, with neither historic castles nor curio shops to investigate, was immensely bored. Delighted he was when finally the family ventured on horseback to nearby Hakone Lake, from whence Mount Fuji could be seen, and even more pleased when the family set off for Nikkō with its magnificent temples and shrines and its beautiful surrounding lakes and waterfalls.

After the sights of Nikkō, the Gambles spent four days in Karuizawa, a mountain village, cool and out of the Tokyo heat. Without a nearby hot springs, the Japanese initially ignored this lovely spot, but for the Western missionaries, it became a popular vacation retreat. In Karuizawa, the Gambles rejoined the Gorbolds and met acquaintances from the Missionary Training School back in Cincinnati. Clarence reported that David and Mary had lunch with Mrs. Toppings, who had "sent Miss Ishahara to the…training school," and all the family had dinner with the MacNairs. Best of all for Clarence was his opportunity to ride off and see the nearby Mount Asama lava beds. On July 27, the Gambles returned to Yokohama with Mr. Gorbold to prepare for their journey back to the States.

xiii

In a final nod to their role as conventional tourists, on July 28th, the Gambles travelled to Kamakura, fifty miles south of Yokohama, the political center of Japan during the twelfth century under the Minamoto. In Kamakura, they walked inside the

Adolfo Farsari
鎌倉 大仏
Kamakura Daibutsu
circa 1890

xxvi Introduction

Daibutsu, the "Big Buddha," today practically an icon for Japan, but popular with the Japanese only after *Yokohama shashin* photographer Adolpho Farsari had made it famous.[10]

The Gambles were not the conventional tourists. Certainly, they had shopped. We know from the writings of Clarence that David and Mary bought porcelain, damascene, kimono, china, swords and sword guards, *menuki* (ornaments from antique sword hilts), gold lacquered items, tortoise shell curios, incense, silver, silk, cloisonné, prints of Japanese children, jewelry, posters, bamboo, bronzes, lace, and probably a great many other things that Clarence does not mention, along with one new trunk. But the Gambles had also come to Japan with purpose, to investigate the return on their dollar, so to speak, and in that connection to educate themselves, visiting schools and meeting with missionaries to understand how was progressing the work of education and Christian endeavor that they were supporting.

Nor was Clarence the average fourteen-year-old. An eager visitor, a good writer, and a keen observer, Clarence was representative of his family, all of whom were equally involved in learning all they could about Japan. Spending time with the missionaries who had been living in Japan and who knew the language and its customs afforded Clarence and Sidney, David and Mary an acquaintance with the culture that the ordinary tourist could not hope to experience. Through their missionary connections, the Gambles were invited into a private home, a rare occurrence in Japan even today. Theirs was the trip of a lifetime, giving all the Gambles a deep appreciation for the riches of Japan and introducing Clarence to a culture and land that, many years later, he would return to with a certain sense of familiarity.

Chamberlain had advice for the visitor to Japan "who desires to travel intelligently" and "to do more than merely wander from hotel to hotel":

> He, therefore, who should essay to travel without having learnt a word concerning Japan's past, would run the risk of forming opinions ludicrously erroneous. In Japan, more than in any Western country,

江南 信國
T. Enami
石臼を引く老女
ISHIUSU O HIKU RŌJO
Old Woman Working Mill Stone
circa 1898

Introduction xxvii

it is necessary to take some trouble in order to master such preliminary information.

Few Western travellers had time or inclination for acquiring such preliminary information, nor did they understand the need to do so. Despite the innumerable travel books being published at the time, Japan remained impenetrable, the average foreigner having no idea of any ignorance.

Francis Hall, *Tribune* correspondent in Japan in the 1860s, would write informed accounts of the Japanese people and their politics and so would others, such as John LaFarge, famous for the Ascension mural in Trinity Church in Boston, Massachusetts, and a student of Buddhism; in *An Artist's Letters from Japan,* LaFarge shows an educated appreciation for its culture and people. Mary Crawford Fraser, writing in *The Diplomat's Wife in Japan*, states, "I would like to understand a little…to make a friend."

Yet, too often,n accounts of travel in Japan were tainted by that mixture of self-importance and snobbery bred into the white man by religious convictions and the "science" of Eugenics, so popular in the last and early decades of the nineteenth and twentieth centuries, respectively. All too typical comments from travelling Americans referred to the Japanese as "conceited, insulting and cringing," "extremely disgusting," "a strange and romantic people" with "slavish, humiliating customs," "sitting amid the terrible shadows of sin." "They have little music of their own…It is noise." Yet the geisha girls were "dear little things…too sweet for words."

As distinct from the many books written with the intent to clarify Japan for the reader from a very personal perspective but one ignorant of the culture of the Japanese, Clarence's observations are made from a standpoint of personal honesty, without a consciousness of the reader's expectations. His remarks, fair-minded and evenhanded, stand in sharp contrast to the harsh and judgmental comments of the worldly Wright.

Clarence & Mary Sidney & David Gamble in Japan
1908

As a perspicacious teenager, Clarence provides a refreshing view of Japan in 1908 and of the traveller's experience there, a view that often manages to slice more deeply below the surface than do texts by older professional travellers. Clarence notes that the Japanese confuse the "l" and "r"; their prices change easily; their music is squeaky; their drama is "very dull," but "I suppose there would have been more to it if we could have understood what they were saying." Clarence looks at what he sees in Japan and may quiz it, but he does not fault it. What he sees is simply "so new and strange."

Clarence's observations are enriched by the photos, which range from beautiful (the seascapes)—to realistic (the hardware store, the *komusō*)—to empathetic (the little girl with baby on her back, eating with her fingers; three little girls at the Christian kindergarten). Several of the photos are especially powerful with a gritty, uncompromising tone: the beggar with his baleful glare; a grandmother, her granddaughter strapped to her back; a woman in *anesan-kaburi*; these individuals stare unsmilingly into the camera, stolid and grounded in their own time and place. Their photos penetrate the impenetrable Japan, reaching beyond language and cultural difference, and speak of the human condition.

It required three days in "hot hot hot" weather for the Gambles to pack. Leaving Japan on July 31 with their extra new trunk, Clarence records from aboard the S.S. *Manchuria* one last glimpse of Mount Fuji. Through his acceptance of the unfamiliar, the liveliness of his prose, and the honesty of the photos, his Journal brings to life the experience of travelling through a Japan that existed in 1908.

江南 信國
T. Enami
富士山から本栖湖
FUJISAN KARA MOTOSUKO
Fuji from Lake Motosu
circa 1912

ENDNOTES

[1] The Thatcher School was founded in Ojai, California, in 1889 by Sherman Day Thatcher as a boys' school that combined academic studies with outdoor responsibilities, especially horsemanship: each student was required to ride and care for a horse during his first year at the school. This policy continues. The school became co-ed in 1977.

[2] Paixhans shell guns, designed around 1823, were the first naval guns to fire explosive shells.

[3] Hannah Sigur, *The Influence of Japanese Art on Design* (Salt Lake City: Gibbs Smith, 2008) 9.

[4] Marked Japanese-derived influence did not, however, appear in the work of the Greenes until after Charles Green attended the 1904 St. Louis Exhibit. For "The Gamble House," *see* Cecil Huggins Gamble, Biographical Notes, 103.

[5] Basil Hall Chamberlain's *A Handbook for Travellers* was sufficiently popular to go through seven editions. Speaking of the monotonous trip of eighteen days from San Francisco to Yokohama, Wright suggests that the time on board ship "can be put to good use if you read your Murray on Japan" (5).

[6] For the year 1908, Clarence kept a diary in a purchased small bound book from January 1 through March 29 (and a few days in August) (D), from which excerpts have been included in this Introduction. During the Orient trip, Clarence wrote, by hand, on stationery of his parents and on hotel stationery an account for each day (with the exception of April 19) of the Japan tour, beginning March 10 and concluding July 31 (S). Sometime later, when he returned to the States, Clarence edited the stationery accounts of the first four weeks in Japan and typed up an edited version (T). He entitled it "MY TRIP TO THE ORIENT: A Daily Journal 1908." The account of the weeks in Japan from June 18 until the Gambles' departure on July 31 exists only on various stationery. The "Daily Journal 1908" entries in this book covering the first four-week stay in Japan have been reprinted from the edited typed version (T) and the second stay of six weeks from the handwritten stationery accounts (S).

[7] Castle & Cooke was founded in 1851 and invested in Hawaii's sugar industry, later other agricultural products, and finally became the forerunner of Dole Food Company.

[8] Rt.Rev. Doremus Scudder was instrumental in organizing the Palama Settlement in the Palama district of Honolulu. Visiting the Settlement and various educational institutions were for David and Mary the high points of their time in Hawaii. Their evangelical fervor had a practical bent that directed their philanthropy. They believed in and supported the community building and educational opportunities offered by organizations such as the Palama Settlement and the international Y.M.C.A. and its branches. The Palama Settlement, until 1906 the Palama Chapel, in addition to maintaining its Pure Milk Depot, had opened the first public health nursing department in Hawaii. The Settlement ran a day camp for children with tuberculosis; a day nursery for working mothers; a night school, where English, American history, civics, and geography were taught; and in 1908 the Settlement built a swimming pool for the Palama community.

[9] Kindergarten Hall was a part of The Elizabeth Gamble Deaconess Home Association, which had been established by James Gamble, co-founder of Procter & Gamble and grandfather of Clarence, in honor of his deceased wife, Elizabeth, to minister to the poor. David Berry Gamble was on the board of directors, and the Association, which also founded Christ Hospital, was and is in the twenty-first century an important part of the Cincinnati civic community. In 1907, The Deaconess Home Association opened The Cincinnati Missionary Training School to prepare Christian women for work as missionaries in home and foreign fields; in this case, Christian women included several Japanese women.

[10] Known as 鎌倉大仏 "The Great Buddha of Kamakura," this bronze statue of Amida Buddha, once gilded, dates from approximately 1252 and stands on the grounds of 高徳院 Kōtoku'in Temple. Over fifty feet tall, its hollow interior allows visitors to walk within it. Only the Great Buddha at Tōdaiji in Nara surpasses Kamakura Daibutsu in size. The large halls that once sheltered it were several times destroyed by typhoons and tidal waves; since the end of the fifteenth century, the Kamakura Daibutsu remains in the open air, massively serene.

To the Reader: While the possible paternalistic aspects of the missionary movement may disturb some readers, we would suggest that, in another age, the reigning values differed from those that direct contemporary society today. The Gambles were always considerate of their employees. The Gambles paid their employees well, and when they left Nagasaki, a nearby observer, seeing the appreciation which the "coolies" expressed as they watched their temporary employers depart, observed "They must have treated those coolies well" (5/2).

THE GAMBLE FAMILY IN JAPAN 1908
Background for the Itinerary

He, therefore, who should essay to travel without having learnt a word concerning Japan's past, would run the risk of forming opinions ludicrously erroneous. —Basil Hall Chamberlain

Basil Hall Chamberlain, whom the reader has met in the earlier pages, advises the tourist that "a word concerning Japan's past" is needed if one is to understand and appreciate Japan. Such is equally the case if the reader is to appreciate the tour of Japan by the Gambles, their choice of cities to explore, and their many visits to temples and shrines.

The temples and shrines of Japan are inextricably interwoven with its history and culture. The earliest religion of Japan, the indigenous faith of the Japanese people, is Shinto; many Shinto shrines in Japan have their beginnings before recorded history. Shinto, which means the way of the *kami*, the gods, sees the *kami* as embedded in the land and in the natural world, the islands comprising Japan under the beneficent rule of Amaterasu Ōmikami, goddess of the sun.

But another system of belief was to challenge the Shinto world view. Around the fourth century, Korean itinerants and Buddhist monks began to reach Japan, bringing Chinese kanji and Chinese culture, the former to give rise to Japan's written language, the latter offering Buddhism, which was seized upon and promoted by Japan's ruling class, presenting Amida Buddha as the personification of infinite mercy and the counterpart to Amaterasu Ōmikami. In 593, Prince Shōtoku commissioned the building, in what is now Osaka, of the Buddhist temple Shitennōji, the first of many Buddhist temples to be built and maintained by the governing aristocracy of Japan.*

Concurrently, a centralized government was slowly being developed. To support its growth, the Emperor Kammu, who died in 806, founded in Nara the first capital of Japan, and Nara shortly became a lively cultural and Buddhist religious center. But the organized Buddhists soon came to threaten the power of the Emperor; hence, the decision of Kammu in 794 to relocate the capital to what is now modern-day Kyoto, out of close reach of the ambitious Buddhists.

*Temples belong to Buddhists, shrines to Shinto.

天鈿女命
AME NO UZUME NO MIKOTO
whose dancing enticed Amaterasu Ōmikami from Heavenly Rock Cave

阿弥陀
AMIDA BUDDHA

So began the Heian period (794-1185), the classical period of Japan's history, when the arts, especially literature, flourished, and when the world's first novel, *Tale of the Genji,* was written. But beyond the enclosed circle of the refined Heian Imperial court, a warrior class along with Buddhism and its warrior monks was steadily increasing in strength.

The Heian period officially ended when Minamoto Yoritomo (1147-1199) set up his military government in Kamakura, away from the enticements of the luxury-loving court in Kyoto. Minamoto Yoritomo became the first *shogun* of Japan, setting the pattern for times to come: a *shogun* as *de facto* ruler of Japan; the emperor, a semi-religious symbol, who could trace his descent directly from Jimmu, the first emperor of Japan, who was in turn a direct descendent of Amaterasu Ōmikami, Goddess of the Sun.

Over the centuries following the Kamakura period (1185-1333), a centralized government controlled portions of Japan, but throughout most of those centuries, Japan was the scene of unceasing warfare between and among rival clans—Minamoto, Hōjō, Fujiwara, Taira—and bitter wars within and among the clans themselves.

Amazingly enough, throughout this continuous turmoil, while heads were—literally—rolling amuck (thanks to the superior swords of the extraordinary Japanese sword makers), the classic arts of Japan grew and developed. The fiercest warrior might be known for his delicate calligraphy and his subtle blending of perfumes. During the Muromachi period (1358-1408), Shogun Ashikaga Yoshimitsu, who built *Kinkakuji*, the Golden Pavilion, brought the Noh theatre to new heights of refinement through his enthusiasm and support, and grandson Shogun Ashikaga Yoshimasa (1435-1490) at his *Ginkakuji*, the Silver Pavilion, popularized the tea ceremony (*chanoyu*), flower arranging (*ikebana*), and garden design. Fabric design, paintings on silk and on sliding door panels (*fusuma*)—all decorative and cultural arts—flourished, and Japan brought forth its unique aesthetic of restrained elegance that we admire today. Meanwhile, the great lords, the *daiymō*, who held small or large territories under their control, were constantly vying to enlarge the same, the Buddhist warrior monks supporting one or the other as possible advantage beckoned, and wars, small and large, raged among the disparate partisans, while the leader of each proposed to be the sole ruler of a unified Japan.

Felice Beato
鎧を着けた武士
YOROI O TSUKETA BUSHI
Samurai in Armour
1860s

xxxii Introduction

In the sixteenth century came a man who was determined to unify and rule all of Japan and whose ferocity and brilliance prepared him to do so: Oda Nobunaga (1534-1582) is known as the first of The Unifiers of Japan. He quelled the warrior monks and subdued challenging *daymō* with ruthless efficiency. When he was assassinated, one third of Japan was under his control. Beyond his extraordinary skill as warrior and tactician, Nobunaga understood the importance of good roads, of local and foreign trade, and of a free market. Because of his foresight, he left Japan with a growing economy.

織田信長
ODA NOBUNAGA

The second Unifier was Toyotomi Hideyoshi (1536-1598), who built on the work of Nobunaga; forbade personal possession of weapons, thus preventing future armed revolts; supported the arts, thereby reaching the people; and was the first to rule over a completely unified Japan.

豊臣秀吉
TOYOTOMI HIDEYOSHI

After the crucial Battle of Sekigahara in 1600, victorious Tokugawa Ieyasu (1543-1616), third of The Unifiers, closed Japan to the outside world; broke up the Buddhists, thereby reducing their power; enlarged on the accomplishments of both Nobunaga and Hideyoshi, and did so so successfully that a Tokugawa would be *shogun* for over two centuries, until 1867, at which time rule was returned to the Imperial Court and the Emperor Meiji.

With the arrival of U.S. Commodore Matthew Perry on its shores, Japan was forced to abandon the policy of isolation set up by the Tokugawa and to move posthaste out of its feudal society status. And this it did, under the new Meiji government to become almost overnight a modern industrialized nation capable of conducting the Sino-Japanese War (1894-95) and the Russo-Japanese War (1904-05). That the United States itself would step in to negotiate a treaty to

徳川家康
TOKUGAWA IEYASU

end the Russo-Japanese War was full acknowledgement by the West that, with the opening of the twentieth century, Japan stood as an equal to the great industrialized nations of the world.

To the Reader: Within "A Daily Journal 1908," the occasional misspellings and accepted nineteenth-century spellings used by Clarence, such as "to-day," "Corea," and "Kioto" have been retained as a gentle reminder to the reader of the era in which they were written. The punctuation has been silently emended by the editor. Citation of references and photo and art credits are to be found in "Sources and Credits."

Introduction xxxiii

THE GAMBLE FAMILY IN JAPAN 1908 ITINERARY

Date	Location	Activities	
4/10	YOKOHAMA	Grand Hotel	T. Enami Studio
4/11		Yokohama Park, Theatre Street, Bluff	
4/12		Church	
4/13	TOKYO	American Embassy	Ueno Park
		Tokyo University	
4/14	YOKOHAMA	Native Town	Hundred Steps
		Benten Dōri	Nursery
4/15	NAGOYA	Tōkaidō	Cloisonné factory
4/16		Nagoya Castle	Atsuta Jingū
		Dairyūji	Gohyaku Rakan
4/17	KYOTO	Kyoto Hotel	
		Damascene factory	
		Chion'in	Hojo Gardens
		Bamboo store	Theatre street
		Kiyomizudera	Higashi Ōtani
4/18		Hozu Rapids	Silk factory
4/19		Nanzenji	Heian Jingū
4/20		Hōkoku Byō	Hōkokuji
		Yamanaka's	
4/21		Shūgakuin (Imperial Gardens)	
		Shimogamo Jinja	
		Fushimi Inari Taisha Procession	
4/22		Kyōto Gosho (Emperor's City Palace)	
		Christian Missionary Kindergarten	
		Oiran Procession (Geisha Procession)	
4/23		Ginkakuji (Silver Pavilion)	
		Tea Ceremony	Bazaar
		Hall of the Butoku Kwai	
		(Hall of Military Virtues Society)	
		Dōshisha University	
4/24		Lake Biwa	Hikone Castle
		Lake Biwa Canal	
4/25		Japanese private home	
		Kitano Tenmangū	Bazaar
4/26		Resting	
4/27		Kakemono store	Cherry Dances
4/28		Kinkakuji (Golden Pavilion)	
		Kitano Tenmangū	
4/29	NARA	Deer Park	Kasuga Taisha
		Tōdaiji	
4/30	KYOTO	Nijō Castle	
5/1		Higashi Honganji	
5/2	OSAKA	Cotton Spinning factory	
		Shitennōji	
5/3	KOBE	Resting	
5/4		Glory Kindergarten	
		Christian College for Girls	
5/5	KOBE	Clarence builds & flies a kite.	
5/6	SHIMONOSEKI	Factories	Steamers
5/7	NAGASAKI	Tortoise Shell Store	Coal Loading
5/8 - 6/17	CHINA & KOREA		
6/18	MIYAJIMA	Trained goldfish	
6/19		Isukushima Shrine	Miyajima Ōtorii
		Senjōkaku Hall	Gojū No Tō
6/20		Photographing	
6/21		Mt. Misen	Misen Hondō
6/22	KYOTO	Train	
6/23		Lunch Mr. Gorbold	
		Japanese Theatre	
6/24	YOKOHAMA	Train View of Mt. Fuji	
6/25		Buy extra trunk	
6/26		Shopping and packing	
6/27	TOKYO	Metropole Hotel	
6/28		Church	
6/29		Tsuda School	Miss Milliken's School
6/30		Shopping	Iris Garden
7/1		Asakusa Park	Poster Shop
7/2		Ōkura Kihachiro Private Art Collection	
7/3	MIYANOSHITA	Fujiya Hotel	
7/4		Resting	
7/5		Walking	
7/6		Shopping	
7/7		Hike to Miyagino	
7/8		Horseback	
		Ōjigoku Hot Springs	Yumoto
7/9	HAKONE	Lake Hakone	
7/10	MIYANOSHITA	Horseback & Kago ride	
7/11		Trains	
7/12	NIKKŌ	Kanaya Hotel	Bullomobiles
		Shinkyō (Sacred Red Bridge)	
7/13		Tōshōgū	
7/14		Kirifuri Waterfalls	Helen Hyde Studio
7/15		Cryptomeria Avenue	
7/16		RAIN RAIN RAIN	
7/17		Chūzenji Falls	Yumoto Hot Springs
7/18		Shopping	
7/19		Jizō zazo statues	
7/20		Rinnōji	Futaransanjinja
7/21	IKAHO	Train	
7/22	YUMOTO	Hot Springs	Daruma
7/23	KARAUIZAWA	Lace shops	Tennis courts
7/24		Missionary reception	
7/25		Mt. Asama Lava Beds	
7/26		Church	
7/27	TOKYO	Japanese restaurant & inn	
7/28	KAMAKURA	Daibutsu	Christian conference
7/29	YOKOHAMA	Packing	
7/30		HOT HOT HOT	
7/31	"Manchuria"	Last view of Mt. Fujij	

MY TRIP TO THE ORIENT
A Daily Journal
1908
by
Clarence James Gamble

The Japan Visit
April 10 to May 8
June 18 to July 31

A

HANDBOOK FOR TRAVELLERS

IN

JAPAN

INCLUDING THE WHOLE EMPIRE FROM SAGHALIEN
TO FORMOSA

BY

BASIL HALL CHAMBERLAIN, F. R. G. S.
EMERITUS PROFESSOR OF JAPANESE AND PHILOLOGY IN THE IMPERIAL UNIVERSITY OF TŌKYŌ

AND

W. B. MASON
CORRESPONDING MEMBER OF THE ROYAL SCOTTISH GEOGRAPHICAL SOCIETY AND LATE OF THE
IMPERIAL JAPANESE DEPARTMENT OF COMMUNICATIONS.

With Thirty Maps and Plans and Numerous Illustrations

EIGHTH EDITION, REVISED AND PARTLY REWRITTEN

LONDON
JOHN MURRAY, ALBEMARLE STREET

YOKOHAMA } KELLY & WALSH, LIMITED { HONGKONG
SHANGHAI } { SINGAPORE

1907

[ALL RIGHTS RESERVED]

Title Page of the Popular 1907 "Murray"

横浜 YOKOHAMA
Friday 1908 4/10

We were awakened this morning at 6 by the gong (very early but still we were glad of it), which was supposed to be half an hour before inspection time. I got up, dressed, and finished my trunk before the second gong sounded and then there was about another half hour before we went to the table. After walking upstairs past the inspecting doctor and back again, we had a fine breakfast. We went aboard a steam launch and were taken ashore to Japan. Of course, we took a jinrikisha to go to the hotel and, as Mother says, we wore a good broad grin all the way. It certainly seems very queer and unnatural to ride in a narrow little carriage all by yourself with a man running in front to pull you."
CJG

人力車
JINRIKISHA
Clarence
James
Gamble
on
Jinrikisha

FOURTEEN-YEAR-OLD CLARENCE JAMES GAMBLE, his seventeen-year-old brother Sidney, and their parents, David and Mary Gamble left San Francisco on the S.S. *Siberia* on March 10, 1908, to visit China, Korea, and, most particularly, Japan. After a two-week stopover in Hawaii, on March 30th, they boarded the S.S. *Manchuria* and reached Yokohama on April 10th. During the eleven days on board ship (a day was lost when crossing the international date line), Clarence, possibly motivated by parental oversight, was keeping a daily journal. Meanwhile, both Clarence and Sidney looked forward to documenting the Asia tour, not only with Clarence's journal entries, but with photographs, for both young men were avid photographers. In preparing for their visit to Japan, the Gambles most certainly studied the 1907 eighth edition of the popular *A Handbook for Travellers in Japan including the Whole Empire from Saghalien to Formosa* by Basil Hall Chamberlain and W.B. Mason, published by John Murray in London. Generally referred to as "your Murray," in the following pages, it is herein referenced as "Chamberlain."

Basil Hall Chamberlain (1850-1935), in his day the foremost interpreter of Japan for the West, was eighteen years old when he left his native England to travel abroad for his health. He arrived in Japan in 1873, quickly became fluent in Japanese, and by 1886 was professor of Japanese at Tokyo Imperial University. In 1890 was published his well-known *Things Japanese* and, in 1891, his first edition of *A Handbook for Travellers.* Excerpts, advertisements, and maps from the 1907 edition of the *Handbook*, along with photos taken by Clarence and Sidney, give us in the following pages a glimpse of the Japan seen by the Gambles in 1908.

Japan 1908 1

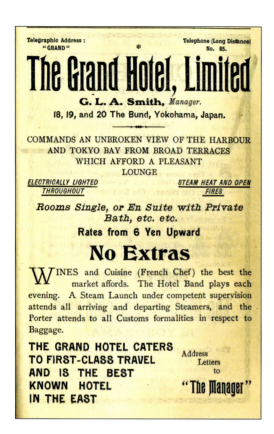

FOUR INCHES OF SNOW *A Handbook for Travellers discusses in its early pages the need for warm clothing and the unpredictable weather of Japan (Chamberlain 7).*

MEASURED FOR SUITS *In Yokohama, "Chinese tailors attend the hotels, and will fit out travellers with duck, crape, and other light clothing, literally between a night and a morning" (Chamberlain 8).*

江南 信國 **T. ENAMI** *Enami Nobukuni (1859-1929) was a military photographer during the Russo-Japanese War, then had a studio on Benten-dori from 1892 to 1929. T. Enami catered to the foreign tourist market; in 1904 his lithographs were sold through Sears Roebuck. His son Tamotsu ran the studio from 1929 to 1945.*

MR. LOOMIS *was an active member in Yokohama of the American Bible Society. In 1905, he writes a letter in support of printing 1,000 copies of a Chamorro (official language of Guam) translation of the Gospel of Matthew.*

横浜 YOKOHAMA
Friday 1908 4/10

The storm of yesterday passed through here and left about four inches of snow. The air was very cold, and the piles of snow on the side of the street did not seem very suggestive of Japan as we had expected to find her. They say such weather is very unusual, and they haven't had anything like it for sixty years. Our rooms are fair but pretty cold, as there is no heat in the fireplace. Their temperature is 58 at present.

"The salesmen here are really bothersome. We were attacked as soon as we entered the hotel by a dozen different agents for tailors and dressmakers. One even came into our room and sat down to show his samples of duck, pongee, and serge. These don't seem very suitable for this sort of weather. We have also received almost a dozen circulars or 'invitations' to visit stores. We did go to one this morning to look at curios. They had every imaginable thing in the store, from small lacquer boxes to a ten-thousand-dollar ivory eagle.

"The 'tiffin' or lunch served at the [Grand] hotel was fair but rather poor when compared to the meals on the boat. Our guide, Jinya, who met us at the wharf, is very nice. He speaks a queer but understandable English, and we expect to like him very much.

"In the afternoon, we went to a tailor to be measured for suits and then to see T. Enami, the photographer that had been recommended to us. We liked his work very much and expect to have our printing done there. We left a few films to be printed and then went to see Mr. Loomis of the Bible society to whom Father had a letter of introduction. He gave us quite a little information. We saw two wooden idols that he had bought in a second-hand store. They were Daikoku, the god of wealth, and Yebitsu, the fisherman's god.

"After dinner, I watched a traveling magician perform on the hotel piazza. He carried his outfit and stage on his back and had two acetylene burners for illumination. Considering the outfit, his tricks were very good."   CJG

YEBITSU *or Ebisu, The Fisherman's God.*

横浜 YOKOHAMA
Saturday 1908 4/11

"We went rikisha riding this morning. First, we stopped at the post office and got some stamps, then went to some small shops where they sold netsukes and other small carvings. A netsuke is a small round carving of almost any design, which the Japanese fasten by a string to their purse and then tuck through their belt to hold the purse securely.

"A ride down theatre street was very interesting. All the theatres had long banners hanging over the street from bamboo poles, and some had the whole front covered with boards giving names of the actors.

"A visit to the park showed us our first cherry blossoms. They were very pretty but not as pink as we had expected. From some of the books on Japan, one might be led to believe that the whole landscape was covered with cherry blossoms and the sky given a peculiar glow on their account, but as we found out, they are to be seen only in parks or gardens where they have been specially cultivated.

"The Yokohama park is a fine playground for children, and we got several fine snaps of them there. (*See next page.*)

YOKOHAMA PARK Chamberlain advises that the best place to view cherry blossoms is the Cricket Ground built behind the Bluff in 1883 by English residents. Clarence writes only of "Yokohama Park."

Tourists, writes Chamberlain, should schedule their arrival in Japan during early April. "If possible, he should be either in Tokyo or in Kyoto during the first half of April to see the lovely display of cherry blossoms, which are followed through the early summer by other flowers - peonies, azaleas, wistarias, irises, - well worth seeing, both for their own sake and for that of the picturesque crowds of Japanese sightseers whom they attract"(8). Camellias, not mentioned by Chamberlain, are a much loved early spring flower and have been cultivated in Japan for centuries. Camellias are an important part of the tea ceremony because of their fragile beauty and because of their lack of odor, which does not interfere with the fragrance of the tea.

椿 **TSUBAKI** *Camellias* This beautiful camellia bush is at Jizo-in Tsubakidera, established in 726 by Gyōki, and is not far from Kitano Tenmangū in Kyoto, which the Gambles visit on 4/25 and 4/28.

Japan 1908 3

横浜 YOKOHAMA
Saturday 1908 4/11

The afternoon was spent in a ride along the 'bluff.' This is the place where most of the Americans live. The climbs are frequent and steep, so we took two men for each rikisha, one to pull as usual and another to push behind.

"We stopped to see one of our 'table-mates' on the 'Siberia' who lived at the top of the bluff and then went past the golf links and race track, for Yokohama can boast of such, to a fine viewpoint, one of the highest places in the city. After admiring the view, we went down to the water's edge and out into the country. Japanese children seemed to be everywhere, sometimes almost blocking the road from side to side. Most of the girls carried babies on their backs.

"The houses were very different from anything we've seen before. The roofs were all thatched, and the ridge was covered with a few rows of tile. On the way back to the hotel, we stopped at some of the smaller shops farther from the center of town than we had been before. We invested in a netsuke after reducing the price to one half what was first asked. Some daffodils and hyacinths displayed on the street seemed to be quite out of place considering the temperature." CJG

子守り **KOMORI** *Babysitter*
"Most of the girls carried babies on their backs."

RACING Horse racing originated in eighth-century religious ceremonies held for the Imperial Court and then became popular among all classes. In 1861, British residents of Yokohama introduced Western-style horse racing to Japan and shortly built the Yokohama Race Club.

横浜 **YOKOHAMA** The city was created by and for the foreign merchants, those eager to seize this new market in a Japan whose trade was newly open to the West. After 1866, the small fishing town and mud flat of Yokohama morphed into a center of business bustle, its ample natural harbor the *de facto* port of Tokyo, which lay twenty miles to the north. The Gambles rode in a "little box-like car" for half an hour to reach Tokyo, where they met Ambassador O'Brien and secured their tourist permits. In this new Yokohama, a wide street on the waterfront known as the Bund faced the harbor. The landing place, the Custom House, the consulates, and banks, all about five minutes from the hotels, comprised the Foreign Settlement. Just outside the Foreign Settlement was the Native Town or Japanese Town, the "real Japanese section of town," where the Japanese lived and which Clarence sees with Jinya. The well-to-do, the foreigners, mostly British and some Americans, lived on the Bluff, which could be reached by "The One Hundred Steps" and overlooked the Mississippi Bay—so named by Perry when he visited Yokohama in 1854. After reminding the foreign visitor of the closing of the Custom House, public offices, and banks on Public Holidays, Chamberlain also warns, "Little business is done at Yokohama during the race meetings in spring and autumn" (3).

横浜 **YOKOHAMA**
Sunday 1908 4/12

"A rainy, foggy, and generally disagreeable day. We decided to go out, nevertheless, so covered rikishas with rubber aprons took us to church. We arrived just as the people were coming out of the Japanese service, changing their shoes that they wore in the building for those for street wear and clattering away. We stayed for the English service, and the guide stayed with us, though I don't know how much he understood. As it was still disagreeable in the afternoon, we spent it in our rooms." CJG

東京 **TOKYO**
Monday 1908 4/13

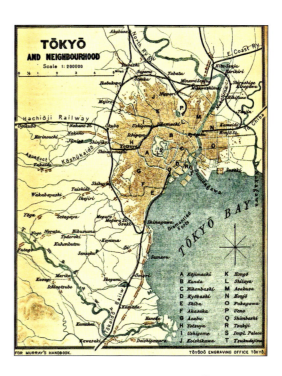

"Still raining and foggy, but we decided to go to Tokyo for the day. A half-hour's ride in a little box-like car brought us to the Japanese city of magnificent distances. Such it really is, for we spent more than half our time getting around the city.

"Our first trip was by rikisha to the American legation to see our ambassador, Mr. O'Bryan. We left the legation in great style, at least for Japan, in a two-horse carriage with a footman perched up behind. As we drove around the palaces and across the city, the footman was kept very busy, for every time we came to a corner, he would jump down to the ground and run ahead and clear the way, shouting 'Hi hi' and even taking hold of the horses' heads to help turn them around the corner. A carriage seems to be quite a novelty in the poorer quarters, for the people would get out of our way in a hurry and gaze after us when we had passed. The rain made the streets very muddy; and as our footman went splashing along, the mud seemed to fly from side to side at the narrow streets. We took our lunch in a small Japanese eating house in Ueno park. We managed to get enough to eat, though the meal was an unsuccessful attempt to serve real European food.

"In the afternoon, we went to the university to try to find Baron Kukutche, to whom Father had a letter of introduction. He was not at the university, but we were given the address of his house and set out to find it. We wound through narrow alleys, sometimes having to retrace our steps or, more properly, our splashes, until we found the house, but the Baron was not at home. The ride back to the station was long and rather damp, but the streets and shops that we passed were very interesting. It seemed a good deal better to be in a carriage where you could talk to someone and laugh over the sights than all by yourself in a jinrikisha. Nearer the station, we saw our first temple. Crowds were passing up and down the steps, even though it was raining. The idols were very large and curious, but we were told that we would see much better ones in Kyoto." CJG

"MR. O'BRYAN"
Thomas O'Brien (1842-1933) was ambassador to Japan from October 1907 until August 1911.

上野公園 UENO KŌEN
Ueno Park is well known as the site of the elaborate Tokuguwa mausoleums. Also there are the Tokyo National Museum, the Zoological Garden, Tokyo University, and other cultural institutions, along with many eating places.

"BARON KUKUTCHE"
Kikuchi Dairoku (1855-1917) graduated from St. John's College, Cambridge, became president of the Tokyo Imperial University, later Minister of Education; finally, president of Kyoto Imperial University.

FIRST TEMPLE *Asakusa Temple. See page 67.*

横浜 YOKOHAMA
Tuesday 1908 4/14

This morning, Sidney and I went with Jinya, our guide, for a walk in the real Japanese section of Yokohama. The streets were flanked by little irregular houses, each one touching the next. Most of them were one and a half or two stories high, and each seemed to be quarreling with his neighbor over the proper height. In the daytime, the front rooms on the ground floor were usually open to the street for use as a shop. The goods were displayed on the floor about two feet above the street level and seemed to take up most of the space.

"As the morning was cold, the woman who was keeping shop would sit with her hands over a 'habachi' [sic] or small charcoal stove until the 'foreigners,' for all Americans and Europeans are called foreigners here, appeared, when she would jump up and bow, talking in Japanese all the time.

"After stopping at one or two shops, we climbed the 'hundred steps' to the bluff. There on a gable of one of the large houses, there was a hideous-looking animal, of which the Japanese imagination seems to be so productive. Some years ago, an epidemic broke out across the street, and a Buddhist priest was called in to investigate the cause.   (See next page.)

金物屋 **KANAMONOYA** *Hardware Store*

薬屋 **KUSURIYA** *Pharmacy*

Western-style Architecture in 1908 Japan

The 'cause' was found to be the evil influence of this animal looking down on the people. To counteract it, two brass cannon were mounted on the tops of neighboring houses and aimed at the source of the trouble. The animal, fearing the cannons, ceased to send sickness on the people, and all was well. The guns and the animal still remain to tell the story of Japanese superstition.

"We visited an extensive Japanese nursery before returning to the hotel.

"In the afternoon, Mother and Father went off with the guide, while Sidney and I went down Benton [sic] Dori, a great street for curios. The Japs have a sliding scale of prices varying according to the customer, and one is seldom expected to pay the first price that is asked. Sidney purchased a lacquered wood netsuke for a little less than half what was first asked for it and, when we asked another shopkeeper what it was worth, he told us just half of that.

"At another store where they could not speak English, we managed to strike a bargain by using signs and showing pieces of money. Farther down the street, we purchased some posters of Japanese war scenes. In one store, I saw them playing Japanese chess. I asked them what it was, and they said, 'shogi' and told me where I could get a set. I expect to have Jinya teach me how to play it." CJG

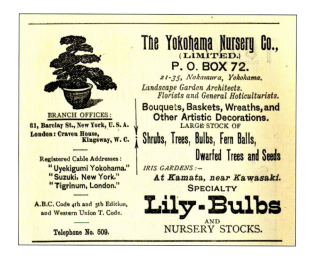

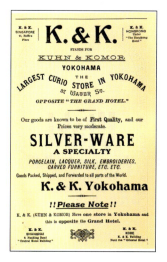

将棋 **SHOGI**
Generals' Board Game, known as Japanese Chess.

弁天通 **BENTEN-DŌRI** *Curio Street*
Curio dealers abound in Yokohama, "especially in Benten-dōri," and Chamberlain lists some of the wares available:

"Photographs of Japanese Scenery and Costumes, Lantern-slides, Books and Maps, Japanese Works of Art, Silk, Embroideries; Silk and Cotton Crapes, Bronze, Toys, Bamboo and Bead Blinds, Cabinets, Artificial Flowers, Lanterns, etc. and much more to be found at numerous Japanese Curio Dealers" (100).

湯と薬屋 **YU TO KUSURIYA**
Bathhouse and Drugstore
The lantern in the upper left indicates that around the corner is a bathhouse. The store fronting the street is a pharmacy.

Japan 1908   7

名古屋 NAGOYA
Wednesday 1908 4/15

We took an early ride to the railroad station in our rikishas. The streets seemed quite different from usual, for many more people were out. The train was quite crowded, and the Gamble quartet had to sit in a place just large enough for three, but that was not the worst part of the trip. We had to live all day in an atmosphere of concentrated tobacco smoke. A man next to us was hardly without a cigarette for five minutes at a time, and across the aisle an old man and a woman kept at it very steadily.

"The scenery was good, though clouds and occasional showers interfered a little. Most of the way, the tracks ran between the sea on one side and steep mountains on the other. One of the latter, we were told, was Fuji, but, unfortunately, it raised its head so high that it was lost in the clouds. There were many rice fields on the hillsides, terraced so that two or three inches of water would cover them. Men and woman were out working in them, getting nearly as wet from the rain above as from the water below. In one or two places, we passed large factories that seemed quite un-Japanese to us.

"At the stations, we heard boys calling out 'bender.' We wondered what it was but found out later when an old couple next to us bought a box from one of these boys and began to eat the contents for their dinner. The box was divided into three trays, one of rice, another of fish and pickles or something of the kind, and a third and smaller one of sweets.

"Our own meal in the European dining car was fairly good and, as no smoking was allowed, we enjoyed a short breathing spell. After lunch, I went into the second-class car to have Jinya show me how to play Japanese chess. It is quite a good game and quite different from our chess.

"We reached Nagoya at four in the pouring rain and went to our hotel in rikishas. Leaving our baggage there, we went out again to see a cloisonné factory. For this ride, we were provided with large yellow Japanese umbrellas to keep off the rain and at the same time let us see something of what was passing. There is no generally observed Sunday in Japan, but instead they have two holidays a month, and today happened to be one of them. We saw only one or two men at work but had the whole process explained to us. We bought two or three of the pieces they had made there." CJG

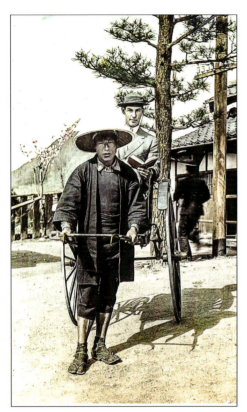

SIDNEY GAMBLE is behind the chairman sitting in the jinrikisha.

CONCENTRATED TOBACCO SMOKE "Europeans usually avail themselves of the first-class railway cars whenever such are provided and ladies in particular are recommended to do so, as not only are the other classes apt to be overcrowded, but the ways of the Japanese bourgeoisie with regard to clothing, the management of children, and other matters, are not altogether as our ways. Smoking is general even in the first-class, except in compartments specially labelled to the contrary; but such are not often provided" (Chamberlain 11).

"BENDER" Clarence is referring to a *bentō*, the Japanese boxed meal.

名古屋 **NAGOYA** A large port city 150 miles southwest of Tokyo on the Tōkaidō.

CLOISONNÉ and porcelain have long been manufactured in the many towns surrounding Nagoya, making the city well known for its cloisonné and fine pottery.

名古屋城 **Nagoya Jō**
Thursday 1908 4/16

The sun was shining brightly this morning when we awoke and gave promise of some good photos. Our first trip was to the Nagoya castle. It was an imposing affair, surrounded by extensive grounds. The space between the outer and inner moats was occupied by barracks. A hundred and fifty steps took us to the top of the castle, where we had a fine view of the surrounding country and several snow-capped peaks in the distance. The castle was very dark, and it seemed almost uninhabitable to us, but we learned that it was only used for living quarters in time of war.

"Outside in a smaller building, we saw the apartments of the shogun, which were used in time of peace. The walls were decorated with paintings of tigers, street scenes, and snow scenes on a gilt background. There was no furniture of any kind, and, in fact, the only thing beside the bare walls was a low shelf about six inches from the floor with a few ornaments on it.

"On the top of the castle, we saw two golden dolphins, each said to be worth forty thousand dollars. One of them had been taken to an exposition in Europe and when coming back, had been sunk off the Chinese coast. It was recovered, however, and restored to its position.

"After watching the soldiers maneuvering in the castle grounds, we went to see a small temple. There they had a collection of about five hundred images of Buddhists, each about two feet high. A whole building was devoted to them, with a little winding walk leading past the long rows of shelves. We had a fine rikisha ride for the rest of the morning, getting some fine pictures with our first good sunshine. (*See next page.*)

SMALL TEMPLE "In northeast Nagoya in a small gallery behind Dairyuji are the Gohyaku Rakan [Five Hundred Rakan], painted carved images of the chief disciples of Buddha, all especially remarkable because each of the five hundred figures is distinctly differentiated" (Chamberlain 238).

名古屋城 **NAGOYA JŌ** *Nagoya Castle* One of the wonders of Japan, with eighteen-foot walls and copper roof, was completed in 1612 to serve as residence for the seventh son of Tokugawa Ieyasu. In 1945, the castle was destroyed in a U.S. air raid. The structure today is a careful concrete reconstruction with air conditioning and elevators. Although most of the artifacts were destroyed in the air raid, the paintings, many by artists of the Kanō school, had been removed and stored in safety. The photo above is a rare photo of the original castle.

GOLDEN DOLPHINS with eyes of silver were made in 1610 by order of famous general Katō Kiyomasa (1561-1611). The dolphins are, in fact, 金鯱 *kinshachi*, mythical creatures with body of dolphin and head of tiger. Measuring eight feet eight inches in height, the gleam of the gold *kinshachi* can be seen from all over the city.

大龍寺 **DAIRYŪJI** (*below*) was built in 1725 by the Obaku Buddhist monk Katsuden and is famous for its statues, some of which were carved by Tametaka Kita, the netsuke carver credited with inventing *ukibori*, a relief carving technique.

名古屋 NAGOYA
熱田神宮 Atsuta Jingū
Thursday 1908 4/16

"In the afternoon, Sidney, the guide, and I went to a large temple. The crowds were very large, as it was a special fete day and there was to be a dance. Goldfish sellers at the entrance were offering tempting-looking goldfish, globe and all, for ten sen, while side shows and toy and candy shops were doing a rushing business.

"The dance was given in the open air on a raised platform. The performers dressed in blue robes with large sleeves and very long trains went through slow twists and turns accompanied by a band of the most squeaky instruments ever invented. Every now and then a large drum was struck to mark some more sudden movement of the dancers. Sidney and I got some pictures by holding our cameras above our heads when we snapped them. A second dance was performed by a single dancer with red and gilt robes and a gold mask shaped like a fox.

"The trip to Kyoto was much better than that to Nagoya, for only one cigarette was smoked all the way. As we traveled most of the way in the dark, we didn't see much of the country." CJG

熱田神宮 ATSUTA JINGŪ The platform in this photo, on which we see the dancers, was built in 1900, the date on the stone column to the left. The original Atsuta structures date back centuries. Those seen by the Gambles had been remodeled in 1893. Most of those were destroyed in World War II, but principal buildings, such as the *honden*, were subsequently rebuilt by 1955.

本殿 HONDEN *Main Hall* and most sacred building of the shrine, in which the *kami* (gods) are enshrined.

神楽 KAGURA *Dancing for the Gods*
In the photo to the left, which is a closeup from the photo above, the robes of the dancers are white. But Clarence noted that the robes were blue. Was this a mistake of the artist who tinted the photo?

Japan 1908

熱田神宮 **ATSUTA JINGŪ** *or* **MIYA** *The Shrine stands near the center of Nagoya in fertile Owari Plain. One of the oldest and one of the most sacred of sacred sites, it dates back to the reign (71-130) of Emperor Keiko and through the centuries has been supported by Oda Nobunaga, Toyotomi Hideyoshi, and the Tokugawa, Japan's most illustrious leaders. A sacred forest dense with Gingko, Japanese Zelkova, and Camphor trees, some of which may be over 1,000 years old, surrounds the Shrine. The Shrine buildings were completely destroyed by bombings of World War II.*

Atsuta Jingū is dedicated to Amaterasu Ōmikami, beneficent goddess of the sun, and is the traditional repository of Kusanagi no Surugi, the sacred sword and one of The Three Sacred Treasures of Japan. Kusanagi was a gift from Amaterasu and is forever imbued with her spirit. Many annual festivals, well over seventy yearly, celebrate the protection of Amaterasu over agriculture in the surrounding area, and her shrine is much visited by local residents and tourists.

KITSUNE 狐
Fox holds a sacred role with the Shinto. The fox is considered the messenger of Inari, the rice god and the god of prosperity.

Japan 1908 11

京都 KYOTO
知恩院 Chion'in
Friday 1908 4/17

This morning, in spite of our expectations, was bright and clear. We took rikishas early to go to a damascene factory, where we saw the process of manufacture. The black and gold pattern is made on a steel base. First, the steel is prepared according to the desired pattern, then the gold is put on where it is wanted. The whole is then covered with a black lacquer that sticks to the steel but is later easily scratched off the gold. All sorts, shapes, and sizes of articles were shown us: hatpins, stickpins, cuff buttons, houses, and chest of drawers. Shortly after we sat down to look at their wares, some very strong tea and a dish of cakes were brought in and set down before us. This certainly seemed a queer custom to us.

"Our next visit was to a large temple. Our rikisha men had large cloth overshoes with them that they slipped over our shoes before we entered the temple. The main deity of this temple was the goddess of mercy or mother of gods. She was surrounded by all sorts of brass lanterns and ornaments. On one side, a man was saying his prayers by beating continuously on a wooden bell. In the back of the grounds were apartments for the use of the members of the Tokugawa family when they came to Kyoto. These were decorated much like those we saw at Nagoya. Just outside these rooms there was a pretty garden where we got some good photos. Farther up the hill on which the temple was located, there was a large bell, so large, in fact, that even six men could not strike it hard enough to get a good tone out of it.

(*See next page.*)

知恩院 **CHION'IN** is described by Clarence as "a large temple" with the main deity being "the goddess of mercy." Chion'in is a Japanese National Treasure and the head temple of Pure Land Buddhism (as opposed to True Pure Land Buddhism) belonging to the Amidist school of Buddhism. Amidism is the most popular of the Buddhist schools in Japan (and worldwide) and is based on devotion to Amida Buddha, the personification of infinite mercy and unchanging love. The Chion'in Amidadō (*Amida Hall*) houses a beautiful golden statue of Amida.

In 1234, when the original temple at Chion'in was built, the common people were being denied the salvation that Buddhism offered because of the intense scholastic learning and the very expensive rituals required. A far-seeing priest, Hōnen (1133-1212), asserted that by simply calling on the name of Amida in faith, an honest man could be assured of salvation, and this was the founding of the Pure Land or Jōdo sect.

Clarence mentions the Tokugawa. All the roof beams at Chion'in are carved with three hollyhock leaves, the *mon*, or family crest of the Tokugawa family, who rebuilt in the seventeenth century the Chion'in structures that stand today. The gate, the largest wooden gate in Japan, was erected in 1619. The squeaky floors inside the temple, the "nightingale floors," were so made to warn the Tokugawa of intruders.

方丈庭園 **HŌJŌ TEIEN** *Hojo Garden* Traditional Japanese garden designed circa 1648, possibly by Zen Buddhist monk Gyokuen (died 1661),

知恩院の鐘 **CHION'IN NO KANE** *Chion'in Bell* was cast in 1633 and at 74 tons is one of the heaviest in Japan. Seventeen monks are needed to ring it at the New Year's ceremony.

徳川家の紋
TOKUGAWA KE NO MON
Three Leaves of Kamo-aoi or Hollyhock.

12   Japan 1908

京都 **KYOTO**
Friday 1908 4/17

On the way to the hotel, we stopped at a bamboo store where they had all sorts of boxes, houses, smoking sets, and such things. We had quite a time there but managed to get away without buying out the entire stock.

"Our cameras worked hard all the morning, for everything seems so new and strange. (*See next page.*)

虚無僧 **KOMUSŌ** *Priest of Emptiness*, seen in the photo to the right, a Zen Buddhist monk of the now defunct Fuke sect devoted to constant pilgrimages. He was a customary figure in Japan from the thirteenth into late nineteenth century, though as this photo indicates, the monks, or ones who appeared as such, existed in 1908 and may even be seen in Japan in the twenty-first century. The komusō wears a basket on his head to signify that he has eliminated his ego; he plays his bamboo flute, the *shaku-hachi*, as a means to meditate and with which to solicit alms.

Under Tokugawa rule, the *komusō* were cleverly used as spies by the wily government and so free to travel, an exceptional privilege at the time. With the Meiji restoration, practice of Fuke Zen was banned, leading to its demise in 1871. Even today, some Japanese recall being frightened as children of the komusō. During the militaristic regime of World War II, men would hide themselves in this convenient apparel. In the twenty-first century, the *shaku-hachi* is played by both men and women in jazz and classical groups and at *shakuhachi* festivals.

商店街 **SHOTENGAI** *Shopping Street*
On the right in this photo are three gas lamps, gas in use in Japan by the early 1870s. To the far left is a restaurant selling Kirin Beer, a German lager-type beer, which began manufacture under the Kirin Label in 1888 with the assistance of German technicians, but whose origins are found in the Spring Valley Brewery established in Yokohama in 1869. Kirin (キリン), the mythical animal on the label, half horse and half dragon, came from China and is a harbinger of good luck.

京都 **KYOTO**
清水寺 **Kiyomizudera**
Friday 1908 4/17

After lunch, we went for a walk down theatre street. The shops looked very gay with banners and goods hung all along the front. Drums and shouting men advertised circuses, theatres, and moving picture shows, while crowds of people stood around the entrance, though we saw few enter.

"Later, we went to another large temple on the side of a steep hill. Judging by the shops at the entrance, one might think that [it] was erected to the patron god of porcelain and china. The people at the temple were of all sorts and sizes, from old men and women down to the babies they carried on their backs.

"Near the front of the building was a tall stone pagoda with a series of small shelves on it. The Japs would throw stones at this pagoda, and if the stones lodged on one of the shelves, they would have very good luck.

"In another part of the grounds was a lovers' shrine. Some kind of an image was inclosed by a lattice, which was covered with bits of paper tied on as prayers. These pieces to be of any value had to be tied on with the thumb and little finger

"In the cemetery nearby, we saw a number of graves surrounded by bits of wood stuck in the ground, which our guide said were prayers. Some of the names on the tombstones were marked in red because the owner of the name had not died as yet. The monument was prepared for the whole family, and the names of those still living were simply marked with red paint.

"On the way home, we found an example of 'English as she is spoke.' A sign read, '*PHOTOGRAPHER AND THIS SHOP IS SUITABLE TO SELL MENY KIND PHOTO GRAPHS OF BEUTIFUL VIEW OR CUSTOMS IN JAPAN AND MENY OTHER COUNTRYS.*' I hope to get a photograph of it some day."*   CJG

The photograph of the shop is on page 16.

土産屋 **MIYAGEMONOYA** *Souvenir Shop*
The building to the left is a tourist restaurant with the restaurant and a souvenir store on the ground floor and a small hotel on the upper level. The signs are for-sale signs of candy, pickles, *udon* noodles, and other such food items. The sign for candy, *mamehiratō*, is the large sign in the lower right; the sign for "tourist hotel" the large sign in the upper right. Such signs and shops were very typical of those on both sides of the approach to many of the Japanese shrines and temples.

清水寺 **KIYOMIZUDERA** is a "large temple" on the side of a very steep hill in the Higashiyama district, not far from theatre street where the Gambles walked after lunch. The approach leading to the temple is jam-packed with shops, including many porcelain and china shops, which cater to the tourist as they have for centuries. Indeed, Kiyomizudera goes back centuries to 778, when Enchin (814-891), founder of Jimon School of Tendai Buddhism, built a small thatched hut to house a likeness of Kannon Bosatsu. The thirty-or-so buildings that now comprise Kiyomizudera date from 1633 and include Jishu Shrine for lovers, dedicated to the deity of love. Kiyomizudera is a UNESCO World Heritage site, but historically it has always been a popular attraction in Kyoto, much visited by tourists, pilgrims, and the ordinary Japanese, which would explain the people "of all sorts and sizes" whom Clarence sees.

宮参りの晴着
MIYAMAIRI NO HAREGI
Special robe worn for the occasion when the newborn child is brought to the shrine to be blessed.

HIGASHI ŌTANI 東大谷

A few blocks north of Kiyomizudera is found Higashi Ōtani, a mausoleum belonging to Zen Buddhists. The temple was founded in 1202 but rebuilt many times over the centuries after destruction by Kyoto's many fires. The Gambles would have passed the Higashi Ōtani on their way back to the Kyoto Hotel from Kiyomizudera.

Japan 1908   15

In the photo left, the signs on the shop are in English and Japanese. The small size of this photo leaves the letters illegible, but see in his 4/17 entry where Clarence quotes the strange English.

"We stopped at the Kyoto [Hotel], which is most Japanese in its furnishing, and has a real American bar-room with a billiard table in it; also, open fires, which are very much needed all over Japan, in the cold chilly month of November."

E.S. Wright,
Westward 'round the World (1908) 21.

京都
KYOTO

高島屋呉服店 TAKASHIMAYA GOFUKUTEN

Below is the Takashimaya Kyoto store in 1908. 飯田新七 Iida Shinhichi (1803-1874) opened his Takashimaya store in 1831, specializing in *gofuku*, Japanese formal wear. Takashimaya became an unlimited partnership in 1909. Today, Takashimaya has stores in all major cities of Japan as well as in Taipei, Taiwan; in Singapore; and in Shanghai, China.

KYOTO HOTEL,
KYOTO, JAPAN.
(Telephone No. 117)
K. INOUYE................Proprietor.
THIS FIRST-CLASS HOTEL
IS beautifully situated in a Garden near the Imperial Park, and is in the centre of the Business District. The Hotel, which is fifteen minutes' ride from the Station, commands an Extensive View of the Mountain and other Scenery for which Kyoto is famous.
Moderate Charges.
A Representative of the Hotel will meet Guests at the Station on arrival of all Trains, and a CARRIAGE will be sent to fetch guests if the Hotel is previously advised.
GUIDES can be engaged at the Hotel.

Banners in the photo above are advertising the sale of kimono in Kyoto, though not Takashimaya kimono.

16   Japan 1908

京都
KYOTO

To the right and just below are Mary and David Gamble seated in jinrikishas, which in April 1908 are being pulled by employees of the Kyoto Hotel, this verified by the vertical row of Kanji and Katakana characters on the uniforms of the four chairmen. Built in 1888, Kyoto Hotel has since been greatly enlarged and is today Kyoto Hotel Ōkura.

When the Gambles saw their first temple in Tokyo and its curious idols, they were told they "would see much better ones in Kyoto." Indeed, in Kyoto are to be found more than two thousand temples and shrines on sites dedicated hundreds of years ago to their sacred purposes. None of the original buildings have survived the fires, wars, and earthquakes that have regularly devastated the city, which has as regularly and splendidly renewed itself. A visitor writes of Kyoto as seen in the late nineteenth century:

> Kyoto is a beautiful city, lying high amid green hills and mountains, near to Lake Biwa, and surrounded by fair gardens and clear rivers whose branches flow down some of the city streets. It...is a bright, cheerful, sunny place of groves, temples, and palaces, squares, and monasteries.

By 1908, this city of groves, temples, and palaces could boast an electric north-south tramway; a canal to Lake Biwa, which provided power and transportation; and a railway connecting Kyoto to Japan's major cities. In 1908, Kyoto, of all the great cities of Japan, remained the most traditionally Japanese, yet in the street were many in Western dress, which the Imperial Family had adopted by 1886. The fine Kyoto Hotel, where the Gambles stayed, kept its furnishings typically Japanese but with a billiard table in its American bar room. Everywhere, shops were being set up with Western-style chairs to cater to the Western tourists. Traditional Kyoto and its picturesque discomfort were surging pell-mell into the industrial age.

The history of Kyoto is very much the history of the nation of Japan, particularly of the arts. Even when the government was for a time set up outside of Kyoto, Kyoto remained the domicile of the Imperial Family and their retinue and the location of state ceremony. Because of this Court connection, Kyoto has historically been a center for the arts and high culture and on the forefront of fashion and change. And so the Gambles found it.

"The way [to Hozu River] is as follows: Jinrikisha from the hotel to Nijō station on the W. side of the city, whence rail to Kameoka, 3/4 hr., and from there on foot or by jinrikisha in about 10 min. to the vill[age] of Hozu. The short railway trip is highly picturesque, the line running along just above the dashing river. The engineering difficulties to be overcome were great, and no less then eight tunnels had to be pierced on the way up the side of the ravine."

(Chamberlain 348)

保津川 HOZU RIVER
Saturday 1908 4/18

This morning, we took our rikishas at ten for a ride through the country. The sun was shining, so we had a good chance for pictures, especially at some of the places where we stopped. One of these was a temple surrounded by beautiful grounds. Most of our trip was through a very pretty region, past lakes and fields, and every now and then a little thatched-roof village. We left our rikishas at a little railroad station where we were to take the train to the top of the Hodzu [*sic*] rapids. Foreigners seemed to be quite a novelty here, for everyone seemed to stare for all they were worth. At one time, there were six women in a row behind Mother, taking in her dress. I set up the tripod in the sunlight and attracted quite a crowd, which Sidney then snapped with his camera.

(*See next page.*)

18 Japan 1908

A twenty-minute ride through eight tunnels and over bridges took us to the place where we were to get our boat. One of our rikisha men had come with us to run to the landing and engage a boat for us. He and several others tried to get off the train while it was still moving, with the result that they all found themselves rolling on the platform. The Japs haven't learned to allow for the motion of the car as yet.

"The ride was grand down the swiftly moving river between the steep green banks. Although the current carried us along at a good rate, we had two men in the bow working with oars. This was to give us headway so that the pilot in the stern could steer us safely over the hills of water and between the rocks. At one place, Sidney and the guide got out and walked a little way to get a picture of us as we came by. We passed several boats being towed upstream by the three coolies that formed the crew. A narrow path had been specially built for their use, part of it of long basket-like cylinders of bamboo filled with stones.

"At the landing place, there were crowds of Japanese out for a holiday, in boats, parading along the streets, usually with American umbrellas for parasols. The European sections of the eating houses were all taken, so we had to sit on the floor by a low table to eat our basket lunch. The meal was fine, for the hotel puts up good basket lunches.

"After dinner, we wandered around awhile, taking in the sights and then, getting in our rikisha which had come to meet us, we started for Kyoto. On the way, we stopped at a silk factory and purchased a velvet picture.

"Before supper, we developed three dozen films and left them to wash until afterwards. When we returned, we found that the maid had turned on the hot water instead of the cold as we had left it, and there was nothing left of the photos. Just imagine our feelings!"   CJG

保津川 **HOZU GAWA** *Hozu River* lies on the outskirts of Kyoto to the west near Arashiyama mountains, running through a picturesque gorge from Kameoka to Arashiyama. In 1606, boats dragged along by ropes, just as those the Gambles traveled on, came into use on the Hozu. In the photo opposite can be seen four men, the lower three men clearly leaning forward as they pull the ropes moving the boat. This mode of transportation continued until the 1950s, and traces of the tracks made by ropes and those pulling on them are today still visible. These river boats made it possible to transport the wood and supplies needed to build the large temples still venerated in Kyoto today.

The ride down the Hozu can take up to two hours, depending on the water level, and passes through some white water and beautiful areas, rich with wildlife and plant life. The river trip is available in the twenty-first century and is especially esteemed for its fall colors, which bring even more tourists than are usual during the rest of the year.

並河靖之七宝記念館 **NAMIKAWA MUSEUM**
The cloisonné factory of Namikawa Yasuyuki (1845-1927) on Sanjō-dōri in Gion, Kyoto, is seen in this 1908 photo. Namikawa Yasuyuki was the Imperial Craftsman for Emperor Meiji. Today, the building is the Namikawa Yasuyuki Memorial Museum honoring the life and art, the cloisonné masterpieces, of Namikawa Yasuyuki.

京都
KYOTO

Advertisement in Chamberlain's 1907 *Handbook for Travellers* for cloisonné in Tokyo made by Namikawa Sosuke (1847-1910), a remarkable artist but one unrelated to Namikawa Yasuyuki.

TAKASHIMAYA ADVERTISEMENT
A Handbook for Travellers

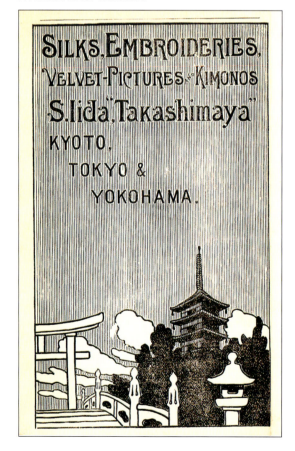

京都 **KYOTO** has historically been a center for the fine arts, famous, as Chamberlain notes, for "its pottery and porcelain, its embroideries, and velvets, and brocades, its bronzes, and its cloisonné" as well as for its shops, which are "perhaps" the finest in Japan (319). On the 18th of April, the Gambles buy a velvet picture in Kyoto, along with much, much else.

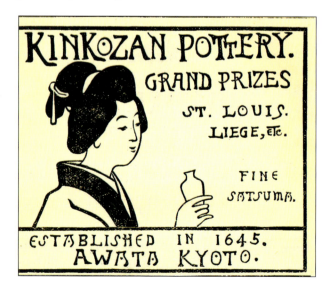

20 Japan 1908

南禅寺 **NANZENJI**

In the photo to the right, Clarence is standing before what appears to be the well-known Tiger and Bamboo *fusuma* (sliding door) painting by Kanō Tan'yū (1602-1674) located in the Hōjō (abbot's quarters) of Nanzenji. The Journal entry of Clarence for 4/19 is missing; it is possible that this photo belongs to that day.

Nanzenji, the Southern Mountain Temple, sits at the base of Higashiyama mountains and is regarded as one of the most important Zen temples in the world. It is home to the Rinzai sect of Zen Buddhism, the sect that pursues the use of *koans*, puzzles that defy normal logic. In 1290, it was the retirement home of the 亀山天皇 Emperor Kameyama (1249-1305), but the palace was plagued by ghosts. After the meditations of Mukan Fumon (1212-1291) disposed of the ghosts, the grateful Kameyama in 1291 gave the Lower Palace to the Rinzai. Destroyed many times by fires and wars, most of the temple buildings seen by the Gambles were constructed in the seventeenth century.

正装 **SEISŌ** *Formal Japanese Attire* worn by Clarence James Gamble

KYOTO 京都
Nanzenji 南禅寺
Sunday 1908 4/19

平安神宮の青龍楼 **SEIRYURO** *Shaden* Main Building of Heian Jingū

平安神宮 **HEIAN JINGŪ** was built in 1895 to commemorate the 1100th year of the founding of Kyoto and to honor both Emperor Kammu (737-806), the first emperor of Japan to live in Kyoto, and the Emperor Kōmei (1831-1866), the last to do so. The latter laid the foundations of the Meiji Restoration. The shrine commemorates as well the 2600th year of the founding of Japan. The *shaden*, main building, is a two-thirds replica of the original Kyoto Imperial Palace destroyed in 1227. Outside the shrine before the main gate and arching over busy Jingū Road is the largest torii in Japan, built in 1920. Surrounding the shrine are beautiful gardens.

五輪塔 GORINTŌ *Five-element Stone Cenotaph* honoring Toyotomi Hideyoshi at Hōkoku Byō is approximately 33 feet high.

豊国廟 HŌKOKU BYŌ With his back to the Gorintō, the man below, possibly Jinya, is enjoying the view that in 1908 left Clarence "fully repaid" for his arduous climb. Today, that view has been lost to a century of foliage growth.

京都 **KYOTO**
豊国廟 **Hōkoku Byō**
Monday 1908 4/20

The sun is still shining, and we are in love with Kyoto. Mother and Father went on a shopping tour with one of the missionaries this morning, so Sidney and I took the guide and went off on a sight-seeing excursion.

"A shrine dedicated to a shogun was built at the top of a flight of 557 steps, and to this we made our pilgrimage. We not only had to work for the view but also had to pay the sum of two and a half cents, but we were fully repaid. On one side we could see the city, a mass of gray tile roofs, and on the other, some beautiful hills and the canal from Lake Biwa coming out of a tunnel.

"Later, we visited a temple to get a photo of a fine old painting, but semi-annual cleaning kept us from even entering. Nearby, there was a large bell weighing about thirty tons.

"In the afternoon, as Mother hadn't finished her shopping campaign, we condescended to accompany her. For several hours, we had a great mixture of porcelain, curios, postals, pictures, silks, and bronzes, and all in such great numbers that they were really bewildering. One curio store, Yamanaka's, was just like a Japanese residence except that they had some chairs that the 'foreigners' could use. In the rear, was a fine garden with bronze deer and fountains and a small temple used as a showroom."   CJG

方広寺 HŌKŌJI A temple in the Higashiyama area of Kyoto with "a large bell weighing about thirty tons." Toyotomi Hideyoshi built the Hōkōji in 1586. It was destroyed by earthquake in 1596 and only the enormous bell remains.

豊国廟 **HŌKOKU BYŌ** as shown in the photos here is the grave site and mausoleum of Toyotomi Hideyoshi (1536-1598), second of The Three Unifiers of Japan and the first to rule over all of Japan. Of peasant birth, Hideyoshi became an adroit ruler, revising the land tax system, devising a code of maritime law, and encouraging foreign trade, as well as supporting the fine arts: Noh drama, classical poetry, and the tea ceremony. Clarence writes of climbing 557 steps to reach the Gorentō, but the exact number is said to be 565.

To appreciate the scale of the monument, note, in the center of the photo on the upper left of opposite page, the figure of a man, possibly Jinya, standing in front of the railing.

In the photo right, tall stone lanterns stand on either side of the path leading from the torii to the 565 steps. Cherry blossoms confirm the April date.

お母さん **OKASAN** Mother

Japan 1908 23

京都 **KYOTO**
修学院 **Shūgakuin**
Tuesday 1908 4/21

Mr. and Mrs. Gamble and their 'two daughters,' for so our permits read, went to visit the gardens of the Mikado. I rode the guide's bicycle most of the way so that I could stop quickly for photographs, and I certainly made use of the chance: Old men and women tottering under heavy loads, Japanese 'hayseeds' from the country with large hats, women pulling heavy carts, and last, but not so frequent, beggars.

(*See next page.*)

籠 **KAGO** *Basket on back of vender selling bamboo baskets.*

PERMITS Some of the sites visited by the Gambles were not open to the general public but were allowed to tourists, who were given special permits by their foreign embassies.

The Gambles took "a little box-like car" to Tokyo and obtained their permits from the then Ambassador O'Brien.

頬被り **HŌ KABURI** *Cotton Toweling for head-and-cheek covering worn by this worker protects against the dust of the road.*

物乞い **MONOGOI**
The "not so frequent" Beggar

The country through which we passed was beautiful with the green and bright yellow of the rape seed plant, but the climax was reached when Mr. and Mrs. Gamble and their 'two daughters' entered the gardens. Small winding paths through bamboo thickets and by the side of little lakes and streams led us to tea pavilions and the apartments of the emperor. On one of the panels in these rooms, an artist had painted a fish so well that at night it would go out into the pool in the gardens and swim away. Another artist had to be called in to paint a net over them to keep them where they belonged. A half-mile walk around the largest lake of the grounds was very pretty." CJG

SHŪGAKUIN 修学院

Gardens of the Imperial Villa or Imperial Gardens comprise a set of gardens referred to as the Upper, Middle, and Lower Gardens, all of which include extended strolling areas around ponds with bridges or waterfalls. In the several small buildings in each garden, many of them tea houses, are fine paintings by such famous artists as Sumiyoshi Gukei (1631-1705) and Kanō Hidenobu (1588-1672). The latter painted on a wooden panel in the Rakushi-ken, a small building of the Middle Garden, the run-away carp Clarence mentions.

Shūgakuin was built between 1650 and 1659 for retired Emperor Go-Mizunoo (1596-1680) but altered in 1883 by the Meiji. Today, Shūgakuin covers 133 acres. The gardens are an important cultural treasure, an area of extraordinary beauty, regarded as the finest in all of Japan.

菜種油 **NATANE ABURA** *Rapeseed Oil* *In the early seventeenth century, merchants in Osaka discovered that oil pressed from nanohana, the Japanese rapeseed plant, burned well in lamps, giving the expanding urban society a dependable source of light late into the night and thus more time for pleasure and work. Rapeseed came into great demand. Soon the fields in early spring were bright yellow as farmers turned to rapeseed as a second money-making crop.*
James McClain, A Modern History of Japan (2002) 60.

墓地 **BOCHI** *Cemetery in Kyoto*

京都北部
Northern KYOTO
下鴨神社
Shimogamo Jinja

糺の森 **TADASU NO MORI** *Forest Where Lies Are Revealed* surrounds the Shimogamo Jinja Shinto sanctuary. It is the vestige of a primeval forest, which may have been burnt by fire but has never been cut and for centuries has been growing naturally.

下鴨神社
Shimogamo Jinja

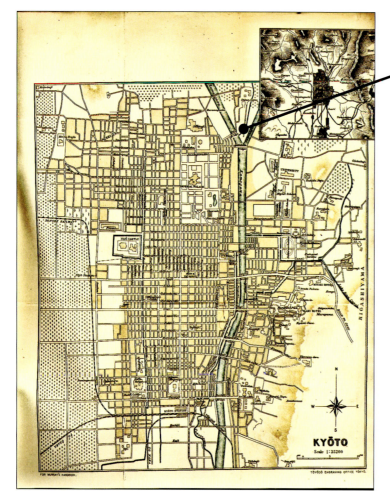

As can be seen on viewing this 1907 map of Kyoto, Shimogamo Shrine lies in the north of Kyoto between the confluence of the Kamo and Takano Rivers. It is believed that before Heian (Kyoto today) was laid out as the new capital, the Kamo River joined the Takano farther south in a location where it would divide the city, thus auguring a future division within the nation. Therefore, the Kamo was diverted to join the Takano at its present location, and Heian was laid out with its northernmost boundary at the new confluence of the Kamo and Takano Rivers. In this improved location, the Shimogamo Jinja is ideally situated to protect Kyoto from malign influences, particularly those from the northeast, the direction of the flow of the Takano and the so-called "devil's gate" direction from whence comes all misfortune. Shimogamo is the "River Confluence" shrine.

マリギャンブル
と子供達
下鴨神社の前

MARY GAMBLE & PARASOL

with children in front of Shimogamo Jinja

京都 **KYOTO**
下鴨神社
Shimogamo Jinja
Tuesday 1908 4/21

"About half way home we stopped at a temple. The gardens were very pretty and the gates about the largest we had seen, but the interesting part came when Mother came in sight of a lot of school children out for a picnic. The Pied Piper couldn't be compared to it. The children came around her in swarms, staring for all they were worth. It was near noon, however, and the prospect of something to eat seemed to furnish a stronger attraction than even the foreigner with roses on her hat and a toy parasol in her hand." CJG

下鴨神社 **SHIMOGAMO JINJA** or *Kamo Mioya Jinja*
As seen in the photo above, Mary is surrounded by the many curious children while standing before a building belonging to Shimogamo Shrine. Shimogamo is part of the Kamo Jinja, a Shinto complex in the northeast of Kyoto, which includes Shimogamo (Lower Shrine) and Kamigamo (Upper Shrine). The two shrines lie three miles apart on the Kamo River.

Shimogamo, one of the oldest Shinto shrines in Japan, is believed to date from the sixth century or earlier, well before 794, the year in which Kyoto was founded and when Emperor Kammu (737-806) arrived at Shimogamo in a grand progress. The Aoi Matsuri, a magnificent historically costumed procession, replicates that progress every year on May 15th, as it proceeds throughout the day from the Imperial Palace to Shimogamo and then Kamigamo.

The Gambles could have left Shūgakuin, which is east of Shimogamo Jinja, and reached Shimogamo before heading south to the Kyoto Hotel.

京都 **KYOTO**
伏見稲荷祭
Fushimi Inari Matsuri
Tuesday 1908 4/21

In the afternoon, we saw a great procession. The gods of one temple were taken from their usual resting place and transported to its branch for a week's stay. First came a lot of men in blue gowns to clear the way, then more trunks and chairs and some pulling a tree covered with paper prayers. After these had passed, there came five finely made brass cars, each jostled around by about sixty men. To carry one of the cars was supposed to be a positive preventative for rheumatism, and there were saki stands for the carriers about every two blocks, so that there was a great crowd of men following and taking turns shaking the car, tipping it, and jostling it around in every possible way. Our cameras were very busy, you may be sure, and we got some fine results."
CJG

伏見稲荷祭 **FUSHIMI INARI MATSURI** *Fushimi Inari Festival*
Its procession featured five *mikoshi*, portable shrines (Clarence refers to them as "brass cars") in which the gods are housed. They were being moved from the Fushimi Inari Taisha at the foot of Mount Inari in southeast Kyoto to their two-weeks' resting place in Otabi-sho, near Kyoto station.

神輿 **MIKOSHI** are exceedingly heavy, each weighing one ton, and do indeed require the help of the many who want to carry them. The procession that the Gambles saw was an annual tourist attraction from 1900 to 1920 and was noted in the Osaka *Asahi Shinbun*, April 22, 1908. On the opposite page is a photo of the procession published by the Kyoto *Morning Sun*, and their photo is similar to that taken by Clarence,

伏見稲荷大社 **FUSHIMI INARI TAISHA**
Its site predates the founding of Kyoto and is the headquarters of the more than 40,000 Inari shrines in Japan honoring Inari, the rice god, the god of prosperity. In Nagoya, the Gambles visited Atsuta Jingū, another important Shinto shrine.

祭 **MATSURI** *Festival* In the upper left photo on the opposite page, the figures wearing blue gowns, *kamishimo*, are leading the procession. Three policeman are in the forefront. Clearly a hot day, some are carrying Japanese parasols to protect against the sun. The large yellow chrysanthemum on the red coverings of the *mikoshi* was the Imperial Crest until 1945. Most of the onlookers wear white as an expression of their devotion. Signs advertise *sushi* and *Uji* tea, high quality green tea grown in nearby Uji since the fourteenth century. Tracks, probably streetcar tracks, are seen in photos below and on opposite page.

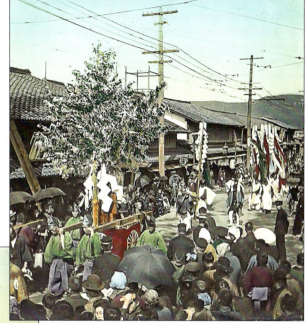

Kyoto Morning Sun April 1908

京都 KYOTO
京都御所 Kyōto Gosho
Wednesday 1908 4/22

Another procession comes off to-day, so, of course, the clouds are in evidence, though not completely shutting out the sun. We visited the Emperor's City Palace in the morning. It was built about fifty years ago and was very much like those we had seen before, only somewhat larger. From there we went by rikisha to a Christian kindergarten. The little Japs look awfully funny running about in their queer clothes, but when they get into American costume, as two of them were, they are stranger yet.

"When we arrived, they were all out in the yard, so we got some fine photos. They all took off their shoes when they went into the house, and the boy with the American shoes had quite a struggle, finally getting another boy to help him.

"The games were very interesting, representing Japanese family life, entertaining company, and farming. Jinya was quite interested, and our five jinrikisha men all looked in through the window to see what was going on. One of the children presented me with a decorated blotter, accompanied by a ceremonious bow."   (*See next page.*)

京都御所 **KYŌTO GOSHO**   *Kyoto Imperial Palace* has stood in the heart of Kyoto since at least 794 AD, the year of the founding of Kyoto and the beginning of the Heian period. The current incarnation of Kyōto Gosho (*Imperial Palace*), which the Gambles visited—fires and earthquakes having destroyed previous structures—was built in 1855. It is surrounded by 27 acres of gardens and park, originally land on which were located residences of the emperor's retinue but which today is enjoyed by the populace for picnics, strolling, and cherry blossom viewing. With the relocation in 1868 of the capital to Tokyo, or Edo as it was then called, the Emperor no longer resides in Kyoto, though official functions, such as the Hirohito coronation, were held there in Shishinden Hall. Directly across from Imadegawa Street on the north side of the grounds is Dōshisha University, which the Gambles visit on 4/23.

靴 **KUTSU** *Shoes* The little boy on the right is wearing American shoes.

幼稚園
KINDERGARTEN

京都 KYOTO
花魁道中 **Oiran Dōchū**
Wednesday 1908 4/22

We had a grand time getting our places for the procession in the afternoon. We were a little late, but by winding through back passages instead of through the crowd, we managed to get to our seats in safety. They were very good ones on the edge of the streets. Opposite us behind a bamboo railing, the space was just packed way back into the homes, and the balconies above looked as though they might break down any minute under the load of people.   (*See next page*.)

花魁道中 OIRAN DŌCHŪ

Procession of the Courtesans The Oiran was a witty and highly educated woman of pleasure, her position a distinctive part of the early Edo period, which began in 1600. Confined to living within the pleasure quarters of a city (in Kyoto the Shimabara), these entertainers were available only to the wealthiest and highest ranking daimyō or overlords of the government. When summoned to an assignation by her patron, the *Oiran*, accompanied by her personal retinue of servants, would proceed through the streets with the mannered gait demanded by the stylized shoes and constraining clothing that were her trademark.

The public walk of the Oiran to her assignation was the beginning of the elaborate procession that the Gambles viewed in 1908. The Oiran Dōchū is no longer presented in Kyoto but now held in Bunsui, Tsubame, Niigata, on the second Saturday in April. Each year, many hundreds of girls from all over Japan vie for a role in this popular event.

"The girls' faces were all painted a ghastly white, and their hair was almost hidden by a mass of silver ornaments."

Line Drawing. Osaka Asahi Shinbun 4/22 1908

"The procession began with a row of girls arranged according to height pulling a wagon filled with flowers. The girls' faces were all painted a ghastly white, and their hair was almost hidden by a mass of silver ornaments. Around their waists were fine silk sashes, beautifully embroidered. The dresses were gorgeously colored in all shades of the rainbow, though red predominated. Behind these girls came a row of about a dozen women. On the dress of one of them was embroidered a shining gold dragon with large porcelain eyes, on another a man on horseback, while a third had a large vase of flowers and some doves. Each of the women had an immense silk 'obi' or sash about a foot wide tied in a bow that almost covered her back. In the hair of each one were about a dozen tortoise shell ornaments and numerous silver and glass hairpins. Behind each one walked a green-robed parasol bearer, though these seemed hardly needed on such a cloudy day."
CJG

銀閣寺（慈照寺）
GINKAKUJI *Silver Pavilion* (慈照寺 *Jishōji*) is found just outside of northwest Kyoto and was built in 1479 by Ashikaga Yoshimasa (1435-1490), grandson of Ashikaga Yoshimitsu, who had built the Golden Pavilion for the same purpose: to serve as retreat after resigning the shogunate. The garden of Ginkakuji was designed by the great Sōami (1472-1525) and is famous for its much-photographed cone of white sand. The garden was the site of the tea ceremony, which Yoshimasa raised to a fine art, prescribing the regulation size of the tea room as 4½ mats and popularizing the concept of *wabi sabi*, the Japanese aesthetic that recognizes beauty in the utilitarian and in the imperfect. Yoshimasa died before the silver foil could be applied to his villa. On his death, the villa became a Zen Buddhist temple.

足利義政 **ASHIKAGA YOSHIMASA**

京都 KYOTO
銀閣寺 Ginkakuji
Thursday 1908 4/23

"Still cloudy this morning with occasional showers. The men of the party went to visit the Silver Pavilion, or 'Gin Kaku-ji.' We all carried large Japanese umbrellas so that we could see what we were passing instead of being shut up inside the rikisha covering. On entering the pavilion, we had to take off our shoes again. Here we had our first lesson in the tea ceremony. The tea is served in bowls with a piece of cake beside each. First, part of the cake must be eaten, not all, for the remainder is to be carried home. The bowl of tea is taken in one hand and turned around three times with the other. The tea must then be drunk in three sips and a half. The ceremonial tea room always has four and a half mats on the floor. Every Japanese room is made so that mats, each three feet by six, will just fit it, and the capacity of the room is spoken of as so many mats. The pavilion contained the usual highly decorated rooms and ornamental carvings.

"The garden was the most interesting part. Here in the pools, there were a number of trained goldfish that swim up to be fed when you clap your hands. Although it was rather cloudy, we got a few good photos. From the Gin Kaku-ji to the bazaar, a sort of exposition sale is held once a year. The admission charge of a cent and a half did not seem very high. Inside, we purchased some chestnut jelly put up in a half round of bamboo. It is called a 'cake' by the Japanese.

"In the afternoon, we went to watch the jiujitsu and fencing practice. A large hall and two or three teachers are provided by the government, and anyone who wishes to may go there for practice or instruction. It was interesting to watch but very bewildering on account of the number of pairs that were wrestling together.

"We went to the house of Miss Denton for supper. She is connected with the Doshisha girls' school. We exchanged quite a lot of information. She told us about Japan, and we told her of America. The dean of the school, a Christian Japanese, was at the supper, and we had an interesting talk with him. He spent five years in America at Johns Hopkins.

"After supper, Mother gave a talk to the girls of the school. After she had finished, her speech was turned into Japanese by the dean. It certainly seemed queer to have the Gamble family sitting on chairs on the platform, while about eighty girls knelt in front of us listening to Mother's speech being given in Japanese. On the way home, we had our first experience in rikisha-riding at night. There was a little Japanese lantern hanging from the shafts to keep others from running into us." CJG

柔術 **JIŪJITSU** Not far from Chion'in and on the way to Nanzenji is "the spacious hall of Butoku Kwai, or the Military Virtues Society, which was founded in 1896, and now numbers over a million members of both sexes and all ages from eight years upwards. Here may be seen almost daily contests of fencing, jiūjitsu, archery, etc." (Chamberlain 343).

DŌSHISHA DEAN

Motora Yūjirō (1858-1912), Dean of Dōshisha University in 1908, is regarded in Japan as the founder of modern psychology. He earned his Ph.D. in 1888 at Johns Hopkins University and in 1890 became professor of psychology at Tokyo Imperial University.

同志社大学 **DŌSHISHA DAIGAKU** Dōshisha University was founded in 1875 by Niijima Jō, or Joseph Hardy Neesima (his American name) (1843-1890), under the auspices of the American Board of Commissioners for Foreign Missions to serve as a Christian university. At its founding, it included a girls' school, a training school for nurses, and a hospital. In 2012, Dōshisha served 24,000 students.

At twenty-one years of age and risking a death sentence by the Tokugawa, Neesima fled Japan to study science and Christianity in America. He became the first Japanese to become an ordained Protestant minister, graduating from Andover Theological Seminary in 1874. When he returned to Japan in 1875, he founded what was to become Dōshisha University and made western education available to Japanese women.

Miss Mary Florence Denton (1857-1947), with whom the Gambles had supper, was born in California and teaching in Pasadena, when she met Congregational missionaries on furlough. Against her family's wishes, in 1888 she went to Japan and for almost sixty years was a vital part of Dōshisha University, vigorously raising funds and teaching English, the Bible, and Western-style cooking. So famous was her marble cake, that when the Empress of Japan visited Dōshisha in 1924, Miss Denton was asked to serve her cake to the Empress. Still at Dōshisha when World War II broke out, Miss Denton refused to leave what had been her home for so many years and was placed under house arrest. Her students, who dearly loved her, defied all the rules and would sneak away to visit her. After she died at the age of ninety, Miss Denton was awarded the third class Order of the Sacred Treasure, and her home became a museum. In 2012, the Denton Building stands on campus bearing a plaque in honor of Mary Florence Denton.

日本庭園
NIHON TEIEN
Japanese Garden

市場に行く人達 **ICHIBA NI IKU HITOTACHI** *Going to Market* The farmer with his basket is on his way to market. To your right is a jinrikisha man, and behind the right shoulder of the farmer can be seen the face and hat of David Gamble.

特別な日 **TOKUBETSU NA HI** *Special Day* "Mother says that it was a special fete day for Father as he was allowed to ride with his wife in a double rikisha."

彦根 **HIKONE**
彦根城 **Hikone Jō**
Friday 1908 4/24

At the early hour of half past seven this morning, we were in our rikishas and started for a seven-mile ride. Our way lay through the country where we passed many of the Japanese coming into market. One of these failed to get out of the way quick enough to suit our runners and had his vegetables spilled in consequence. The last part of the ride was down a steep hill through a narrow street, where the pedestrians had to flatten themselves against the wall to escape being run over as we came tearing by.

"At nine o'clock, we took a little steamer on Lake Biwa and after a beautiful ride of three hours, we landed at Hikone. We at once set out in rikishas to see the castle. Mother says that it was a special fete day for Father, as he was allowed to ride with his wife in a double rikisha.

"Sidney's man made a mistake and started to take him to the station. Sid knew that he ought to go to the castle and began to consult his guide book to see what he should do. Jinya finally found him by asking two policemen where he was and riding fast after him on his wheel and managed to get him started for the castle. From this building, we had a fine view over the lake and of snow-capped mountains in the distance.

"The castle itself was much like the one at Nagoya, only smaller and not so highly decorated. Leaving it and walking down a steep path, we came to a tea house that was formerly the apartments of the owner of the castle. Here we ate the lunch that we had brought with us from the hotel. We had a beautiful room to ourselves with a good view out over the lake.

(*See next page.*)

The furnishings of the room were very interesting, and we took a number of photos of the interior.

"After lunch we wandered through the garden that surrounded the house and then went to the station where we were to take the train. Soon after we had sat down in the tiny room known as the first-class waiting room, the windows and doors were crowded with spectators. Most of them were students evidently off on a day's trip together. One of them, to show his knowledge of English, asked us, 'You talk English?' and 'Where you go?' A policeman had to clear the way for us when we were ready to leave the waiting room. It seemed almost as though there was a sign that said, 'First-class caged animals being transported under convoy' from the way the people stared at us.

"A half-hour's train ride along the edge of the lake brought us to the head of the canal that led to Kyoto. We hired a small boat and crew and started on our journey. The first two miles were in a tunnel under the range of hills that surrounded the lake. A short distance from the entrance, we found ourselves in total darkness, relieved now and then by the light of a torch on some boat traveling upstream. These were being pulled along by their crews, who hauled on a rope attached to the side of the tunnel.

"It was weird to see the faint lights grow brighter and brighter and then flash by us, giving us a momentary glimpse of the boat and its contents. Beyond the tunnel, the ride was beautiful. The canal wound along the side of a row of hills, which were lighted up by the pink of the setting sun. At the Kyoto end of the canal, we were met by our rikishas and taken back to the hotel."   CJG

MARY GAMBLE
Wearing the same hat and dress as in the photo seen on the opposite page, it would appear that this photo of Mary Gamble was taken during the trip to Hikone Castle.

彦根城 **HIKONE JŌ** *Hikone Castle* stands on the southeast shore of Lake Biwa, just a short trip from Kyoto. Awarded to 井伊直政 Ii Naomasa (1560-1602) after the Battle of Sekigahara in 1600, the castle was until 1874 home to fourteen generations of the Ii family, who traditionally held the position of Chief Minister for the Tokugawa during their years of rule. Construction of the castle took twenty years and was completed in 1622 by the son 井伊直勝 Ii Naokatsu (1590-1662). Under plans of the Meiji, it was to be dismantled; fortunately, the emperor requested it be saved. It remains one of the finest examles of an original construction castle of the feudal period of Japan. With its moats, guard houses, walls, and gates, this beautiful castle allows visitors a glimpse into feudal Japan.

Especially unfortunate is the loss of the photos taken by Clarence and Sidney of the interior and furnishings of the castle rooms, which CJG writes "were very interesting." In 2012, the furnishings are no longer seen within the castle.

Japan 1908

四人の姉妹 **YONIN NO SHIMAI**

Four Sisters in the photo above are wearing their very best kimono. The older girls wear special hair decorations, all in honor of the American guests.

男子生徒 **DANSHI SEITO** *Boy Student*

京都 **KYOTO Saturday 1908 4/25**

A shopping tour occupied the morning. We had lunch at the Gorbolds. Mr. and Mrs. Hale, two missionaries, and Mr. Green, a teacher in a commercial school, were there also.

"In the afternoon, we went with Mrs. Gorbold to call on a Japanese family. We had to leave our shoes at the front door, of course. First, we were escorted into what might be called the reception room. This was without furniture, except for a circle of mats on the floor. The only ornaments on the walls were a kakemono or picture (there is never more than one in a room) and a board over the door on which was written a number of characters. We tried to find out what these meant but were told only by whom they were written. On a shelf at one side of the room was a beautiful lacquered box containing writing materials and a gold lacquer cigar box.

"As soon as we were seated, a bowl of tea and a piece of paper with a little candy on it were placed in front of each of us. The candy was made in the form of iris blossoms. According to the Japanese custom, it is not polite to eat these at once. They must be wrapped up and taken home. We were allowed to take the tea, however, but this was almost too bitter to touch.

(See next page.)

After we had admired everything in the room, we went out into the garden. This was very pretty. We took a picture here of the children of the family. There were four girls and one boy. The oldest daughter was married. She was practically the hostess.

"After we had seen the garden, we were shown into a room where there was a piano. Mother was asked to play a piece, which seemed to be much appreciated. The children of the family gave us two Japanese songs with a one-finger accompaniment on the piano.

"Refreshments were served in this room, also. This time, they were tea and cream puffs. The hostess, through Mrs. Gorbold as an interpreter (all our conversation had to be carried on in this way), asked us if we wouldn't eat these there and not take them home. There were no forks, so as you may imagine, we had a time in eating them, and I'm afraid I nearly disgraced myself. The little girls of the family had the hardest time of it, but managed to get some of it in the right place. Let us hope that the next foreign visitors will not be placed in a like predicament.

"Before we left, Mother was presented with a doll dressed in the court clothes of some centuries ago. I wonder if this is the usual thing for a call. Although we said that it was time for us to leave, we were taken into the ceremonial tea room where some tea was made for us in the prescribed style. This time, a maid mixed it in our presence with slow and precise movements. When we left, we carried with us the cakes that had been placed before us when we came, and quite a bundle they made.

(*See next page.*)

雛祭り **HINAMATSURI** Doll Festival on the 3rd of March is a day celebrating girls, such as those at play in this photo to the right. Around the middle of February, a platform of multiple tiers is set up in the home and on it are arranged *hinaningyō*—dolls dressed in the ancient Japanese court costume of the Heian period (794-1192) representing the Emperor, the Empress, and their retinue, including musicians, along with furniture and accessories belonging to the Imperial Court. The custom of exhibiting dolls grew out of the ancient belief that dolls possessed the power to contain bad spirits and would prevent the bad spirits from hurting those who owned the dolls.

On March 3rd, the girls dress in their very best and visit their friends. A special meal is served: *hishi mochi* (diamond-shaped rice cakes) and *shirozake* (white rice wine), along with sushi rice topped with raw fish called *chirashizushi*, and a salt-based soup containing clams in their shell.

ままごと遊び
MAMAGOTO ASOBI
At Play with Bows
These little girls wearing traditional Japanese dress will celebrate Hinamatsuri.

Japan 1908 39

鳥居
TORII

京都 **KYOTO**
北野天満宮
Kitano Tenmangū
Saturday 1908 4/25

On our way home, we went to the Kitano temple where Mr. Gorbold was doing some preaching from a tent. It was a special festival for the temple, and the grounds were crowded. Small booths selling pipes, toys, hair ornaments, and many other things were packed close to each other on both sides of the approach to the temple. Around Mr. Gorbold's tent, there was an especially large crowd listening to the preaching through the megaphone and buying the testaments and tracts that were offered for sale. The main part of the crowd went up to the temple, threw their coppers into an immense box, clapped their hands, said their prayers, and went away. (*See next page*.)

"KITANO TEMPLE"
Kitano Tenmangū is a shrine, not a temple. Clarence was apparently unaware of the distinction.

40 Japan 1908

"A medicinal cow was one of the attractions of the place. We saw several people go up to this stone cow. They would rub the part of their body that was in trouble and then rub the corresponding part of the cow and then themselves again. This was supposed to cure the disease, but we thought that it would be more apt to spread it." CJG

NOTE In the lower left of the photo above, a man, who may be Jinya, stands beside the stone cow. This gives an idea of the size of the statue.

NADEUSHI 撫牛
Stroking Cow

北野天満宮 **KITANO TENMANGŪ** was built in honor of the scholar and literary man Sugawara Michizane (845-903), whom university students worship as their patron of learning. Sugawara, a trusted favorite official of Emperor Uda (867-931), was maliciously slandered, leading to his exile from Kyoto to Kyūshū, where he died. Following his death, the home provinces suffered severe storms and earthquakes, and those who had slandered him met with unusual deaths. The populace became convinced that the cause was the angry spirit of the unjustly exiled Sugawara. Finally, Kitano Tenmangū was built to appease his wrathful spirit. In August 987, the first Kitano *matsuri*, a festival celebrating the grain harvest, was held; it continues yearly to this day. Similarly, a flea market and bazaar are on the grounds of Kitano Tenmangū on the 25th of each month, as they has been since long before the visit by the Gambles in 1908. Kitano Tenmangū is very much a destination for those who believe in the healing power of the "medicinal cow," which Clarence mentions.

三光門
SANKŌMON
Gate of Three Great Lights
Central Gate of KItano Tenmangū

Japan 1908

京都 **KYOTO**
Sunday 1908 4/26

"Felt rather tired this morning, so spent most of the time resting. In the afternoon, I did some reading and writing." CJG

京都 **KYOTO**
都おどり
Miyako Odori
Monday 1908 4/27

"Father, Sidney, and Jinya went off to Yamada this morning, leaving Mother and me to shift for ourselves. I started off alone in the morning to do some shopping. The rikisha boy was directed by the clerk, and we (for he followed me everywhere) got along finely. I didn't know how to ask the price of the things I wanted, so the rikisha boy would suggest that the shopkeeper would show me the price in money. The little china stores where I stopped were queer in their arrangements but in their stock were not very different from some of the cheap stores in our country.

"In the afternoon, Mother and I went on a shopping tour with Mrs. Gorbold, first down theatre street, which is one of the sights of the city. We stopped at some of the little shops that are crowded in between the theatre entrances to get some samples of hair ornaments. Later, we went to a kakemono store. Here a great number of the Japanese wall pictures were for sale. With the Japs, as with us, the name of the artist and the age of the picture seem to count for more than anything else in determining the price of the picture.

"At about six, we went to see the cherry dance. First, all the 'foreign' visitors were seated around a large room behind little low tables. Tea, the usual bitter Japanese kind, and bean cakes were served. The first cup of tea was made in the slow ceremonial way, and then the other bowls were brought in quickly by little girls, who were being trained to become geisha dancers. After tea, we went across a rustic bridge into the theatre proper. Benches were provided for us in the 'dress circle,' but it was much more interesting to sit farther forward on the floor where we could get a good view of the Japanese audience below us in the pit. This was rapidly filled and, when it seemed impossible for any more to crowd in, the dance began. On either side of the audience sat the orchestra. One lot had drums, cymbals, and gongs which they used at different times, while those on the other side had banjo-like instruments. The movements of the dancers were quite pretty at times, and their gorgeous costumes, all alike, were quite striking.

都おどり **MIYAKO ODORI**
Cherry Dances "No one visiting Kyoto during the cherry blossom season in April should fail to see the *Miyako Odori*, a fascinating kind of ballet given every evening from 5 to 10 o'clock at Hanami-kōji, near the Gion-za Theatre" (Chamberlain 320).

"The method of changing the scenery was interesting. A street scene was turned over to become a house with a veranda and a flight of stairs down which the dancers came at their appearance. The house disappeared by being hauled up out of sight to reveal a beautiful garden. Later, a board at the front of the stage swung back with a bang, and a row of chrysanthemums grew up with many stops and jerks. A fringe of pine boughs was lowered and raised at intervals. The last scene was the prettiest. The entrance to a castle was raised and turned flat, revealing hundreds of candles hanging down from the sky. A beautiful cherry tree lighted by red torches occupied the center of the stage." CJG

The shop below is selling tea and sweets. Cherry blossoms indicate the photo was taken in the spring.

山田 **YAMADA** hosts travellers to the city of Ise, where lying on its outskirts are some one hundred and fifty-five Shinto shrines. Included is Jingū, the Ise Grand Shrine, the most sacred shrine in Japan. For many, to achieve any success in life depends on at least one pilgrimage to Ise to invoke the protection of Amaterasu Ōmikami, ancestor of the Mikado, and Toyouke Ōmikami, the goddess who cares for Amaterasu Ōmikami. In 1907, more than a half-million pilgrims were visiting Ise annually.

As with all temple towns, the sacred does not inhibit the secular, and the inns and tea houses in the area were very lively, "especially at night." Part of the pilgrimage in 1908 involved viewing sacred performances, such as *Ise Ondo*, a graceful dance of great antiquity. Unfortunately, writes Chamberlain, *Ise Ondo* "is generally to be witnessed only at houses of a doubtful character " (301-302). Yamada was a rigorous day's journey from Kyoto, and remaining at the Kyoto Hotel and its metropolitan comforts must have seemed much more preferable to Mary than elbowing crowds of pilgrims and putting up with what were probably the less-than-comfortable appointments of Yamada inns.

外宮 **GEKŪ** *Gekū* is the common name for Toyouke Daijingū, one of two groups of buildings comprising Jingū, the Ise Grand Shrine. Gekū, the outer shrine complex, is dedicated to Toyouke Ōmikami, goddess of agriculture, who brings food to Amaterasu.

Naikū, the inner shrine, is dedicated to the sun goddess, Amaterasu Ōmikami, whose serene light blesses all indiscriminately. For 1300 years, the shrines have been rebuilt every twenty years in accordance with the Shinto ritual of renewal, exactly reproducing the original buildings.

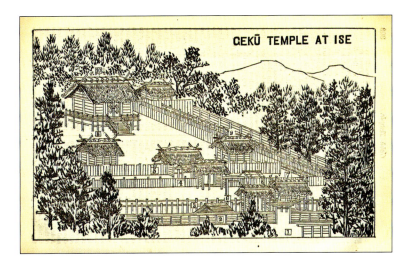

夫婦岩 **MEOTO IWA** *Wedded Rocks* lie south of Nagoya along the coast of Futami, Mie, close to Jingū, the Ise Grand Shrine. These great rocks celebrate the sanctity of marriage and so are "wedded" and tied together. The larger represents Izanagi, the husband; the smaller, Izanami, the wife, who according to the myth are the earliest *kami*, deities who gave birth to the Islands of Japan. On the larger rock rests a *torii*, a sacred gateway. A *shimenawa*, a heavy rope of rice straw weighing over a ton, joins the rocks and is renewed three times a year.

Viewing the rocks at sunrise, the sun appears between them and sometimes in the distance can be seen the shadow of Mount Fuji. The photo right would have been taken by Sidney, who went with David to Yamada, while Clarence and Mary remained in Kyoto.

ISE 伊勢
MEOTO IWA 夫婦
Wedded Rocks

京都 **KYOTO**
金閣寺 **Kinkakuji**
Tuesday 1908 4/28

Mother and I ventured out alone this morning. Our coolies were instructed at the hotel, and we set off at a good pace to the Golden Pavilion. After one or two stops for photographs, we reached our destination in safety. At the entrance, we bought our admission tickets, had our shoe covers put on, and started in. We didn't know exactly what we were to do. We wandered through a little gate that we found open and then decided to wait for a guide. Suddenly, a girl came down upon us from somewhere and with frantic motions shooed us back through the gate and motioned to some benches where we were to wait.

"After some other people had appeared, our guide, an old man, came in and took us through the building. Around a little veranda and through rooms we went, accompanied by the singing of the old man, who was telling the histories of the rooms, as near as we could judge. The numerous kakemonos, though not very interesting to us, were to the Japanese old and valuable works of art, no doubt.

"In one place, almost enclosed by the irregular house, was a pine tree trained in the form of a boat. I thought that I would take a picture of it, but as soon as I got out my camera, the guide began calling something to me as fast as he could. Fearing I had done something wrong, I shut up my camera as quickly as possible and started along. The guide kept pointing to a little ridge in the garden, and I finally understood that he wanted me to take the picture from there. I took off my cotton overshoes and obediently went out where the guide pointed and took the photo. Although I delayed the procession, Mother thinks that they were fully repaid by the interest of watching me.

"At the end of the tour, tea and cake were served. We were all seated in a line and a small tray passed to each one. We didn't care for any tea and so shook our heads when the boy offered us some, but he kept kneeling in front of us until we helped ourselves.

"Refreshments over, we were ushered into the garden, where we saw the Kinkakuji, or the gold pavilion itself. It isn't gilded all over as you might expect from the name, but only the walls of the top room and the underside of the eaves are covered with gold paper.
(*See next page.*)

金閣寺 陸舟の松
KINKAKUJI RIKUSHU NO MATSU

Boat in Pine Tree at Kinkakuji In the photo left, the base of a boat can be seen amidst the lower branches of the pine tree at Kinkakuji (鹿苑寺 *Rokuon-ji*). Pine trees symbolize longevity, and the boat will take the soul to heaven.

While we were in the garden, a Jap that looked like a student stepped up to us and asked, 'You spik English?' We admitted that we did, and he apparently wished to continue the conversation further. We didn't know what he wanted, so I'm afraid we didn't do our share.

"On the way back to the hotel, we saw a temple that looked interesting, so we decided to stop. We found that it was Kitano, the one we had visited on Saturday, but how changed! None of the booths or the crowds were visible, and it looked like an entirely different place. On one side of the temple was a large box filled with little strips of bamboo on which were some characters. We found out afterwards that these were used to count the number of times a devotee walked around the temple. He would pick out as many sticks as the number of times that he wished to make the tour and then drop one each round until they were gone. On the sticks were written names, and the owner of the name shared in the benefit to be gained from the circular promenade.

"In the afternoon, we visited the exposition again, this time going into the art gallery where old kakemonos and screen paintings were exhibited. I purchased a globe of goldfish. For the sum of two and three-fourths cents, I secured three goldfish, a small globe, and a net to hang it up with."
CJG

金閣寺庭園
KINKAKUJI TEIEN
Kinkakuji Gardens

金閣寺 **KINKAKUJI** *Golden Pavilion* A large palace complex built in the last decade of the fourteenth century by 足利義満 Ashikaga Yoshimitsu (1358-1408), third Ashikaga Shogun. Yoshimitsu was a vigorous leader, who curtailed piracy and restored trade with China after a six-hundred-year lapse. The political stability that he brought allowed development of a luxurious court life; enriched cultural advances in Noh theatre, garden design, fine painting; and the building of great temples and palaces, the one most famous today, the Kinkakuji. Buddhist monks filled court positions. After Yoshimitsu died, his magnificent villa, emblematic of his ambition and career, was converted into a Zen Buddhist temple.

The grounds feature a beautiful garden whose design remains completely unchanged from its original, with a lake surrounded by pines, and within the lake small islands of pines and flowering lotus (*junsai*). Of the many complex buildings that once existed, there remains only the three-story villa, now the Pavilion, which draws its name from the gilded third floor. The Gambles saw the Pavilion after its restoration of 1906. In 1950, a deranged monk set fire to the Pavilion, and it was totally destroyed. In 1955, it was reconstructed in accordance with the original design of Yoshimitsu. The deranged monk's story is the basis of a novel by Mishima Yukio, *The Temple of the Golden Pavilion*.

奈良 NARA
東大寺 Tōdaiji
Wednesday 1908 4/29

"We met Mrs. Gorbold at the station at nine this morning and, after an hour's ride on the train, arrived at Nara. We engaged rikishas and started off to see the temple. On the way, we stopped to feed the turtles. The food that is sold near the pond is very light and floats high up in the water. It is great fun to see the turtles pushing it around trying hard to get a bite. In time, it gets water-soaked, and then they can swallow it very easily.

"At the entrance to the temple, we fed the deer. Here again, there is specially prepared food, this time rice cakes containing a good deal of salt. We picked out a place to eat our basket lunch, and then I started back to the station to meet Father, Sidney, and the guide. I bought a platform ticket and then asked for a train coming from Yamada. This came in but failed to bring the people I wanted.

"As I was on the platform and yet didn't get on the train, the guards were quite excited. I finally found a guard that could talk English and explained my case to him. The conductor said he had seen some foreigners get off at Kidzu.* The station master at Nara then telephoned to Kidzu that there was a boy lost and asked them to tell the party of Americans there. It seems that Jinya expected to get on the train that was to have brought us to Nara. We had taken an earlier train, however, and so we both missed each other. They arrived at last, and we were united for dinner.

"After our refreshment, we visited the big things of Nara, the big cryptomaria [sic], the large temple, the big buddha, and the big bell. We also saw an immense number of stone lanterns erected by wealthy persons as a monument to themselves. There are said to be about three thousand in all. One of them is over a thousand years old."
CJG   *Kizu Station *Junction for numerous railway lines.*

奈良公園と鹿
NARA KŌEN TO SHIKA
Nara Park and Deer

奈良公園 **NARA KŌEN**
Famous in 1908 as well as today in the twenty-first century for its many deer roaming freely throughout Nara Park

奈良 **NARA** Twenty-six miles southeast of Kyoto lies Nara, the capital of Japan from 710 to 784. During the Nara period, Buddhism, with support from the government, became well established, and with its establishment, the arts, crafts, and literature, including early Japanese poetry, blossomed. The well-known temples and shrines of Nara date from its beginnings in 710, and in the twenty-first century, many of the shrines and temples along with the Kasugayama Primeval Forest are a UNESCO World Heritage Site.

The Gambles first fed the turtles, then the free-roaming deer for which Nara Park is famous. An ancient myth tells of a white deer bringing the god Takemikazuchi to guard the city of Nara, and so the deer came to be considered messengers of the gods, sacred animals—perhaps regarded as less than divine by the tourist, who endures bites and forceful nudges from the sacred animals so very aggressively demanding the deer biscuits that are expected.

Within Nara Park is 東大寺 Tōdaiji (*Great Eastern Temple*) established in 752 to serve as central administrative temple for the state sponsored Buddhists. There are "the big things of Nara." The largest wooden building in the world until 1998, Daibutsuden (Big Buddha Hall), was reconstructed in 1698 and is two thirds the size of the original Daibutsuden. Within it sits Buddha Dainichi, the Daibutsu, the "Big Buddha," a fifteen-meter (approximately fifty-foot) high gilt bronze—now quite black—statue, the largest statue in the world of Buddha Vairocana. The making of the statue consumed most of Japan's available bronze at the time and nearly bankrupted the economy. The "big bell" that Clarence writes of is also at Tōdaiji and is one of the three largest bells in Japan. When struck with the large timber that functions as a striker, or mallet, the sound of the bell is said to last for two minutes and can be heard four miles away.

Around 春日大社 Kasuga Taisha stands the Kasugayama Primeval Forest, a sacred old-growth forest where cutting has been forbidden since 841, now closed to the public. Evergreen broad leaf trees grow there, oak and beech, as well as the Japanese cedar, the "big cryptomaria" [sic]. The Japanese cedar are commonly planted around shrines and temples throughout Japan, and Clarence writes again of cryptomeria when the Gambles are in Nikkō.

Kasuga Taisha—*taisha* referring to the oldest architectural style of building shrines—is one of the great shrines of Japan, founded in the early sixth century by the Fujiwara to protect the city of Nara. The stone lanterns—some say as many as three thousand—that line the pathway to Kasuga Taisha and the bronze lanterns that hang from the eves, hundreds and hundreds of them, have been donated in faith and gratitude throughout the centuries by devout worshippers.

不動 **FUDŌ** *God of Wisdom*
Chamberlain identifies Buddha Vairocana with Fudō, personification of purity and wisdom, the flames surrounding Fudō representing wisdom (46).

春日大社 石灯籠
KASUGA TAISHA ISHIDŌRŌ
Kasuga Grand Shrine Stone Lanterns
A few of the "immense number" of stone lanterns

Japan 1908   47

THE GAMBLES ON THE ROAD David is behind Mary, as we can see by his hat, and Sidney appears to be last. No doubt Clarence took the photo.

京都近郊 KYOTO Environs

巡礼 JUNREI *Pilgrims* These pilgrims are wearing straw sandals and loose jackets and carrying the pilgrim's staff. Their pilgrimage could take two days or two weeks.

"Most Japanese villages undertake annual pilgrimages, more or less extended according to the means at command, to the sacred mountains and holy places of Japan, or at least of the immediate vicinity. Everybody cannot go, and therefore delegates are chosen each year to represent the community, and to offer worship on its behalf. The expenses of these pilgrimages are borne by the whole village in common.

"The pilgrims are dressed in cheap white cotton garments which can easily be washed, tight fitting trousers, shirt, and a loose jacket which can be tucked into the girdle. On their heads they have a broad, stiff hat of straw, which affords a splendid shade against the sun; on their backs, a light piece of matting, which protects them from rain by day, and at night serves as a bed. Their luggage is strapped on behind and in front, in two small bundles, the one in front being often wrapped in oil-paper and bearing the name or mark of the particular shrine to which the pilgrims have given their confidence. In the right hand is the pilgrim's staff of white wood, round the left wrist a rosary, and attached to the girdle a small bell which tingles as they go. Their feet are shod with *waraji*, the simple straw sandal, which can be bought anywhere at the cost of one of the smallest copper coins issued from the Imperial Mint.

"The pilgrims travel by train, by coach, by jinrikisha even, when fatigue compels them to do so; but they are supposed to travel as cheaply as they can, and mostly go on foot. They work their way from mountain to mountain. They will begin, for instance, with Mount Tsukuba, the solitary two-peaked hill near Mito, which legend connects to the first creation of the Japanese archipelago ... At a little shrine near the top they will pray. ...When you next see them they will be swarming out from the railway station at Nikkō.... Then they will climb to Chūzenji....When you meet them again it may be [they] are now on their way to Fuji."

Arthur Lloyd, "The Village Pilgrimage,"
Every-day Japan
London: Cassell and Company (1909) 145-156.

京都 KYOTO
二条城 Nijō Jō
Thursday 1908 4/30

Mr. and Mrs. Gamble and the two daughters went out again today, this time to visit Nijo castle, another palace. The chief difference from the other palaces that we have seen was in the highly ornamented ceilings and the numerous tigers. The latter were in every imaginable place and position, grinning, sleeping (at least their eyes were closed), flying, jumping, fighting, or making their toilets.

"Later in the morning, we stopped in at a small shop where we picked out a few good sword guards and menukes. The latter were small ornaments taken off the hilts of old swords. Our offer of half the price that was asked for them was immediately accepted, much to our surprise.

"We also saw some samples of gold lacquer work. This must be very tedious work, as they say the wood must be lacquered and polished forty times before it is finished. It is hard to tell what work is really good and what is poorly done. Some time ago, the rich men of the land would keep good workmen on their payrolls continuously to make this lacquer ware for them. Time was of no importance to them, so they always did their best work. Since the introduction of the tourist, quality has become of less value and quantity of a great deal more.

"In the afternoon, Sidney and I went off on a shopping tour by ourselves. We have learned the Japanese numbers now and a few other expressions so that we can do our shopping without an interpreter. Later, Father and Sidney went to see the cherry dance."   CJG

福禄寿
FUKURYOKUJU
*God of Long Life & Happiness
One of the Seven
Gods of Luck*

二条城 **NIJŌ JŌ** *Nijō Castle* Tokugawa Ieyasu (1543-1616), third of The Unifiers, ordered construction of Nijō Castle, and it was the setting for the official recognition of the Tokugawa takeover in 1603 and the site of their resignation from power in 1867. In 1626, extensive renovations were made for the visit of the Emperor Go-Mizunoo (1596-1680). These renovations secured in the Ninomaru Palace a treasure of brilliant paintings from artists of the Kanō school, which somehow survived the fires that destroyed other of the castle buildings. Clarence was fascinated with the paintings of the tigers, but also to be seen were vivid artworks of birds, trees, and flowers, as well as rich but subdued mountain and water scenes. The extraordinary art continues to attract tourists to this day.

S. HAYASHI, fourth-generation art and rare antiquities dealer, soft-spoken and well known in Kyoto. His shop was mentioned online as open at 39, Furumonzen-dori in 2008. This S. Hayashi advertisement was included in the 1907 *Handbook for Travellers*.

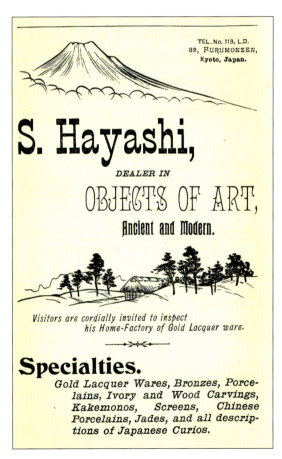

Japan 1908

京都 **KYOTO**
東本願寺 **Higashi Honganji**
Friday 1908 5/1

T he whole morning was spent in getting our wardrobes and our many purchases into our trunks. In the afternoon, when things were pretty nearly cleared up, we went to Hongwanji [*sic*], the largest temple in Kyoto. The main room of this temple contains over a thousand mats or eighteen thousand square feet. Jinya says that the farmers near Kyoto will work hard and live on a very little that they may bring their savings to the temple. Generally, they give about fifty dollars a year. One of the curiosities of the temple is an immense coil of rope made of human hair. Thousands of women are said to have contributed their hair to make this rope with which the parts of the temple were hoisted into place. In front of the temple is an immense court with a large bell, some pretty lanterns, and a fountain in the shape of a lotus leaf.

"On the way home, we stopped at the Gorbolds for a few minutes. I have had a seal made with my name written in Japanese characters on it. Here it is. Can you read it?" CJG

クラレンス ギャンブルス

東本願寺 **HIGASHI HONGANJI** *Eastern Temple of the Original Vow of Jōdo Shinshū Buddhism* (*True Pure Land Buddhism*). *Jōdo Shinshū has historically inspired great devotion from its followers, even as Jinya says.*

Lafcadio Hearn visited Higashi Honganji in 1895 for the dedication of Goei-dō, the Founder's Hall, seventeen years in construction and one of the largest wooden buildings in the world. Hearn wrote admiringly of the "hard-working peasants" who had built Goei-dō through their own physical exertions and their hard-earned donations of money. After describing its dimensions, "one hundred and twenty-seven feet high, one hundred and ninety-two feet deep, and more than two hundred feet long"; the size of its beams, "forty-two feet long and four feet thick"; and pillars, "nine feet in circumference," Hearn continues: "For no small part of the actual labor of building was done for love only; and the mighty beams for the roof had been hauled to Kyoto from far-away mountain slopes, with cables made of the hair of Buddhist wives and daughters." One such cable, preserved in the temple, is more than three hundred and sixty feet long and nearly three inches in diameter. The need for the ropes of human hair arose when conventional ropes became unavailable and the devout were determined to continue without interruption the construction of the temple.

In Kyoto, "Honganji" is the collective name for the two major branches and temples of Jōdo Shinshū Buddhism. Higashi Honganji is headquarters of the Otani branch; a few blocks to the west stands Nishi Honganji, The Western Temple of the Original Vow. This organizational split dates from 1602, when Shogun Tokugawa Ieyasu perceived the great popularity of Jōdo Shinshū among the populace as a threat to his government and ordered the massive organization to divide itself into two, thereby reducing its power.

鐘撞き堂と手洗鉢
KANETSUKIDŌ TO CYOUZUBACHI
Small Bell Tower & Purification Basin Lotus-leaf-shaped structure in the photo left is part of Higashi Honganji.

侵雪橋
SHINSETSUKYŌ
Snow-Capped Bridge

渉成園
SHŌSEIEN
Pond Strolling Garden

SHŌSEIEN 渉成園
also known as
KIKOKUTEI 枳殻邸

東本願寺庭園
Higashi Honganji Teien
Higashi Honganji Gardens

銅灯籠 **DŌU TŌRŌ** *Copper Lantern*

傘をさす紳士 **KASA O SASU SHINSHI**
Gentleman with Paper Umbrella

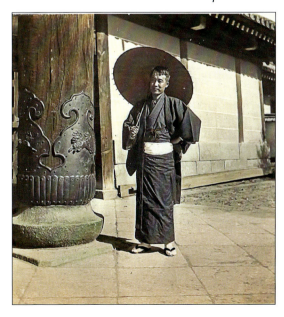

東海道 **TŌKAIDŌ** *East Sea Road* started at Kyoto and ran along the eastern seacoast of Honshū to Tokyo, then called Edo. The Tōkaidō came into existence after the Tokugawa government demanded that every *daimyō*, every great lord, travel to Edo every other year to reside there for a full year, travelling each time with a stipulated number of attendants. In the case of one lord of the Maeda clan, that *daimyō* traveled with approximately 10,000 retainers. The Tōkaidō was in constant use, not only by the great lords and their retinue, but by the common people: merchants, pilgrims, farmers, and tradesmen—pretty much all of Japan. It took these foot travellers twelve to thirteen days to reach Tokyo from Kyoto; in 1903, with the railway, the trip was made in fifteen hours.

The Tōkaidō Railway followed most of the route of the Eastern Sea Road; the first stretch was begun in 1872 and finished in 1889. On 7/15, when the Gambles take the train from Yokohama to Nagoya, Clarence describes the route of their train as it follows the Tōkaidō: "Most of the way, the tracks ran between the sea on one side and steep mountains on the other."

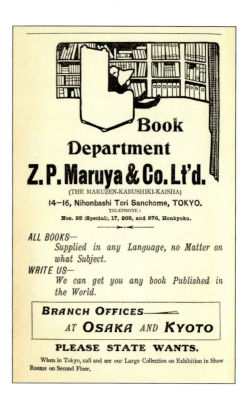

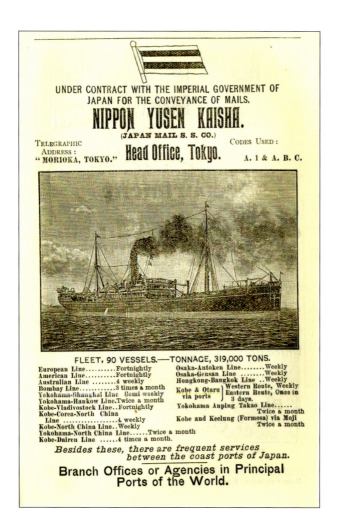

大阪 **OSAKA** long a cultural and commercial center, located about three-quarters of an hour from Kyoto on the Tōkaidō and, along with Tokyo and Kyoto, one of the three most important cities in Japan. In 1860, with the opening of Japan to Western trade, Osaka became the site of many factories, including many cotton mills, built to supply the new markets. By 1907, Osaka was a thriving and gritty industrial center, "a dirty and smoky city." But the tourist in 1908 also found there many fine shops, such as Yamanaka's and other curio dealers, some of whom specialized in Satsuma porcelain.

Clarence writes of the temple Shitennō-ji, which lies in downtown south Osaka. It was founded in 593 when Buddhism was being introduced into Japan. In 1907, a large new stone dancing stage had been laid, and behind it stood a large bronze bell that had been cast in 1902, sixteen feet in diameter at the mouth, weighing over 155 tons, said in 1907 to be the largest bell in the world. Nearby stands the pagoda of five stories.

大阪 OSAKA
四天王寺 **Shitennoji**
Saturday 1908 5/2

Packing is all done now, and we are on our way to China. The rikisha men that we have had for the last two weeks escorted us onto the station platform. As we got into the train, they bowed and smiled and again when they saw us through the window. One of the ladies in our car, a resident of Kyoto, said that those coolies certainly must have been treated well.

"Osaka, where we arrived after an hour's ride, is a dirty and smoky city of rough streets and long distances. One of the missionaries met us at the station and took us to a cotton spinning factory. We were shown through some of the quarters where the three thousand girl employees are housed.

"Each girl is allowed a space six feet by three for sleeping. About twelve girls occupy each room at night and twelve more in the daytime. A large court is provided for recreation, and there are schoolrooms and teachers for those that desire them. One room is devoted to a store for dress goods and hair ornaments and another for a hospital.

"The girls work in twelve-hour shifts, being allowed one hour for lunch and recreation. The wages are from ten to thirty cents a day, four of which are paid for board and lodging. The superintendent told us that the board really costs them seven and a half cents, but they gave the difference to the girls as a part of their wages. How would it seem to live on four or even seven and a half cents a day in the United States?

"After lunch at the missionary's house, we started off to see the temple. Here we had our first sight of a pagoda. There was also a large bell near the temple cast in memory of the soldiers that died in the Russian war. This did not look very well, as it was covered by a scaffolding so that they could carve the names of the fallen upon it. The many cobblestone streets and the rikishas without rubber tires made riding in Osaka rather hard.

"Another hour on the train took us to Kobe, where we once more met Jinya."   CJG

四天王寺 **SHITENNŌJI** Largest temple in Osaka as well as the oldest temple in Japan. It was founded in 593 by Prince Shōtoku (573-621), who promoted Buddhism in Japan. Its buildings, including the five-storied pagoda, have been reconstructed many times, always in accordance with their original design, and have given their name to the Shitennōji temple style of architecture.

MADO NO SOUJI 窓の掃除
Washing Windows

Japan 1908   53

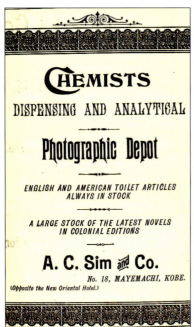

神戸 **KOBE** was founded in 1868 as a Foreign Settlement, when, after two centuries of isolation, Japan opened trade to the West. Kobe quickly became a leading port of Japan, preferred because of the dryness of the air and its proximity to such desirable points of interest as Kyoto, Lake Biwa, and Nara.

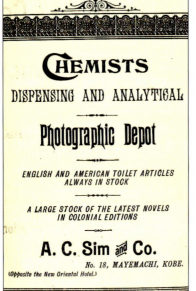

神戸 **KOBE**
Sunday 1908 5/3

"Was spent mainly in resting. We did some reading and a good deal of writing in the afternoon."   CJG

神戸 **KOBE**
Monday 1908 5/4

"We visited the 'Glory Kindergarten' this morning. Here we saw the children at work on their little gardens. Although it was cloudy, we managed to get some very good photos of some of the boys. A short distance from the kindergarten was a Christian college for girls. We were shown all around this place. The equipment seems very good and well kept up. Returning to the kindergarten, we saw the closing exercises. Umbrellas and the tall rainy day shoes were much in evidence, and they were needed, for it started to rain as the children left.

"Miss Howe, the kindergartner, took us to see a girls' public school. Here the schools for the girls and those for the boys are always separated. The building seemed very different from those we have at home. In general plan, it is like a figure eight, for it is built around two courts.

"We had lunch at the home of Miss Howe and an interesting talk with her afterwards. On the way back to the hotel, we stopped at a florist's where they had an exhibition of peonies. In the pouring rain, we had to get out of our rikishas and splashed through puddles of water to the little building where the flowers were growing. At the entrance, there was a sign that informed us in large capitals that 'VISITORS ARE REQUESTED NOT TO ACCOMPANY DOG IN GARDEN.' As we didn't have any dog to accompany, we managed to get in all right.

"It is time for the 'Mongolia' to leave now, but she has not arrived as yet. I suppose we will have at least another day in Kobe."   CJG

Chamberlain recommends a visit to Kobe for the following specific items:

"The pretty basket-work sold at Kobe is made in Arima. The 'Kobe beef' highly esteemed all over the Far East, comes mostly from the province of Tajima to the N.W. The finest sake in Japan is manufactured at Nada, about 2 miles E. of Kobe" (308).

54   Japan 1908

神戸 KOBE
Tuesday 1908 5/5

The 'Mongolia' has arrived after a delay caused by fog. There was good sunlight this morning, so I started out to get some photos. I also decided to get materials to make a kite to occupy some of the spare time. At one shop, after much inquiry, I managed to get some string. At another, I got a roll of Japanese writing paper. I had a good deal of trouble in getting the sticks but finally found some at a bucket factory. They use bamboo strips here for binding the buckets together. You may imagine what a time I had finding and purchasing all these things when I could not say anything except to inquire the price. The string was the priciest. I found a likely store and then had to draw a picture of a kite and string and point to the latter before I could make my want known. Soon after lunch, I took the completed kite out in front of the hotel and soon had it flying nicely. I was immediately surrounded by a mob of children and grown-ups. Sidney got a good photo of the curious crowd. I put some pieces of paper on the string to send up to the kite. This seems to be quite a novelty to the natives, judging from the way they looked at it, laughed, and even shouted when the paper reached the kite. It seemed to be a very amusing sight to them. At about five, we went aboard the 'Mongolia' and found our staterooms. Jinya came aboard with us and stayed until the next launch went ashore. The ship left the harbor at ten." CJG

端午の節句 **TANGO NO SEKKU** *Boys' Day*, the fifth of May (now Children's Day), when all over Japan are seen *Koi Nobori*, carp swimming through the air. Carp streamers made of paper or cloth catch the wind and are flown outside the homes of families with sons, the number of carp corresponding to the number of sons. The largest carp at the top of the bamboo pole represents the oldest son, the smaller carp below representing progressively the younger sons. Because the carp is regarded as a powerful, aggressive fish, capable of surmounting swift-running streams and great obstacles to reach its destination, it is considered the suitable symbol of the type of manhood desired for sons.

Boys' Day is celebrated with figures of heroic warriors placed in the *tokonoma* in the home. The children receive traditional delicacies such as *Chimaki*, sweet rice dumplings wrapped in iris or bamboo leaves, or *Kashiwa Mochi*, rice cakes with sweet bean paste wrapped in oak leaves. The exact origin of Boys' Festival is unknown, but it may have had its beginnings as far back as the sixth century, or it may be attributed to the celebration of the victory of Hōjō Tokimune (1251-1284) over the invading Mongols on 5 May 1282.

Carp Streamers **KOI NOBORI** 鯉幟

下関 SHIMONOSEKI
Wednesday 1908 5/6

We awoke this morning to find ourselves steaming past little islands dotted with houses. Until about four o'clock, when we passed through the straits of Shimonoseki, we were in sight of land all the time. In the straits, we saw a great many steamers at anchor and large factories on the shore. Although the place was probably strongly fortified, we could see no evidence of any forts."* CJG

*Forts *Japan was believed to have built many forts during the Russo-Japanese War of 1904-05.*

Japan 1908

長崎 NAGASAKI
Thursday 1908 5/7

After the usual medical inspection and our breakfast, we hurried out on deck to see Nagasaki and the beginning of coaling operations. Scaffolding was being put up on the side of the ships with steps about three feet apart. Large coal barges were towed to the side of the ship, and boat loads of men and women came out from the shore. The loading of the coal was all done by hand. Straw baskets were filled on the barge and then were passed up the lines of men and women, who stood on the scaffolding. Up and up they came, handed rapidly from one to another, until the person at the top of the line dumped the contents into the hold and dropped the empty basket back to the barge.

"In some places inside the ship, the coal chutes did not empty into the hold. Here the coal was caught in baskets, and men with two of these full baskets hung from a pole would walk to the center of the steamer and drop the black diamonds to their final destination. Here are some of the figures of the operation: *(See next page.)*

長崎 NAGASAKI From the sixteenth through the nineteenth centuries, Nagasaki was the open port through which, first, the Portuguese, then the Dutch conducted trade between Japan and the rest of the world. It was also the point of entry for the evangelizing Jesuits, who arrived in south Kyūshū in 1549 and who left Nagasaki a permanent Catholic center. With the Restoration of the Meiji, Nagasaki rapidly built up its heavy industry, especially shipbuilding, with Mitsubishi the primary contractor for the Imperial Japanese Navy.

石炭の積み荷
SEKITAN NO TSUMINI *Loading Coal*

Generally, there were about thirty-five people to each barge. Their wages averaged six cents a day. In two hours and a half, they could load twenty tons of coal, sometimes passing as many as sixty baskets a minute. Twenty-two barges were being unloaded at once.

"At about nine, we went ashore to visit some of the curio shops. Nagasaki is very well provided with rikishas. Almost every step you take and certainly every time you stop, a rikisha man offers his services. Often they say 'Mogi? Want go Mogi? I can take Mogi.' Apparently, Mogi is one of the chief attractions of Nagasaki. It is a little town on the sea coast.

"We went to the post office and then to some of the tortoise shell stores. The latter are very numerous. They offer everything imaginable for sale that can be made from real or imitation tortoise shell. We returned to our boat by hiring a sampan, or one-man power launch.

"We found that the curio sellers had invaded the steamer and tried to waylay people all over the deck. As the day progressed, their prices gradually descended, but as a whole, their things were very poor." CJG

門司区 **MOJI** A small town on an island about four miles from Nagazaki with a port vital to coal shipping and transportation of troops during the Russo-Japanese War. Currently, the historic buildings of Moji are of great interest and a draw for tourists.

長崎 **NAGASAKI**
Friday 1908 5/8

"At five last night, we passed out of the Nagasaki harbor and started on our way to China." CJG

SEKITAN NO TSUMINI 長崎の波止場
Loading Coal

KIKŌYA 亀甲屋
Tortoise Shell Store reads the sign on the shop in the photo below. The store is selling 下駄 *geta*, wooden sandals, and 足袋 *tabi*, toesocks.

Japan 1908   57

CHINA and KOREA

The Gambles next spent eighteen days in China, where these photos of Clarence (to the right) and Sidney (lower left) were taken. The family traveled by houseboat from Shanghai to Hangzhou, where, escorted by Rev. Robert F. Fitch, they toured Hangzhou Presbyterian College and the new Y.M.C.A., and they met with Presbyterian missionaries. On returning to Shanghai, they visited more schools, a rescue home, and the Shanghai Y.M.C.A.

Once again they sailed through the Shimonoseki Straits, landing in Fusan, Korea, where they were met by Dr. Charles H. Irvin. The party traveled to Seoul and later Pyongyang and met again with Presbyterian missionaries in Korea and visited Presbyterian mission schools and hospitals. After a stay in Korea for a day short of three weeks, on 18 June the Gambles returned to Japan.

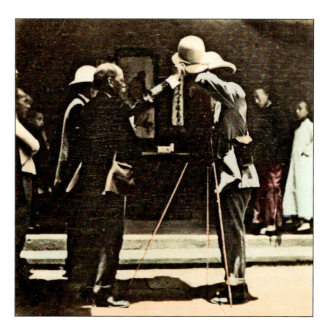

宮島 **MIYAJIMA**
Thursday 1908 6/18

"Jinya met us in the pouring rain and accompanied us to the train. We reached Miyajima still in the pouring rain at about two and were soon established in our room. Such luxury! We are 'out of season' and, therefore, have a double room apiece (though I regret to say we have each a private bath), all opening onto a long porch.

"The main building in which we have our rooms is built like a palace or temple, though it is quite Europeanized on the inside. Still our rooms show the Japanese style a great deal, ground-glass windows just like the paper ones, sliding doors, and rustic-looking fireplaces with a great Japanese picture at the opening.

"The scenery is fine. We are right in the woods with a view of the sea, reminding us very much of the Tree Tops.* A small stream runs between our building and the dining room and offices, widened out into a goldfish pond. The goldfish are trained, as we find all well-bred Japanese goldfish should be, to come when you clap and eat bread when you choose to throw it to them."   CJG

*Tree Tops *Summer home of the Gambles in Harbor Point, Michigan.*

宮島 **MIYAJIMA**
Friday 1908 6/19

"We visited the temple this morning and saw the torii one sees so much in Japanese pictures. Shops are on all sides of the streets leading to the temple, and all sorts of things are displayed to catch the tourist: toriis, puzzles, canes, boxes, cups, and more than anything else, hair ornaments and chop-sticks.

"In one place, a woman sells rice on little trays to feed to the pigeons. When she sees a party of tourists approaching, she rings a cracked brass bell, which brings the pigeons flying from all sides, and then she hustles out with her trays, which she sells at the rate of half a cent apiece. The pigeons soon fly up and perch on the tray and on your arm and though they sometimes eat the rice, they spend a good deal of their time in fighting for a good place. Once, I had eleven birds on the tray, which is about 4 inches square, and my hand and arm.

"The temple has a long winding corridor for an approach, and shopkeepers try to catch your eye and pocket money all the way along.

(See next page.)

フェリーを待つ人々
WAITING for the ferry to Miyajima

宮島 **MIYAJIMA** is the common name of Itsukushima, meaning "Island of Shrines," and is an island of twelve square miles just off the coast of Hiroshima, its beauty so awe-inspiring that for thousands of years none dared to live on it lest the gods be offended.

厳島神社 **ITSUKUSHIMA JINJA** is a large complex of red lacquered shrines begun in the sixth century. Its present design is based on that of 1168. So as not to disturb the gods by breaking the soil, the shrine was built out over the water and, at high tide, Itsukushima Jinja appears to float on the sea.

宮島大鳥居 **MIYAJIMA ŌTORII** is one of the largest and most famous *torii* in Japan, and when framing Misenyama, one of the most photographed. Ōtorii sits on the tidal flats before Itsukushima Jinja, appearing at high tide to float on the water, welcoming the spirits of the departed.

Japan 1908   59

千畳閣 **SENJŌKAKU** *Hall of a Thousand Mats* accommodates only 857 tatami mats. Toyotomi Hideyoshi ordered its construction but died before the hall was completed. Its purpose: chanting sutras for war casualties.

しゃもじ **SHAMOJI** *Rice Scoops* made of wood, whose taste does not affect that of the rice and are said to have been invented by a monk who lived on Miyajima.

五重塔 **GOJŪ NO TŌ** *Pagoda* Vermilion-painted with five (not six) stories, built in 1407 to house a Buddha statue. In 1868, the statue was moved to Daiganji, next to Itsukushima Shrine. Gojū no Tō stands next to Senjōkaku.

We found a great lot of letters from home waiting for us here when we arrived here, and we have had a fine time reading them.

"Up on the hills beyond the main temple where there is not much to see is a large 1,000 mat room. For some reason or other, it seems to be the fashion to write your name on a rice paddle used ordinarily for dishing out rice and put it up on the walls or columns of the room. On one side of the room was a pile of spoons about five cords, I should say, which had been taken down to make room for newer ones, and beside the walls being covered, the central columns were padded with about three feet of spoons tied on with heavy ropes.

"Nearby was a pagoda of six stories, which we passed on our way home, thereby avoiding the shops, which Father thinks are quite dangerous.

"At about noon, we took a steam launch for a trip around the island. The scenery was fine, islands on every side covered with trees and dotted here and there with forts. There are about seven steep valleys on the island, each one having its village. At the third one of these, we stopped and ate our lunch in an old temple. While there, we saw four Jap torpedo boats maneuvering, clouding up the sky with their smoke at the same time.

"Farther round the island, we saw a number of sailboats with their baggy sails sailing sideways, pulling fish nets with them. On returning to the hotel, we went out a short way in a rowboat to catch some fish. We managed to catch one about three inches long, which our attendant told us was a 'kiwgo' or 'kisu' fish. Having had so much luck, we decided we wouldn't wait for any more and so returned to the hotel.

"That night, we saw all the stone lanterns along the shore lit for a new arrival and the sum of three dollars. It was beautiful. About 400 tiny lights in a long curving row were lit, one after another, and burned for over an hour, though we didn't stay to see them go out."   CJG

鱚 **KISU** *Japanese Whiting* A common fish, with soft, not fatty flesh, especially tasty in summer.

TORPEDO BOATS Japan had built a large navy during the Russo-Japanese War (1904-05).

宮島 **MIYAJIMA**
Saturday 1908 6/20

"Photographing occupied the morning, as our permits are here now, and we went over about the same ground as yesterday.

"In the afternoon, I wandered up through the woods for quite a distance, then out to the shore part way around the island and back to the hotel, then down to some of the shops." CJG

宮島 **MIYAJIMA**
Sunday 1908 6/21

"Jinya and I went to the top of the island this morning, a distance of two miles, up 2,250 stone steps. We passed three little Japanese maids, who invited us into their three little tea houses to sit down and rest, but the fourth and last was too much for us after a mile and a half of climbing, and we just had to sit down and dispose of a couple of large-sized oranges.

"Just below the top is a small temple from which one has a fine view over the right side of the island opposite the hotel and the sea and other islands beyond. On the very top was a large temple, where a Buddhist priest was preaching. Jinya took out a copper, tossed it into the money box, and taking off his hat, put his hands together, said a prayer. This is the first time we have seen him do anything of the sort, and it was quite a surprise. I suppose though that he thought that he might as well get the benefit of the long climb.

"The view was fine, but as it was getting late, we couldn't stay long and had to start down again.

"Jinya applied at one of the tea houses for a girl to help in his house in Kyoto. He wanted a country girl, as 'the city girls, they know too much.'

"In the afternoon, I felt rather tired, so didn't do very much but lie down or read." CJG

Sailing Boats **HOKAKEBUNE** 帆掛け船

弥山本堂 **MISEN HONDŌ** *Main Hall of Worship* A large Buddhist temple founded in the early ninth century on the very top of Mount Misen, the highest mountain of Miyajima, rising to almost 2,000 feet above sea level. On the way to Misen Hondō are other small temples. Climbing Mount Misen is a popular tourist activity.

京都 KYOTO
Monday 1908 6/22

We packed all morning and left at two in the pouring rain. The ride to Kyoto was tiresome, to say the least. The smoking was awful, and we couldn't have the window open much on account of the rain. The car was crowded, and the hand baggage took up most of the floor space and what was worse than all, we didn't get to Kyoto until 1:35 a.m.

"About eight, the man sitting in the same division with Mother evidently felt rather tired, so stretched out so far, in fact, when he dosed off that he poked Mother with his toes. She finally had to get a umbrella to protect herself, much to the discomfort of the sleeper. Luckily, however, we had about two hours sleep before we reached our destination, as a number of people got off at Kobe, and we all had a chance to stretch out."   CJG

京都 KYOTO
Tuesday 1908 6/23

We finished up odds and ends of shopping. Mr. Gorbold came over to lunch, and after talking a short time, Mother and Father went upstairs to lie down and Sidney and I went to Mr. Gorbold's house with him. He wants us to stay with him until Friday and go into the country with him on a tour with a stereopticon. I think it would be great, but I'm afraid we haven't time

"About five o'clock, we went to a Japanese theatre. The theatre lasted from two in the afternoon to eleven at night, having in that time about seven different disconnected acts. When we arrived, a lot of court men were sitting in a semi-circle, while the chief man and another would drink saki, keeping up a sort of dialogue between them, finally ending up with a fencing match. I suppose there would have been more to it if we could have understood what they were saying, but as it was, it seemed very dull and uninteresting. The second scene was a little more lively. A boatman's daughter met a daimyo and his wife and sent them across the ferry against the will of her father, who had been paid to refuse to ferry them. The boatman stabs his daughter, though not fatally, and she finally cuts her throat.

"The scenery is arranged on a circular platform, which is turned when a change is wanted. The daimyo and his wife come onto the stage by a raised platform through the pit.

"The central figures, the boatman and his daughter, are followed in all their movements by a candle held by a man with a long stick. To open a door of five or six sliding sections, the actor gives it a slight push, and men behind rapidly take it away. The asides or thoughts of the actor are read out by a man at the side of the stage and accompanied by appropriate(?) [*sic*] motions of the actor, and any sudden move or notable word or deed is accompanied by the banging of two blocks of wood. Altogether, the acting seemed very crude and queer."   CJG

STEREOPTICON First slide projector, the "magic lantern," introduced in 1850, projected photographs onto glass.

巡礼
JUNREI
Pilgrim awaiting alms

横浜 **YOKOHAMA**
Wednesday 1908 6/24

"The trip to Yokohama was one of the finest rides we have had. The weather was fine, the sun shone all the way, and there was no fog in sight, so we hoped to see Fugi. At about three in the afternoon, we ran through a tunnel, and the porter telling us to look out on one side of the car, we saw the mountain for the first time. It was grand. The snow came down about half way in the crevices, and in some places there was no snow clear up to the top. Soon after we saw it, a bump appeared on one side, and before it disappeared, we saw the same bump on the other side of it, showing that we had gone half way around it. We took two or three pictures of it, but except in one taken just as the sun set behind the mountain, Fugi looked so much like the sky that they aren't worth much. Mother says that she hopes to see it again, but if she doesn't, she'll be satisfied." CJG

Monk **SŌRYO** 僧侶
The red necklace, which is a string of prayer beads, and the bowl he is carrying identify this man as a monk.

横浜 **YOKOHAMA**
Thursday 1908 6/25

"We had to buy a second extra trunk, as the one we got in Kyoto is to be general hold-all on some of our side trips." CJG

横浜 **YOKOHAMA**
Friday 1908 6/26

"We spent the morning visiting some of the Yokohama stores. I got all my Korean and Chinese prints, and they are fine. Mother had a great time in two or three silk stores, and Father and Sidney went to the bank and SS offices. The afternoon was spent in listing up and redistributing our numerous dutiable articles and leaving." CJG

SS OFFICES *Steamship Offices* The Gambles would sail from Yokohama to San Francisco on the S.S. Manchuria, which was leased by the Pacific Mail Steamship Company.

東京 **TOKYO**
Saturday 1908 6/27

"Still raining a little. We finished up the last things and got off for Tokyo at two. Our hotel in Tokyo, the Metropole, is not as comfortable as we expected, as we will probably change to another under the same company on Monday.

"We found a surprise waiting for us when we went down to supper, for we found the Tartars that were on the 'Mongolia' from Shanghai to Kobe sitting at the next table. They still had the same pajama-like suits, and the same comical expressions were to be seen. The woman had more hair ornaments than before, and the boy wore the purple suit with yellow stripes." CJG

東京 TOKYO
Sunday 1908 6/28

"Mother and Father, following the good example we set them in Corea, went to church and arrived there not only after the benediction but at the wrong church. However, Father discovered a friend of his, Miss Vale, who had been at Wesleyan College in Cincinnati. Sidney and I took life easy in the morning, but the whole family went out to English service in the afternoon."   CJG

東京 TOKYO
Monday 1908 6/29

"Regular Tokyo weather or at least our idea of it. We drove in the pouring rain, this time in a closed carriage. We have a footman again, though he is not half as funny as the one we had before.

"First, we visited Miss Treuda's [sic] school. She was formerly at the head of the government school for peeresses [sic] but left that to start one of her own. She is a perfect wonder at teaching English, and I thought at first that she must be an American dressed in Japanese clothes. We found out that she had been in America ever since she was eight years old. The school was fine with a good building and faculty. We couldn't see much of the girls though, for they were all having examinations.

"We next went to [a] school in which Miss Milikan is interested.* Here we started in at the primary and went up, each class going through their 'stunts' for us. Very often when some slip was made, the girl would retire and whisk the end of her sleeve over her face to hide her confusion. This shows another use of the long pocket-like sleeves.

"Later on, the Gamble family was marched up onto the platform, and the whole school marched into their seats in the assembly room. Then followed songs by the school and, as usual, Father, much to his delight, was asked to make a speech. I forgot to tell how he had to explain Ivory soap-making to the girls.   *(See next page.)*

* Miss Milikan. *See* page 104, Line Notes "A Daily Journal 1908, p. 65. Elizabeth Patton Milliken.

津田 梅子 **TSUDA UMEKO** (1864-1929), whom Clarence refers to as "Miss Treuda," was sent by her father when she was six years old to America with the Iwakura Mission, which departed in 1871. On her return to Japan in 1882, she had all but forgotten her Japanese language and how to adjust to the demeaning position that Japanese society accorded to women.

After working as a tutor and then in a girls' school, where the girls were trained to be obedient and subservient rather than educated and lively, she returned to the United States and attended Bryn Mawr College. She saw the need to educate Japanese women into intellectual rigor and along Western lines. In 1900, in Kojimachi, Tokyo, she founded the Women's Institute for English Studies and offered young women a rounded liberal arts education. In 1903, the school was officially recognized. In 1905, Tsuda became the first president of the Japanese branch of the Tokyo Y.W.C.A., a position that no doubt helped to bring her to the attention of the Gambles.

After World War II, the name "Woman's Institute" was changed to Tsuda College; in 2012, it is one of the most important colleges for women in Japan. Tsuda opposed woman suffrage but was adamant in her belief that women in Japan deserved an education equal to that given men.

The school is half English and half Japanese: that is, they study their lessons in English in the morning and in Japanese in the afternoon. One of the more advanced classes thought they would like to ask us questions, so when we went in, Father was prepared to answer them. First came, 'How did you like your trip?' and then as if by a prearranged scheme, for there was a lot of giggling, 'Tell us how you make soap.'

"We tried to take one or two flashlight groups of the girls, as the day was very dark, but I'm afraid they all moved.

"We went to Miss Milikan's for lunch, and there we met a Japanese teacher, Miss Mitano, who is going to America with Miss Milikan in a few days. After lunch, we saw the graduating class of the school we visited this morning. They are under Miss Milikan in a boarding school.

"On the way back to the hotel, we stopped at the house of Miss Hyde, a painter. Here again, my Japanese came in handy. Miss 'Haida' was out, so I asked, or rather put two words together, and asked, 'What hour?' and managed to understand the reply, 'Six.'"
CJG

ELIZABETH PATTON MILLIKEN CLASS
Above is the graduating class under Elizabeth Patton Milliken, who may be standing in the back row second from the right.

HELEN HYDE (1868-1919) American print maker, who lived in Japan from 1899 to 1914, learned the Japanese art of woodblock color print making, working closely with skilled Japanese carvers and with the foremost Japanese printer, Morata Shōhirō.

The Gambles met Hyde in Tokyo, but she also had a home in Nikkō, where anyone who could afford to would go to get away from the summer heat of Tokyo. Clarence records visits with Helen Hyde in Nikkō on July 14, 15, and 22. On the fourteenth, Mary and David purchased some of her prints, but these have vanished from The Gamble House along with any information about them.

The subject matter chosen by Helen Hyde for her prints and art was often mothers and children. Arriving in Paris in 1891 for three years of study, she was immediately in touch with the work of Mary Cassatt and the craze for *Japonisme*, both of which informed the Hyde *oeuvre* for her lifetime. Prior to study in Europe, she had attended the best art schools in the United States. Helen Hyde won many awards throughout her lifetime and remains a popular artist. To the left, she is seen in her Tokyo home around 1905.

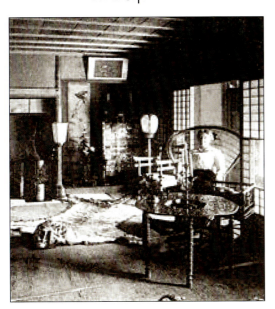

菖蒲 **SHŎBU** *Iris are much loved in Japan.*

蓑 **MINO**
*Straw
Raincoat
worn by
Clarence*

東京 **TOKYO**
Tuesday 1908 6/30

"We went on a shopping tour this morning. One of the stores where we stopped is fitted up a good deal like our large store, but one of the queerest things about it was that it was such a mixture that we all had to have cloth coverings put over our shoes as we entered.

"Later, we received quite a recommendation for the store. One of the salesmen that attacked us in the hotel assured us that any other store 'except just me' would have told you that was silver 'except me & Mitsukoshi,' which was the name of the store. Why that was picked out I can't say, but you see it was and by an eminent authority, too.

"In the afternoon, we went in the carriage to an iris garden about six miles outside of Tokyo. The blossoms were very nearly gone but were still very beautiful.

"We had been wanting very much to get a picture of a Japanese straw raincoat, so when I saw one hanging out to dry, I asked Jinya to see if I couldn't put it on. As soon as I started to do so, one of the men ran round the corner of a building and soon returned with about two dozen girls, whom I had seen weaving hats. They seemed to enjoy the joke immensely, but when we pointed the camera at them, it was great fun to see them run.

"I hope the picture will turn out well, as I had the straw raincoat, the large straw hat, and a Jap spade."   CJG

東京 **TOKYO**
浅草公園 **Asakusa Kōen**
Wednesday 1908 7/1

"Still we have Tokyo weather. Mother and Father went off somewhere in the carriage, and Sidney and Jinya and I went out to Asakusa Park near the temple we went to on our first visit to Tokyo.

"The crowds seemed to be still visiting it and throwing their coppers into the large money box. The little toy store was still there, though it didn't seem that they could possibly make enough to keep going. What interested us the most, however, were the poster shops. All available space on the floor and walls was covered with pictures, posters, or kakemonos. It was queer to notice that a piece of tissue paper was always pasted over the face of the emperor whenever his picture was hung up.

(See next page.)

It does seem as though it would never stop raining. All day, it has been coming down steadily, and walking is rather unpleasant.

"A man attacked us after lunch and wanted to show us some curios. He spread them out all over the room, on the desk, on the table, and on the beds, and as we didn't want to buy them, he left them there until night, as we were his first customer of the month and he was very anxious to sell so as to have good luck.

"Just as I was going down to the carriage, a young-looking salesman spoke to me, said that he was a student and worked only in vacation time. He wanted me to come to the silver shop where he worked— 'no matter if you buy or not, you see, master think I do good work.' As luck would have it, the silver store was one of the places on our list for the afternoon, and we met him there again. After we had bought something, he said that he would like to give me a copy of a book written by Togo and would bring it and some cloisonne he had made <u>himself</u> to the hotel in the evening. The cloisonne is fair, but how could a student get time to make them?

"The first salesman that I spoke of has been back again, this time bringing about seven swords with him. Such a time as we had getting rid of him. He talked most of the time for over an hour, and then we had to leave him in the room and go down to dinner." CJG

東郷平八郎 **TŌGŌ Heihachirō** (1848-1934) Father of modern Japanese Navy, hero of the Russo-Japanese War. The book would have been about Tōgō, not by him.

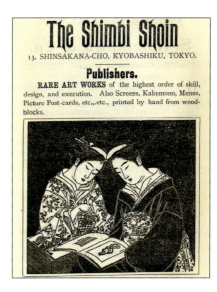

SENSŌJI 浅草寺
Asakusa Kannon Temple
Oldest Buddhist temple in Tokyo, until its destruction in World War II. The colorful reconstructed temple remains popular and is surrounded by a centuries-old shopping area thronged by pilgrims and tourists alike. Every May, the area is the scene of the four-day *Sanja Matsuri*.

Wall Hanging **KAKEMONO** 掛物
A Japanese silk or paper scroll, usually long and narrow in shape, with a roller at its bottom edge.

浅草公園 **ASAKUSA KŌEN** *Asakusa Park* was "laid out in 1885 as a recreation ground for the people. On one side is the Hanayashiki, originally a flower garden but now much more of a zoo, while over against the Hanayashiki is the fishpond teeming with goldfish, with a tea-house and a bridge, and in summer an arbour of trailing Wistaria beautiful to look upon. Beyond the lake on one side is the Aquarium; on the other the great Theatre Street, with its row of "Dime Shows" where you can see a constant succession of feats of jugglery and acrobatic performance. Archery, which is always a favourite pastime with the Japanese, has a special corner for itself, and, if you are fond of exercise you may climb to the top of the twelve-storied tower, from which you can get a very comprehensive bird's-eye view of the whole city. Everywhere you will find the place swarming with itinerant vendors and hawkers with most varied assortments of goods, and you will be obliged to keep a smart look out for pickpockets....The headquarters of the [Thieves'] Guild are said to be in this district,...and it is only a very short distance from [Asakusa Park] to the great Yoshiwara, the largest and most famous of the prostitute establishments in Japan."
Arthur Lloyd, "Tokyo's Four Great Parks,"
Every-day Japan (1909) 230-31.

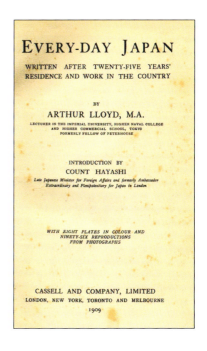

大倉喜八郎 ŌKURA KIHACHIRŌ (1837-1928)

was an entrepreneur, who founded the Ōkura *zaibatsu* (business concern), and a philanthropist, who created the Ōkura Shōgyō Gakkō, which became Tokyo Keizai University. He was greatly distressed at the increasing export of Japanese art treasures and began his own personal Oriental art collection. In 1917, he donated his entire collection, the land, and the building to found the Ōkura Shūkokan, the first private art museum in Japan. Only the art in storage survived the Great Kanto Earthquake of 1923, but the new earthquake-proof building was opened in 1928 and museum holdings augmented by son Ōkura Kishichirō. The Ōkura Shūkokan stands next to Hotel Ōkura Tokyo, part of the Ōkura Hotel Chain established in 1978, and is a designated cultural asset of Japan.

CLARENCE & DAVID GAMBLE & FRIENDS

東京 TOKYO
Thursday 1908 7/2

Still raining though not very hard. Sidney and I went out for a short time to get some postals, but Mother and Father were courageous enough to be out all morning visiting schools.

"In the afternoon, we went with Mr. Fujiwara, the agent for Ivory Soap, to see a collection of old curios made by a private gentleman. The collection was immense. A large three-story building was just packed with images, statues, china ware, lacquered boxes, or swords. A large part of the building had once been a temple, which Mr. Okura had bought. There was a large collection of deities from Japan, China, Tibet, and Corea. One pair of them was over twelve feet high, while the smallest were less than a quarter of an inch. One whole room was filled with Japanese lacquered medicine cases. The one considered the most curious represented a man in a dream. Standing at full height, you could not see his face, as it was covered with an opaque-looking pearl fan; but when you stooped down low, the fan became perfectly transparent. The next-to-the-largest clear quartz ball in existence is in the next room, while farther on is a room full of carved lacquer work.

"A young Japanese lady is studying archeology in the museum, and she showed us around, later taking us into the living apartments, where we were served with tea and cake. The apartments, or as much as we saw of them, were furnished entirely in European style, though you could see many Japanese touches.

"Our sword friend was back twice this evening, wanting to know if we wanted to take a pair of swords. The pair in question was 'lowest price $200 to start in with.' At present is quoted at $250. If we were only going to stay here a week or two, he might be willing to give us the swords, if he keeps on at the present rate of reduction." CJG

宮ノ下 MIYANOSHITA
Friday 1908 7/3

Off on the train again this morning, though only for an hour's ride. We were thankful enough for this, however, as the smoking on the car was awful. Arriving at our station, we took a small streetcar for another hour's ride. The scenery was fine. We followed a stream up for about two miles, crossing it about five times, then off through two little towns to the terminal at Yumoto. From here, we went four miles uphill in a rikisha. The rain had exposed the stones in the road, and we were pretty well shaken up.

"The [Fujiya] hotel is in the center of the village of Miyanoshita, though a little above it. Our rooms are in the second annex, as the hotel has been added to a great deal and is now built in a semicircle. Perhaps in a few years, it may complete the circle. We all spent the afternoon in our room sleeping to make up for the strenuous exertions in Tokyo, though towards evening we walked through the village to see the shops."   CJG

富士屋ホテル **FUJIYA HOTEL** began its operations in Miyanoshita, Hakone, in 1878. Founder 山口仙之助 Yamaguchi Sennosuke (d. 1915) was visiting the West as an individual at the same time that the Iwakura Mission was on tour (1871-1873). Upon his return to Japan, Yamaguchi determined to open a hotel with Western-style accommodations. Two destructive fires later and after building a temporary Japanese-style inn, he saw completed in 1891 the main Victorian-style building of the Fujiya Hotel. In 1906, two Victorian-style cottages mentioned by Clarence had been built near the main building. Charlie Chaplin, Frank Lloyd Wright, and the Imperial Family were some of the many famous to stay at Fujiya, and Basil Hall Chamberlain was in residence for twenty years.

HAKONE-YUMOTO STATION was opened in 1888 for the Odawara Horse-drawn Railway.

宮ノ下 **MIYANOSHITA** The site of several onsen, hot springs, in Hakone, which in 1907 could be reached from Tokyo within a few hours. The hot springs and its proximity to Tokyo made Miyanoshita the ideal location in which to open the Fujiya Hotel to accommodate both Western and Japanese visitors.

**宮ノ下 MIYANOSHITA
Saturday 1908 7/4**

"We were pretty disappointed in not having even a smell of firecrackers all day. We did up a number of shops for our morning's work and rested for the afternoon. So far, there seems to be almost nothing doing here, though I suppose if we can get up our courage to go for a trip in spite of the clouds, it may be a little more interesting."   CJG

**宮ノ下 MIYANOSHITA
Sunday 1908 7/5**

"Usual program through the morning, reading, writing, and sleeping, varied a little in the afternoon by a walk along the road upstream. We passed several fine waterfalls, which made us wish very much for a bright day and our cameras. The shopkeepers all along the way tried their best to catch us in their nets, but we managed to escape and are safely back to the hotel."   CJG

**宮ノ下 MIYANOSHITA
Monday 1908 7/6**

We spent the morning on the shops again, this time doing the other end of town. The shopping isn't very interesting to you (suppose though it may be next Christmas), so I'll skip it and go on to the afternoon.

"Sidney and Father being in the house interested in books or cards and Mother lying down, I started off by myself and climbed the hill behind the hotel. It takes a half hour of steep climbing, but the view when you get to the top, 'nothin finer, baring the fog' or rather the clouds. The sign at the foot of the hill said that there was a fine view of Fuji and refreshment such as tea, beer, lemonade, and cake. There was a tea house at the top, but no one was there. You may be sure I never would have gone up if it hadn't been for Fuji and the beer. I was very much disappointed."   CJG

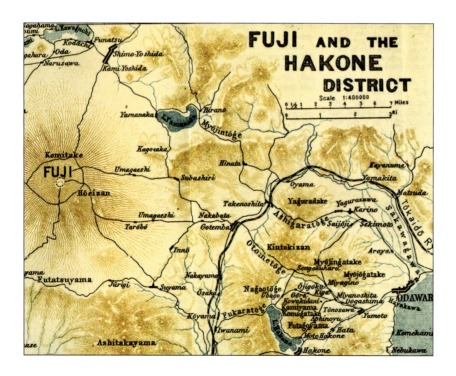

箱根 **HAKONE** is the name of both a town and of a mountainous region in Kanagawa Prefecture at the foot of Mount Fuji. This hot springs and resort area, so close to Tokyo and Yokohama, with its fine view of Mount Fuji, its spectacular waterfalls, and its many *onsen*, has since the beginning of the Edo period in 1600 been the most popular resort area in Japan, a convenient and desirable destination for the Japanese vacationers and then later for Western tourists.

宮ノ下 MIYANOSHITA
Tuesday 1908 7/7

This morning we actually started off on a trip. Father, Sidney, and I put on straw sandals and started off on foot, while Mother followed on a four-man chair. We went up the same hill I climbed yesterday and stayed for a time at the same tea house. Then, instead of finally coming down the same way we went up, we climbed up higher and finally came out of the trees onto a grassy plateau set out with rows and rows of small pine trees. From here, we had a fine view of the ocean with small boats near the shore. As far as we could see, there was a line of breakers on one side and a row of hills on the other.

巡礼
JUNREI
Pilgrim

"Going down on the other side of the hill, we came to a little cascade and with it was, as usual, a tea house. We have gotten into the habit of drinking 'oyu,' or hot water, and it is really quite refreshing. From there, we returned, circling the hill and coming in to the hotel at the back.

"In the afternoon after a short shower had passed, I started off again. Going upstream for about two miles, I crossed over at the town of Miagina [*sic*] and came back on the other side of the river. Opposite to and a little above the hotel is a small tea house. Here I stopped for a few minutes and had some 'yu' and crackers. While waiting there, I actually saw Fuji a little at a time as an opening in the clouds passed over it. I returned to the hotel from there by a steep zigzag path down into the canyon and then up a flight of steps on the other side."   CJG

宮城野 **MIYAGINO** Clarence spells it "Miagina," a village built on both sides of a stream a short distance from Miyanoshita. Chamberlain writes about (note also his reference to feeding goldfish) "principal short walks from Miyanoshita: To Kiga, distance 9 chō, say 1/4 hr.:--no climbing, tame fish to feed with cakes at the favorite 'Gold-fish Tea-house'. That ravine spanned by a bridge soon after starting is called Jakotsu-gawa, lit. 'Stream of the Serpents' Bones,' from some white stones popularly believed to be the bones of dead serpents. A little way up is a waterfall, and the hot water which supplies the village can be seen issuing from the rocks in several places. --Equally flat and pleasant road 8 chō further up the valley of the Hayakawa to Miyagino, a vill[age] built on both sides of the stream" (140-148).

[8 chō = 900 meters or .6 mile]

CLIMB Chamberlain suggests this walk, which is very close to that taken by Clarence:

"Climb half-way up Sengenyama, the wooded hill immediately at the back of the Japanese wing of the Fujiya Hotel. It is a steep pull of 25 or 30 min. to the tea-shed, some 700 ft. above the village, whence view of upper half of Fuji. This walk may be continued along the ridge" (149).

大地獄 **ŌJIGOKU** *Big Hell*, today known as Ōwakudani. The area is bare, rough, and rocky, for no plants can live near the heavy emissions of hydrogen sulfide gas; but, as Clarence notes, one can hard boil eggs.

黒卵 **KURO TAMAGO**
Black Eggs
Boiled in the hot springs, eggs turn turn black. Eating the black eggs is believed to increase longevity.

湯本 **YUMOTO** in 1907 was a small cluster of both houses and hotels catering to those visiting the many *onsen*, hot springs, in the area.

子守りと 日傘
KOMORI TO HIGASA
Baby Sitter with Paper Parasol

湯本 **YUMOTO**
Wednesday 1908 7/8

We had our first horseback ride in Japan this morning. Father rode, or rather bounced, in a four-man chair, and Sidney, Jinya, and I went on horseback to the Ojigoku hot springs. There were a number of places in the rock where steam came out in clouds, though it didn't compare with the Yellowstone.

"One of the chairmen had brought some raw eggs with him to cook. He tied them up in the end of a towel and dropped them into some boiling water. In a few minutes, we had some nice hard-boiled egg to refresh us after our ride.

"In the afternoon, Jinya and I went to Yumoto on horseback. We saw an ingenious pipe hoist when we were half way down. A Japanese company wanted to bring water down from the mountains to generate electricity. The question was how to get the pipe to the top. An inclined board was built half way, and the pipe was fastened onto a cable and pulled up. This then was lifted in the air and, suspended on the cable, was carried the rest of the way. Each section of the pipe weighed a long ton and was carried by twenty men to the boat at the incline and then hassled up 800 feet. We saw a small waterfall and then returned to Miyanoshita."   CJG

箱根 **HAKONE**
Thursday 1908 7/9

A fine semi-sunshiny morning for our trip to Hakone. Mother and Father went in chairs and the rest of us on horseback. After an hour's ride up over a range of hills and down on the other side, we came to Lake Hakone* and had a fine view of Fuji. We were afraid it was going to disappear before the chairs arrived, but it didn't, and we saw it for most of the afternoon.

"Soon after lunch, we started off again for two miles and a half more. From the hill, we had a fine view over the country. We could see the ocean on both sides of Japan, and Hakone Lake between. Fuji seemed to rise higher in the clouds as we went higher and to be way above everything when we reached the top. On the way back, we stopped at one or two of the shops, but they seemed rather unattractive.

"We had hoped to have a sail on the lake, but by the time we got back, there was almost no wind at all and, of course, sailing was out of the question."   CJG

*Hakone Lake *Ashi* or *Ashinoko* Lake

箱根 HAKONE
Friday 1908 7/10

"We were wakened at five o'clock to look at Fuji. Luckily, by just turning over in bed, we could see it, so for about an hour I would look at it between dozes until it was hidden and then, my conscience being clear, I slept until eight.

"Our horses had gone back to Mayanoshita [sic] for the night and didn't appear for a long time after we were ready to start next morning. Finally, one came, so Sidney took that, and Jinya and I took chairs. After about three miles of bouncing and thumping in the four-man chair, I changed with Jinya and tried the two-man chair or 'kago.' In this, though the position was very uncomfortable as I had to lie down and keep my legs crossed Turk-fashion, there was much less bumping, and I liked it better than the other.

"After lunch, I went out to get one or two pictures and then climbed the hill back of the hotel again. From the top, I had a fine view of Fuji for about half an hour.

"Just before supper, I tried the hotel swimming pool and found it fine and much less warmer than I had expected, because a small stream of hot spring water ran into it."   CJG

FUJISAN 富士山
Mount Fuji,
The highest mountain in Japan, about 68 miles southwest of Tokyo

日光 NIKKŌ
Saturday 1908 7/11

"Well, all our packing is done at last, and we are off for Nikko. Our half-hour's ride in a rikisha, though in fine sunshine and beautiful scenery instead of the usual scenery, was somewhat uncomfortable. The bumping, jolting, tipping, bouncing, and shaking were awful.

"Our ride from Yumoto on the train was fine. The sun was bright, and we had a fine chance for pictures.

"For some reason, the streets of the villages that we passed were all decorated with flags and paper lanterns, and the people seemed to be out in full force.

"From Kodzu we saw Fuji just managing to get her head above the clouds. In the station, we had a view of her from the inside, or at least the postcard said, 'Fuji from Fuji liver.' The Japanese do mix their l's and r's, but this is the first time I've seen it done in print.

"We arrived at Nikko in the pouring rain and dark after changing cars three times and waiting over two hours in station."   CJG

Chamberlain warns, "Avoid the native *basha* (carriage) if you have either nerves to shatter or bones to shake; and be chary of burdening yourself with a horse and saddle of your own in the interior, as all sorts of trouble are apt to arise with regard to shoeing, run-away grooms (*bettō*), etc. Such, in a few words, is our advice, founded on long personal experience. Other possible conveyances are pack-horses (but the Japanese pack-saddle is torture), cows, the *kago*,—a species of small palanquin, uncomfortable at first, but not disliked by many old residents,—and lastly, chairs borne by four coolies; but these have only recently been introduced from China, and are not found except at Miyanoshita, Nikkō, and a few other places much resorted to by foreigners" (10).

国府津 **KŌZU**   (CJG writes "Kodzu") is about 50 miles from Tokyo. Kōzu Station opened in 1887.

日光 NIKKŌ
Sunday 1908 7/12

"We have two fine rooms with a little enclosed porch in front of them, from which we can watch the river and the bullomobiles going up or down on the other side of it. On one side, we can just see the end of the red bridge, and going up the opposite hill is a mysterious and dark-looking avenue of cryptomaria [*sic*] trees.

"We ventured out to church in spite of the threatening skies and though it poured while we were there, we went and returned in safety.

"On the way back, we had a near view of one of the bullomobiles with a waving white awning supported by four bamboo sticks. At every step, it waved forward and back in time with the bulkhead." CJG

TWO FINE ROOMS The Gambles stayed at the Kanaya Hotel from the eleventh to the twentieth of July 1908.

BULLOMOBILES The train line to Nikkō was built in 1890, but the trains were first pulled by bulls, or cows. In 1908, the Nikkō Electric Railroad Company was established so that electric power would be used instead of bulls, but apparently the changeover had not occurred when the Gambles were in Nikkō. The bulls were an alternative to the horses used by the Odawara Horse-drawn Railway, which opened its Hakone-Yumoto station in 1888.

神橋 **SHINKYŌ** *Sacred Red Bridge* or *Mihashi* crosses the Daiyagawa, a river, forty feet wide, that separates the town from the shrines of Nikkō.

杉 **SUGI** *Japanese Cedar Tree*, or **CRYPTOMERIA** (though not of the *Cedrus* but of the *Cypress* family), a conifer found in great groves throughout Japan and at many of the shrine and temple sites. The trees can reach up to 230 feet in height. The wood is strong but lightweight, waterproof, and resistant to decay, the ideal building material for the prototypical Japanese house.

日光 **NIKKŌ**, which means sunlight, is a city (a village in 1908) and a resort area, whose origins are found in the establishment of the temples of Rinnōji in 766 and of Chūzenji in 784. The temples originally drew many of the devout as residents, but with the completion in 1617 of Tōshōgū, the mausoleum of Tokugawa Ieyasu, and in 1653 of Taiyūin Reibyō, that of grandson Tokugawa Iemitsu, many more Japanese and foreign tourists came to Nikkō.

日光 金谷ホテル **NIKKO KANAYA HOTEL** In 1871, 金谷善一郎 Kanaya Zenichiro, a musician of Tōshōgū Shrine, invited Dr. James Curtis Hepburn (known for Hepburn Romanization system) into his home. That private invitation was the beginning of the Cottage Inn, the first of its kind to cater specifically to Westerners, whose ways were then so foreign to the Japanese. Nikkō, cool during the summer months, with its many hot springs and beautiful cryptomeria groves, surrounded by spectacular waterfalls and majestic mountains, drew many Westerners, and in 1878, author Isabella Bird was a guest of thr Inn. In 1890, after completion of the Nikkō Line of the Japanese National Railways, the Kanaya Hotel, a continuation of the Cottage Inn, was opened with thirty rooms. Always progressive, in 1914 the Kanaya purchased a fleet of Fords, the first automobiles seen in Nikkō, and promoted the Nikkō municipal streetcar line. Shozo, second son of Zenichiro, married into the Yamaguchi family and became Managing Director, later President, of the Fujiya Hotel. During World War II, the Kanaya was occupied by school students, then the United States military. But to this day, its fine reputation as a premier hotel lives on.

日光 NIKKŌ
東照宮 Toshōgū
Monday 1908 7/13

We all went to visit the temples for which Nikko is famous. The temples are not here opened free to the public, as they are elsewhere, but a charge of 40 cents is made for admission to the three main areas. We went only to the largest one this time, but it is quite enough to occupy a morning.* It was built originally as a Buddhist temple with large house-like gates and highly decorated interior but was later changed to a Shinto Temple with a torii as well as the largest Buddhist gates and Shinto ceremonials and decorations. As we entered, we first passed through a Shinto torii made of stone, then an immense gate with two large bright red guardians, as our guide said, 'to keep out bad animal.' Next came a smaller gate followed by a torii. Beyond this is a group of buildings, the sacred stable for the sacred horse, a bell and a drum tower, a museum and the hall of the dragon, also a bell and lantern made of bronze and presented by the Korean emperor. On the stable is the original of the three monkeys, which we have seen in every curio store and every shape, form, or position until we wish they had never existed. The museum contains relics of the principal nobles that lived about the time of the founding of the temple. Here were fine specimens of swords, guns, trunks, traveling chairs, and armour.

三猿 SAN'EN
Three Monkeys Mizaru, Iwazaru, Kikazaru of Tōshōgū: see no evil, speak no evil, hear no evil.

"Opposite this was the hall of the dragon, so called because of a large dragon painted on the ceiling. Standing under the dragon's head and clapping our hands, you could hear a loud rattling, almost like a growl, coming from the ceiling above. This noise could not be heard or made when standing in any other part of the room.

"Going farther on between a number of bronze lanterns, we came to the last gate, the finest of all. I will not attempt to describe the ornamentation, so you will have to wait until I can show you the photo for that. One interesting fact is that on one of the pillars, though having the same figure carved on it as the others, has it inverted. The structure was considered so perfect in other respects that this was put in to prevent exciting the envy of the gods.

"There is nothing very extraordinary in the temple itself except that the wall decorations were much richer than usual and there was more lacquer work on the walls. Behind the temple and up a winding flight of steps covered with the green moss that grows so thickly on all the stonework, there was the tomb of Ieyasu, one of the first men of great fame in Japan.

"In the afternoon, we started out on a shopping tour. We thought the best plan would be to go down to the lower end of the line of shops and work our way up. The last curio place is called The Nikko Prefectural Bazaar and is established to 'prevent the charging of extortionate prices by the Nikko merchants.' The fact is, however, that these same Nikko merchants are almost the only ones to exhibit there and, of course, a commission is added to their price. The various wares for sale are numerous and all interesting, so that instead of spending the afternoon in visiting all the shops, we spent it in that one only." CJG

徳川 家康 **TOKUGAWA IEYASU** Third of The Unifiers of Japan after Oda Nobunaga and Hideyoshi Toyotomi. Ieyasu was founder and first shogun of the Tokugawa shogunate, which ruled Japan during the Edo period, 1603-1867.

*largest one *Nikkō Tōshōgū, shrine dedicated to Tokugawa Ieyasu and his mausoleum.*

日光 NIKKŌ
霧降の滝 Kirifuri no Taki
Tuesday 1908 7/14

霧降の滝 **KIRIFURI NO TAKI** *Kirifuri Waterfall* Shown above in the print "Shimotsuke Kurokamiyama Kirifuri no Taki" ("Kirifuri Fall at Mount Kurokami in Shimotsuke Province") by Hokusai Katsushika (1760-1849). The Waterfall is probably less known for its own stunning grandeur than for this famous *ukiyo-e* print. Today, copies of the print are to be found on tote bags, T-shirts, skateboards, switch plates, and much, much more.

Father in a rikisha and Sidney, Jinya, and I on horseback went to the Kurifuri [*sic*] waterfalls, a ride of three miles. As usual, a tea house is placed so as to get a good view, and the little maids come out to meet us saying, 'Good-morning,' or 'Ohio.' As soon as Father arrived at the tea house, which by the way, is quite a distance from the falls, we started down the quarter-mile descent to the base of the lower falls. The water of the stream drops down 110 feet and then, stopping for a moment in a small pool, slides gracefully down over 140 feet of smooth, almost polished, rock to the bottom. The descent was very easy and the cool, moist air at the bottom invigorating, but the climb up was not quite so easy.

"About half way back to the hotel, as we were passing two rikishas, Sidney's horse got a little frisky and, going too near the rikisha, caught the mud guard and ripped it off, bolts and all. Startled by the noise, the horse thought that it might be a good idea to go down the hillside and get away from it, but Sidney managed to stop him and get back to the road again.

"In the afternoon, by invitation we went to take tea with Miss Hyde, the artist. She gave us a great deal of information on the different storekeepers in town. When we asked her if they could be trusted, she said, 'Well, they are all rascals, but I like them in spite of it.' She told one or two stories about them, how one man took a Russian out into his fireproof storehouse or garden and brought out an old dust-covered sword that had belonged to his grandfather (we've heard stories before about grandfather's swords), and he told how he hated to part with it (actually shedding tears) and that if his dear father were alive he could never sell it, but he was reduced to such straits, etc. The Russian was much affected and bought the sword for 75 dollars. Later, he was showing it at the hotel, and another man stepped up and said that it had been offered to him for forty.

"There have been three fires in Nikko, one of them only last May, and every time they stopped at the same man's place, and twice it was proved that he had bought up the firemen to stay by his place and protect it. 'All's fair in love, war, and curio selling' must be one of their teachings over here.

"Miss Hyde also showed us some of her prints of Japanese children and, of course, we had to get some." CJG

HELEN HYDE
Honorable Mr. Cat 1904

日光 NIKKŌ
Wednesday 1908 7/15

When Nikko was first built, a great many people made donations or helped to build it. Those who were too poor to do this planted cryptomaria [sic] trees along the road leading to Nikko, and now their contribution seems to be the greatest of all. We went in rikishas and on horseback six miles down this beautiful avenue to the next town and then back to the great tall cryptomaria trees and the small groups of thatched, roofed houses, with here and there a waterwheel. Did not look very much like our country, for sure.

"In the afternoon, Miss Hyde went with us to the various curio stores that were not such awful rascals as they might be, but I don't think the trip is of much interest to you, especially after it gets onto paper, so I'll go on to…" CJG

日光 NIKKŌ
Thursday 1908 7/16

Before today, the rainy season has been a succession of showers and cloudy days, but today it started in good earnest and kept it up steadily for over twelve hours, so we couldn't do more than go out to a postcard store near the hotel or stop in at the salesroom in the hotel. Three times a day, as we walk from the dining room to the office, we are attacked by the shopkeepers, who have brought their wares up for display. 'Won't you come in.' 'Look at my table, please' or 'Pleese, meesee, come in' and, of course, we can't resist. There is a considerable variety for the first day or two as all the storekeepers do not come at once, but after that, you get to know all the displays pretty well. The monkeys are always in evidence, on postal cards, carved in wood, ivory, or silver. All silver or metal here is 'hand carved, no cast' or 'fine hand work.' Perhaps it was stamped by hand, but I doubt it." CJG

SUGI NAMIKI 杉並木
Cryptomeria Avenue

Another version of the donation story relates that a poor daimyō could not afford the gift of a stone lantern for the funeral of Tokugawa Ieyasu. The daimyō asked permission instead to plant an avenue of Cryptomeria. The avenue of Cryptomeria is said to be forty miles in length and continues to awe in the twenty-first century.

踏車
FUMIGURUMA
Treadmill worked by young man to draw water

雨 **AME** *Rain* When the attractions of Nikkō are mentioned, those who are familiar with the area will point out that the rainy season can bring a great deal —really "buckets"—of rain.

中禅寺 CHŪZENJI
Friday 1908 7/17

The first bright day we've had. I skipped down before breakfast and took some fine pictures of the bullomobiles with their waving awnings. Soon after breakfast, we started off in our usual manner on horseback and in rikishas for an eight-mile ride to Chuzenji. We followed the bullomobile railroad for about two miles at first and then, turning off, followed the Nikko river, crossing it several times. At present, the stream is rather small, but if it ever fills its bed, as they say it does, it must be far from small.

"At the halfway tea house, while we were waiting for the rikishas to come up, we met Mrs. Smith, one of our table companions on the 'Siberia.' From the halfway station on is a continuous hard climb.

"At one of the tea houses, a rikisha boy urged Jinya to take the short cut, saying that he could save over a mile and a half that way, but never expected to see us go that way because it is supposed to be too steep for horses. Jinya took the short cut and, of course, we followed, but it was very steep. In one place, our horses had to go up some steps cut in the rock and, in others, they slipped badly in the mud, but we reached the road again in safety. A tea house keeper at the top of the short cut said that she had been there six years and that we were the first ones she had seen come up on horseback.

"About a quarter of a mile from the mouth of the lake where the town is situated, the river drops over a precipice and reaches a pool 980 feet below about five seconds later. We got a fine view of the fall by going down the side of the canyon a short distance to a platform, which is the sole property of the tea house at the top.

"We ate our lunch at the hotel and then started off a short time later to see a cascade three miles farther on, and from there, the rikishas turned back, and the horsebackers went on four miles farther to Yumoto (hot springs). This is also on a lake, and in several places hot muddy water can be seen bubbling up near the shore.

"The water from the lake slides down over a hundred feet of rock at an angle of 70 degrees from the horizontal, and it makes a great sight from the top or from the bottom.

"My horse had been acting well all day, so I didn't expect him to mind a little calf held by a man at the side of the road. But as the horse came up, the calf jumped suddenly, and the horse did the same in the opposite direction. I, not being accustomed to such sudden movement, thought I'd stay where I was, with the result that I soon landed in the road on my back. Aside from that, I was none the worse for my twenty-two-mile ride, but poor Jinya! He could hardly walk, and then he still had a ride of eight miles ahead of him." CJG

中禅寺湖 CHŪZENJI-KO *Chuzenji Lake* Highest lake in Japan at nearly 4200 feet above sea level, a clear and transparent body of water surrounded by deciduous trees that riot in color with autumn and so a lake much visited for its beauty in the fall of Japan. The lake is popular year round for hiking the encircling trail and for boating on its surface.

働く女達 HATARAKU ONNA TACHI *Working Women*

日光 NIKKŌ
Saturday 1908 7/18

"Our ride back to Nikko was not quite so pleasant as the day before, as instead of sunshine we had a thick mist to start out in and later pouring rain, but we reached the hotel about twelve o'clock entirely dry except our shoes.

"Our raincoats were a sight, soaking wet and splattered with mud.

"In the afternoon, we went out to one or two shops and started packing up once more." CJG

日光 NIKKŌ
Sunday 1908 7/19

"Raining all morning, so we didn't venture out. In the afternoon, we walked up the river a short distance to see the uncountable Chuddasso, so called, because there are so many of them and so much alike that the count never comes out twice alike. They are made of stone and are about forty in number, though there used to be more before the last great flood." CJG

Jizō.

"**CHUDDASSO**" is the attempt by Clarence to spell 地蔵座像 Jizō-zazō, the name for Jizō seated on a lotus flower, the beloved Japanese deity who works to ease the suffering of the living and the pain of the dead consigned to hell. Jizō Bosatsu (bosatsu is an enlightened being who chooses to stay on earth and relieve suffering rather than live in eternal bliss) is closely associated with Amida Buddha and Pure Land Buddhism and, even in the twenty-first century, is a popular god in Japan. In Nikkō, just upstream from the famous Shinkyō, the Sacred Red Bridge on which only the emperor is permitted to tread, may be found a great number of stone statues of a seated Jizō—some with red cap, some with red cap and red bib, some with neither. Their backs against the hillside, the Jizōsan sit along the far side of the path that follows the curves of the Kanmangafuchi Abyss and gaze across the path into the churning waters. (*See photo on page 96.*) Clarence notes that many more Jizō statues once existed but that many were destroyed in a flood. Legend also says that the statues change places from time to time and can never be seen twice in the same location.

地蔵 Jizō is usually portrayed today as standing, a sweet, simplistically smiling figure, sometimes cartoon-like, often with red hat and bib. Jizō statues are frequently placed in cemeteries, offering blessings to the dead, while the living—anyone with a problem—can find help through a benevolent Jizō.

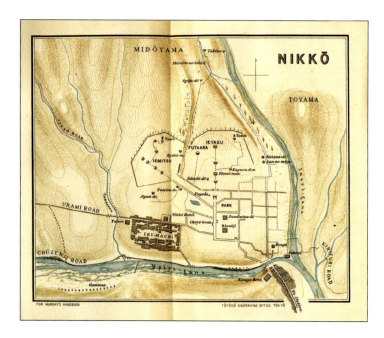

THREE TEMPLES A combination ticket covered entry to Rinnōji, Futarasanjinja, and Tōshōgū.

輪王寺 **RINNŌJI** was founded in 766 by Buddhist monk Shōdō Shōnin (d. 817), who climbed the great summits surrounding Nikkō and brought to the area Buddhism. Rinnōji is to be reached by a long flight of steps.

二荒山神社 **FUTARASAN JINJA** Founded in 767 by Shōdō Shōnin, stands within a grove of cryptomeria and is known for its many stone lanterns. It owns Shinkyō, the Sacred Red Bridge, whose creation is also attributed to Shōdō Shōnin.

日光東照宮 **NIKKŌ TOSHŌGŪ** and the shrines and temples of Nikkō became known to both the Japanese and the Western tourist through the Yokohama Shashin photographer Adolfo Farsari.

日光 NIKKŌ
Monday 1908 7/20

Our admission tickets to the three temples had expired after their five days, but we managed to find five tickets that had been used for the main temple only.

"One of the temples we visited was placed at the top of a long flight of moss-grown stone steps and among a grove of cryptomaria [sic] trees. A service was in progress here as we came up. While we were waiting, the young man that we met at the Gales in Seoul stepped up and spoke to us. We found that he is a Y.M.C.A. teacher in Hachiman, a short distance beyond Hikone on Lake Biwa. He studied for an architect and was at Dr. Gales' to look over some plans.

"The priests of the temple seem to be mixed as well as the decoration, for in the service the Buddhists recited the words while the Shinto priest furnished the music.

"Going down by a staircase at the side of the temple, we looked down on a regular forest of stone lanterns, all covered on the top with about two inches of thick green moss.

"We went to a panorama near the temples, where we saw the various shoguns of the Tokugawa family painted in some important scene of their life and then, in the upper story, the battle by which they first gained their power.*

"In the afternoon, we went to get some photos near an old temple. Here we met a priest whom we had seen at the row of Buddhas yesterday. He invited us to come up to his temple and have some tea. This we did and had quite a talk on maps, admirals of our navy, where we came from, etc. We finally managed to get away and down to the shops to finish up some odds and ends.

"One of the waiters of the 'Manchuria,' who is cleaning up here in the dining room now, said, 'You lite too much. By by you go clazy. You blarne all play out.' At times, I think that it might be true. Another boy says, 'You lite vely fast. You vely clever. How many years you been to school?' My fountain pen and the speed of my writing seem to be the wonder of the time. And then beside that, I can actually read Chinese, for I can tell what the characters on the chessmen are. 'You go Chinese school, boy?' 'No.' 'Then where you learn read?'

"I find that though I played the [chess] game only once before coming on board, I have beaten almost as many times as I have been beaten." CJG

Battle of Sekigahara, 21 October 1600

80 Japan 1908

伊香保 IKAHO
Tuesday 1908 7/21

Off again. After six-hour train ride, we all piled into a private horse car that was almost large enough to hold us and our baggage and started off at full gallop. I'm sorry to say though that this lasted only long enough to get out of town. When we slowed down to a steady trot, the car had a flat wheel and the rails weren't quite as smooth as they might have been. Also, the horse was in the habit of going first to one side and then to the other, giving the car a jerk and a bump every time. You can guess that we were thankful when those three hours were over.

"According to Jinya, this was a great country for 'riris' or 'reerees.' Can you guess what he meant? We saw one or two orange ones and some even on the roofs of the houses but not in the abundance we had expected. An hour and a half of rikisha riding was better than the tramcar but nothing to boast of for smoothness and comfort.

"Our rooms are in semi-Japanese style and made to shut up air tight with paper screens. Luckily, the ones opening into the main hall are stuffed with newspapers to keep the light out and the shadows in. In the window side of the rooms is a public passage way, which can be cut off from the rooms by the air tight screens. We got them to screen off our section of the passageway, and so we didn't suffocate." CJG

鐘撞き堂
KANETSUKIDŌ
Small Bell Tower with sign that reads, "Please don't ring the bell"

伊香保
IKAHO

Famous for its hot springs and for its main street, which comprises a series of wide and deep stairs that climb up the mountainside on which the town is situated. In 1908, Ikaho was a short day trip from Tokyo and well worth the visit. At 2500 feet above sea level, the nights are cool, mosquitoes are few, mineral springs abound, as do wild flowers and birds all summer long. Houses on the west side of the main street border on a great ravine, through which rushes a foaming torrent, and from every standpoint are endless views of vast valleys and majestic mountains.

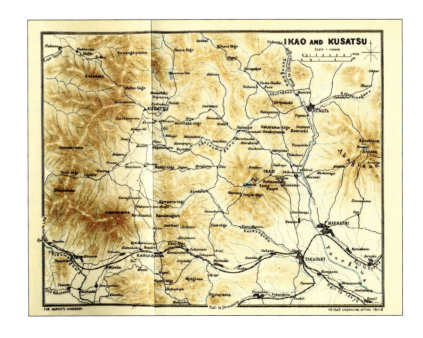

布袋 **HOTEI**
God of Abundance
One of the Seven Gods of Luck

達磨 **DARUMA** *Daruma Dolls*

BODHIDHARMA
A sixth-century Buddhist patriarch and the Buddhist monk who meditated for nine years until his arms and his legs rotted away and dropped off, hence, the armless and legless *daruma* doll. Bodhidharma also plucked out his eyelids in a fury after falling asleep during meditation. Then his eyeballs fell out, leaving him blind, and so Daruma dolls are sold blind.

伊香保と湯本 IKAHO & YUMOTO
Wednesday 1908 7/22

Father and I walked a short distance from our hotel in Ikao [*sic*] to Yumato, the third town of that name that we have visited, and saw the hot springs there. Then coming back to the hotel, we started off downhill again in our rikishas. On leaving the hotel, we were presented with half a dozen postcards. Two of the subjects pictured were 'A hat spring' and 'The glshing place' besides 'All eight of telegraph wires in Ikao.'

"After another three hours on the horse car, we reached the town where we were to take our lunch and the train and transferred our baggage to a small tea house.

"Miss Hyde told us of a custom for business men to get a daruma, one of these fat red men that always stand up again when you knock them down, without the black spots painted in the eyes, in other words, a blind one. They tell him what they want and promise to give him his eyes when they succeed in getting it. We found a large daruma in the tea house with only one eye. When Jinya asked them why it was, they said they'd forgotten but finally confessed.

"We arrived at Karuizawa at about five and were met by Mrs. Gorbold at the train, and she escorted us to the hotel." CJG

YUMOTO Chamberlain lists five towns named Yumoto in *A Handbook for Travellers*.

達磨 **DARUMA** A popular Japanese talisman for good luck. Usually made of papier mache, the figurine, or so-called *daruma* doll, is weighted at the bottom, so that when knocked over, it always returns to upright, this reflective of the success that comes through persistence despite adversity. The Japanese phrase 七転び八起き *Nanakorobi Yaoki* (seven times down, eight times up) encapsulates this type of persistence.

The doll is usually sold without eyes at the first of the New Year. The owner of the doll will paint in one eye with a New Year's goal in mind. Whenever the doll is seen with the missing eye, the owner is reminded of the incomplete goal. When the goal is achieved, the second eye is painted in. This is a part of Japanese culture, and a politician, for instance, may call for votes so that he can paint in the second eye of his *daruma*.

Daruma refers to Bodhidharma, the monk who founded Ch'an (Zen) Buddhism. The Daruma-dera (Temple of Daruma) lies in the city of Takasaki, lying north of Tokyo. An annual Daruma Doll Festival is held in Takasaki, which is believed to be the birthplace of the *daruma* doll. Part of the New Year's celebration includes 達磨供養 *Daruma Kuyō*, The Burning of the Old Dolls, on the night after New Year's Day, and purchasing a new *daruma* doll for the New Year.

軽井沢 **KARUIZAWA**
Thursday 1908 7/23

"We stopped at all the shops on the street in the morning, and Mother went wild over the lace in the five or six lace stores. In the afternoon, we went to the tennis courts, the social meeting place of Karuizawa." CJG

軽井沢 **KARUIZAWA**
Friday 1908 7/24

"I spent [the day] mainly at the tennis courts with some of the boys I met here. We went to the Gorbolds' for dinner and afterwards to a reception in the auditorium." CJG

姉さま被り と 前掛け
ANESAMA KABURI TO MAEKAKE
Head-covering of Cotton Toweling and Work Apron worn by working woman

石灯籠 **ISHITŌRŌ**
Stone Lantern

軽井沢 **KARUIZAWA** A British theologian, Alexander Croft Shaw, discovered how delightfully cool was Karuizawa during the summer. At approximately 3200 feet above sea level, Karuizawa offered to his missionary friends a welcome escape from the sweltering heat of Tokyo. More missionaries and then more Westerners followed him, and Chamberlain in *A Handbook for Travellers* complains of "the cheap wooden houses of the summer residents" and notes that there are no hot springs or mineral baths to attract the Japanese. Up until about 1910, Karuizawa was considered a summer resort for foreigners and Westerners, particularly the Western missionaries, which explains the visit of the Gambles to Karuizawa. But after 1910, the Japanese, too, began to appreciate the summer cool of Karuizawa. The town lies at the foot of Mount Asama, which is a semi-active volcano, and so is recommended as the starting point for excursions into the Mount Asama lava beds and on to the sides of the volcano itself.

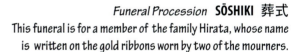

Funeral Procession **SŌSHIKI** 葬式
This funeral is for a member of the family Hirata, whose name is written on the gold ribbons worn by two of the mourners.

浅間 ASAMA
Saturday 1908 7/25

"At seven o'clock this morning, several of the inhabitants here and I started off for the lava beds near Asama, a semi-active volcano near here. Soon after we left the town, the fog in which we started changed to a heavy rain. I had given up the idea of taking an umbrella because I thought that it would be too hard to manage while trotting or cantering. The horses were the poorest we have had, as they walked all the time and very slowly at that. I could have managed an umbrella easily and wished very much that I had taken one. The boys who were walking soon passed us and arrived at the tea house about half an hour before we did. The water started to go through my raincoat, and the saddle got very hard, so I got off and walked for the last two of the nine miles.

"We stopped at a tea house nine miles from Karuizawa to dry off, and some ate their lunch. Then leaving some of our baggage there, we went on three miles farther to the lava beds. These are large masses of broken rock piled up every which way with large cracks and holes between. It forms a strip almost a mile wide of the roughest possible ground, and sharp-edged rock are about the only things to walk on.

"Asama, from which the lava came, showed up finely, as the rain had stopped, and the sun was trying hard to get out. On the edge of the lava flow is a small cave almost filled with ice and with a small amount of water running through it, and here we all had a fine ice cold drink.

"By the time we got back to the tea house, the sun had come out, so we ate the rest of our lunch out in a small summer house by a stream. The ride back was fine. The sun was out, and Asama was sending out small clouds of steam. Half the way, we rode on the division between two provinces, which was marked by a cleared area 30 feet wide, dug out to about three feet below the surface of the surrounding land. The remainder of the distance, we went through thick woods or down steep ravines until about a mile from Karuizawa, where we struck a fine macadam road and followed it to the stables.

"The rest of the family had been to Mrs. Toppings for lunch. She is the one that sent Miss Ishahara to the kindergarten training school in Cincinnati. We all went to the MacNair's house for dinner and had a fine time there, though I had to retire early, as you can imagine that I felt somewhat tired after the twenty-four mile ride." CJG

KINDERGARTEN TRAINING SCHOOL Clarence is referring to the Cincinnati Missionary Training School, where the Gambles had met Japanese women at Kindergarten Hall.

草鞋 **WARAJI** Sandals made from rice straw are being sold by this vendor.

浅間山 **ASAMAYAMA** Mount Asama The most active volcano on Honshū, the main island of Japan, rises over 8,000 feet above sea level. In 1783, the volcano erupted over a three-month period. Referred to as the Tenmei eruption, it destroyed a large primeval forest and several villages on its north side. Eruptions are noted as long ago as 685 and have occurred with frightening regularity, sometimes annually, throughout the subsequent centuries. The surrounding lava beds of barren rock became a popular tourist destination, along with the welcoming springs of fine cold water to refresh the travellers.

軽井沢 KARUIZAWA
Sunday 1908 7/26

"The sun is still out and getting somewhat warm, warm enough to make me very glad to take the morning quietly. We managed to get out to church though and then went over to the Gorbolds for dinner.

"Late in the afternoon after it had begun to cool off a little, Mr. Gorbold and I walked to a large spring near what once was the main road of Japan." CJG

MAIN ROAD *Nakasendō* Approximately 332 miles in length and an alternate trade route to the Tōkaidō, with a station at Karuizawa.

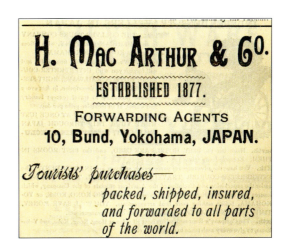

東京と横浜 TOKYO & YOKOHAMA
Monday 1908 7/27

"Mr. Gorbold, having business in Tokyo, went with us on the train. We arrived in Tokyo at about four, and as we had not yet had a good Japanese meal, he took us to a Japanese inn. There, taking off all our shoes at the front door, we put on half-slippers and were escorted to our rooms. We had to take off even the slippers before entering this sanctuary, but we went in and made ourselves comfortable on the floor. Two sides of the room were open, the paper screen being slid back. The third was half door and half plain wall, and the fourth had the closet and bureau combined, occupying one half the space, and the mantel, a small shelf about six inches high, holding a flower basket and curiously colored stone in the shape of Fuji and, above it, a kakemono made of a dozen or so slaps of a brush.

"The supper was served in our rooms at seven. First came a fish soup containing a big chunk of fish and a few vegetables. Next came the dinner, half a fish nicely cooked and ready to break with your chopsticks; raw fish, which in spite of all ideas and prejudices on the subject is fine, and a spicy sauce to dip it in; a vegetable mixture: uly (pronounced "riry") root, Japanese potato, and some greens; and as many bowls of rice as you wish. The meal was all very good, except the vegetables, which the Japs never cook half enough.

"We took the train to Yokohama soon after supper, and sending Mother and Father off to the hotel, Mr. Gorbold, Sidney, and I went to a Japanese inn. Our beds were composed of a quilt about an inch thick to lie on, as many of these as you wanted to suit you (in our case none, on account of the heat), a clean kimono to sleep in, and as we didn't bring our pillows with us, a couple of mats for our head." CJG

ULY *Lily Roots* A popular Japanese food

印半纏 **SHIRUSHI BANTEN** Company-issued jackets are worn by the Yokohama workers below.

Japan 1908 85

鎌倉 **KAMAKURA** lies on the east coast of Japan, today less than an hour south of Tokyo. In 1908, tourists came to see the shrines, temples, and historical monuments that date back to the Kamakura period (1185-1333) and before, but most particularly to see the Kamakura Daibutsu, the fifty-foot-high bronze statue of Amida Buddha at Kōtoku'in. Visitors can walk within the hollow statue. See photos xxvi, 88, and note 9 page xxx.

鎌倉 KAMAKURA
Tuesday 1908 7/28

"For breakfast, we had seaweed soup, a Japanese omelet, and vegetables and rice. We met Father and Mother at the station and went by train to Kamakura to spend the day. We saw and went inside the Daibutsu or Big Buddha and then off to see a conference of Christian women, and after calling at three houses and taking two trolley rides, we found that they had gone on a 'picnic,' as this was their last day. At the last house where we stopped, we saw two girls scurry out of the way with glasses of suspiciously looking brown liquid. Mr. Gorbold said, 'This can't be the place. Look at them drinking beer.' But it was the place after all, and one of the girls was the one that had asked Father how to make soap when we visited the school in Tokyo. After we had left the house and were waiting at the station, the two girls and a maid came down and brought us some of the same brown liquid, which turned out to be iced coffee made from wheat, so it was all right after all. By taking an earlier train than we had expected to, we reached Yokohama in time for lunch. We left Mr. Gorbold on the train, as he was going to Tokyo."   CJG

源頼朝 **MINAMOTO NO YORITOMO** (1147-1199) entrenched in Kamakura, far from the intrigues of the then capital of Kyoto, set the course of Japan history for the next seven hundred years. Kamakura, with hills on three sides and the sea on the fourth, offered natural fortifications to a fledgling government. Yoritomo married wisely, and Hojō Masako brought him the support of the Hojō clan. Yoritomo ruled efficiently and ruthlessly; he had his two brothers assassinated. His twenty-year military rule in Kamakura gave rise to the *samurai*, the warrior caste, to feudalism and its accompanying values, which would govern and dominate Japan until the mid-nineteenth century. Not until Toyotomi Hideyoshi disarmed the citizenry and Tokugawa Ieyasu seized the shogunate in 1600 would Japan know less than continuous warfare throughout its land.

横浜 YOKOHAMA
Wednesday, Thursday, Friday 1908   7/29, 7/30, 7/31

"Were spent in shopping, packing, perspiring, and trying to keep cool. We felt very much inspired to adopt the Japanese costume and came as near as possible to it while in our rooms, but still we were hot hot hot. At sunset on Thursday, we had a fine view of Fuji from our window, and on Friday afternoon, after we had gone on board the 'Manchuria,' we could see the tip of it until dark, and after supper as we sailed away, its dark form was still visible. And now my story, together with our visit to Japan, must end."   CJG

AFTERWORD

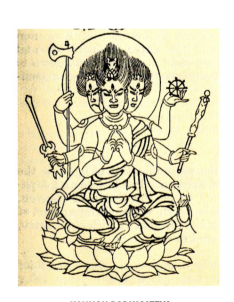

KANNON BODHISATTVA
Goddess of Mercy and Compassion

JAPAN
2012

LOVE STONE
This stone is called "Love-fortune-telling" stone. If you walk safely from this stone to the other with your eyes closed, for once, your wish'll be granted soon. If you can't, it will be long before your love is realized. And it is said taking advice requires you to have someone who'll help you achieve your love.

AFTERWORD
Japan April 2012

But it was Japan...the mysterious land from my childhood....
I loved the cherry blossoms in bloom around Osaka castle....
adored the simple aesthetics of old Japanese houses with their
tatami *floors and sliding* shoji *doors.*
　—Michael Ward, "Last Train to Takatsuki"[1]

Were the Gambles to return to Japan in 2012 and revisit the sites of their original itinerary, their nineteenth-century eyes would find much to wonder at. Immediately, not to be met by *jinrikisha*, but to have a choice of train, bus, van, limousine, or taxi! They would certainly choose a taxi, where they would meet welcoming Japanese courtesy and a driver speaking some English; the ride would be smooth, and the cleanliness and the pristine white pique embroidered covers on seats and head rests would delight them. They would be dazzled by the complex public transportation system of trains, trams, buses, subways, and ferries that connect all areas of the cities and all parts of the prefectures and the nation (as well as the bicycles, motorbikes, scooters, and motorcycles that are available). Any of these choices would offer great comfort compared to the "bouncing and thumping" of a *kago* or the lurching of a wagon drawn by a skittish horse, though they would still find that, at times, many connections are necessary to get from here to there, as did Tsutae-san, my expert *Jinya* of 2012, and I discovered after four changes of train and two taxis on our trip from Nikkō to Ise.

Travelling with a boxed lunch in a basket is no longer necessary. The *bentō* (boxed lunch), now usually arranged on a plastic tray, is sold at stalls and shops and at the ubiquitous convenience stores in every train and subway station and bus depot, but the traditional Japanese *bentō* sits squeezed amidst an array of Western goodies that includes everything from Snickers to chips, pretzels, cookies, and every other kind of packaged snack imaginable. Fast food places offering hamburgers, pizza, and soft drinks abound. Speciality bread shops and bakeries featuring French pastries and decorated cakes are in the train stations that merge into malls and on into the streets of the cities. Pickle shops must be sought out. In Tokyo, in 1908, Clarence noted, "We managed to get enough to eat, though the

京都駅
KYOTO EKI
Decorated
Bakery
Easter Cake
*Kyoto
Train Station*
April 2012

TSUTAE と特急
LIMITED EXPRESS
パーサー
Tsutae &
Limited Express
Attendant
長崎 Nagasaki
April 2012

名古屋城
NAGOYA JŌ
Nagoya Castle
April 2012

meal was an unsuccessful attempt to serve real European food." Such is no longer the case. Today, in the major cities of Japan, real European food and Western junk food fairly crowd out traditional Japanese fare.

Disembarking at Yokohama (instead of flying into Tokyo), it would be raining; otherwise, to the Gambles nothing would be familiar, for Yokohama was fairly leveled by the 1923 Great Kanto earthquake, scarcely a building of the then energetic international port city left standing. The Hundred Steps to the Bluff, where the foreigners lived; the wonderful Grand Hotel, which overlooked Yokohama Harbor where the Gambles and the Western tourists stayed—all obliterated. The rebuilt Yokohama was subsequently destroyed by World War II bombings, as was much of Tokyo, which the Gambles visited on the fourth day after their arrival in Japan. Tokyo remains even today the "Japanese city of magnificent distances," as Clarence called it, but the Kanto earthquake took down vast swaths there as well, and the densely packed, fast-paced technological metropolis that is Tokyo today fairly overwhelms visitors of the twenty-first century, let alone those from the nineteenth and early twentieth.

Nagoya, their next stop, is home to Mitsubishi. During World War II, Nagoya was the site of Mitsubishi Aircraft Engine Works and the center of Japanese aircraft and weapons manufacturing. Its many factories and war industries, along with the railroad freight yards and its spacious port, made Nagoya a prime target for Allied precision bombing and for firebombing. Nagoya Castle, which the Gambles found "an imposing affair" in 1908, was

90   Japan 1908

a military command post in the 1940s and a specific Allied target. Subsequently rebuilt, the Nagoya castle facade appears much as did the original. Not so the major buildings of *Atsuta* Shrine (which dates back to *circa* 686 A.D.), most of which were destroyed. The 1950s constructions are nothing like the buildings that the Gambles saw. Still, from the photo taken by Clarence and Sidney on page 10, the Gambles would recognize the dancers with their great sleeves in ceremony, just as I did when I visited *Atsuta* in April 2012. And the photo on page 9 of *Dairyūji*, which houses the carved statues of the five hundred *rakan* (Buddhist disciples who attained nirvana) could have been taken in 2012. Since its erection in 1875 in northeast Nagoya, *Dairyūji* has somehow remained unscathed by earthquake and fire and untouched by World War II.

林 本工所
HAYASHI MOTSUKOSYO
Hayashi Woodworking Shop
高松
Takamatsu
April 2012

On reaching Kyoto, the Gambles would be confronted by multi-storied office buildings towering over multi-lane boulevards. But behind these busy thoroughfares that channel Kyoto's heavy traffic may be seen some semblance of 1908 Japan in its small burrowing alleyways. Here are mini-streets, streets barely wide enough to accommodate the width of a car, lined with people-sized buildings, and sometimes the original *machinami,* a term that means "city rows" and which refers to the narrow wooden houses, sometimes as slight as eight meters wide but forty meters or more deep. "Bedrooms of eels" they were jokingly called by their residents, the rising merchant class of the Edo period, who built to avoid the taxes that were assessed on the basis of street frontage. With the family shop in the front room opening on to the street, the living quarters stretch back, sometimes including an interior garden, into the untaxed meters of house behind. Today, if not *machinami,* these small streets are packed with two- or three-story high buildings that house restaurants and art galleries, antique shops and convenience stores, even a small private shrine with an offering of fresh flowers.

祠
HOKORA
Small Shrine
Kyoto 京都
April 2012

Japan 1908 91

賓頭盧
BINZURU
東大寺
TŌDAIJI
奈良 Nara
April 2012

修学旅行
SYUGAKU RYOKŌ
Student Field Trip
金閣寺
KINKAKUJI
京都 Kyoto
April 2012

In Kyoto and throughout all Japan, the Gambles would recognize the temples and shrines they had visited a century ago, but now, on entering, instead of cloth overshoes, they would be handed plastic bags in which to carry their shoes as they walk and observe. They would see the great national treasures of Japan, some recently restored, some gently modified, and others standing in their unsullied magnificence just as they have stood for centuries. *Ginkakuji*, the Silver Pavilion, has been carefully returned to the original vision first held by Ashikaga Yoshimasa in 1482; *Kinkakuji*, the Golden Pavilion, was completely but carefully rebuilt after being destroyed in 1950 by arson. The buildings of *Shimogamo Jinja*, as we learned from a priest at its sister shrine, *Kamigamo Jinja*, have been refurbished in a more decorative style over the decades, yet continue to be distinctly recognizable. *Tōdaiji* in Nara appears untouched since its latest incarnation in 1709, and the sacred deer could be the same as those the Gambles fed in 1908.

Over all, souvenir shop and visitor information buildings are new and comfort stations happily updated, but otherwise the sacred buildings belong to the ages. Behind the bemused Kamakura Buddha, the *Daibutsu* dating from approximately 1252, the surrounding arcade has been newly constructed, as has the walkway beside the ocean with its shrines and temples leading to *Meoto Iwa*, the Wedded Rocks, where *Izanagi* and *Izanami* stand yet amidst the roiling waves, their tie faithfully renewed throughout the year with a ton of new straw rope. *Chion'in, Kiyomizudera, Higashi Ōtani, Heian Jingū, Hōkoku Byō, Nanzenji,* and the great temples and shrines of Nikkō and of Miyajima, all seen by the Gambles, remain unmistakably themselves and are much visited, not only by tourists, but by Japanese from all walks of life and especially by troops of school children on field trips, ensuring that the next generation has an understanding of their rich heritage.[2]

So it is with the gardens, which today can appear much as in Clarence and Sidney's photos and where we could often duplicate their shots. *Higashi Honganji* is under major construction until 2013, but *Shōseien,* its nearby garden with the famous bridge *Shinsetsukyō,* is unchanged. In *Shōseien,* we were free to stroll about at our leisure, but through the splendid Imperial Gardens, *Shūgakuin,* we were marched in carefully conducted tours led back to back throughout the day. Although a special permit from your Ambassador is no longer required for admission to the Imperial Gardens, an appointment to do so must be made in advance. The buildings of the Imperial Gardens and the tea pavilion (where the Gambles saw the paintings of Kanō Hidenobu, whose fish was so realistic that it escaped every night, until a second artist painted a net to restrict its swim), are no longer open to the public, but the gardens continue to awe. Similarly, neither the interiors of the Golden Pavilion nor of the Silver Pavilion, wherein the Gambles were served tea and cakes, are open to the public, as they were to the Gambles in 1908.

Hikone Castle, one of the few original castles remaining in Japan, may be entered. Its bare wooden walls, great wooden trusses, and enormous structural beams are sufficiently impressive so that what furnishings might have existed are not missed. For the trip to Hikone Castle, the Gambles took a steamer, but steamers are no longer allowed on Lake Biwa; in our century, Hikone Castle must be reached by train.

To the west of Kyoto, it is still possible to ride down the Hozu Rapids. Today, the men pushing against the bank and steering with great oars are assisted by gasoline engines, somewhat different from

侵雪橋
SHINSETSUKYŌ
Snow-Capped Bridge
渉成園
SHŌSEIEN
東本願寺
HIGASHI HONGANJI
Kyoto 京都
April 2012

彦根城の梁
HIKONE JŌ NO HARI
Hikone Castle Truss
April 2012

Japan 1908　93

京都 ホテル
オークラ
KYOTO HOTEL ŌKURA
April 2012

日光 金谷
ホテル
NIKKŌ KANAYA HOTEL
Front Desk
April 2012

the work of the men whose strength alone towed the boats, while they trudged along the tracks, still to be seen today, beside the river. Today, the passengers include as many foreigners as Japanese, but in 1908, in describing their arrival at the top of the Rapids, Clarence wrote, "Foreigners seem to be quite a novelty here." While Mary Gamble stood and waited for the ride downstream, "six women in a row behind [her were] taking in her dress."

In Tokyo, on the second of July, when the Gambles went "to see a collection of old curios made by a private gentleman," they could not have known that the private gentleman was Ōkura Kihachirō, whose "collection of old curios" would become the basis for the *Ōkura Shūkokan*, the first private art museum in Japan. In the Great Kanto Earthquake, all art on exhibit was destroyed; a new earthquake-proof museum was rebuilt in 1927, and *Ōkura Shūkokan* is today a Registered Cultural Property. Along with his interest in art, Ōkura Kihachirō founded what would become the Ōkura Hotel Chain, and that Chain today includes the Kyoto Hotel where the Gambles stayed in April of 1908.

In 2012, the now Kyoto Hotel Ōkura would not be recognizable to the Gambles. A massive renovation in 1994 added seventeen stories to the building that opened its doors in 1888 and created an elegant lobby reminiscent of the 1920s. The Fujiya Hotel in Hakone, Miyanoshita, which has hosted so many celebrities and dignitaries, including the Emperor and Empress of Japan, would also be a surprise, with its many additions registered as important cultural assets, its Flower Palace and Kikka-so Inn, and its private baths fed by natural hot springs. But the Kanaya Hotel in Nikkō, sister hotel to the Fujiya with an equally impressive guest list, standing as it does atop its hill where there is no room for additional construction, is its original self; and the front desk at which David Gamble signed the register for rooms 55 and 56 on July 11, 1908, remains unchanged. In keeping with maintaining its traditions, Inouye Makiko, the great-granddaughter of Kanaya founder Kanaya Zenichiro, is president of the Kanaya Hotel.

The schools that the Gambles visited have over the century thrived. Although *Dōshisha* University, in Tokyo, in the wake of anti-Western sentiment in the 1880s was forced briefly to close its nursing school, it today runs an integrated educational system with a Christian focus that covers from kindergarten through professional graduate courses, along with many international exchange and visitor programs. Mary Denton, with whom the Gambles had supper at *Dōshisha*, is remembered with the Denton Building and a plaque attesting to her memory.

The Gambles also met "Miss Treuda," as Clarence spells the name, at her school in Tokyo. Tsuda Umeko had taken the radical step in 1900 of opening a private educational institution for women. By 1905, her school, *Joshi Eigaku Juku*, had been granted government authority to issue teaching certificates. In 1908, the Gambles thought the school "fine with a good building and faculty." Today, Tsuda College, with its emphasis on language learning, has graduated over 27,000 students and, in 2010, celebrated its 110th anniversary.

清水寺
KIYOMIZUDERA
Kyoto 京都
April 2012

In Kobe, the Gambles met educational pioneer Annie Howe, who showed the Gambles her famous Glory Kindergarten, then took them to a "Christian college for girls," and finally to lunch. For forty years, Glory Kindergarten was a pioneering influence on the kindergarten movement in Japan, until for economic reasons, it was merged with what is today Kobe University, but which in 1908 was Kobe College and most certainly the "Christian college for girls" that the Gambles visited with Annie Howe.³

高徳院
KŌTOKU'IN
鎌倉
KAMAKURA
April 2012

The Gambles came to Japan as eager tourists but also in the cause of Christianity. They were sincere, kind, concerned, and earnest. As Mary Gamble wrote to son Clarence some years later in July 1921,

> The task of Christian people and the church in this restless, hungry, demoralized world seems perfectly tremendous....I don't believe anything but the principles of Jesus can bring order or lasting peace.

Japan 1908 95

人力車
JINRIKISHA
京都 Kyoto
April 2012

地蔵座像
JIZŌ-ZAZŌ
日光 Nikkō
April 2012

In the twenty-first century, Christian missionaries continue to be active. I had only just arrived in Japan, when I met an eighty-year-old American, who had been living and working in Japan as a missionary since her early 20s and was now writing a book about her life there. But Mary Gamble would be disappointed to know that Christians constitute only about one percent of the Japanese population today —although seven prime ministers have been Christians—and that the Christian calendar has little bearing on Japanese life.

Yet nothing would surprise and amaze David and Mary Gamble more, even Mary Gamble herself, who by 1920 was an outspoken advocate of forthright sex education for children, as much as the part son Clarence took in changing in Japan entrenched government policy on abortion and birth control. It was Clarence Gamble whose largess funded clinical studies that convinced the Japanese Diet to make birth control legal in Japan and, most importantly, to fund government clinics that offered health care and birth control to Japanese women.

The Westernization and industrialization of the world has swept the globe, and Japan is no exception. Where once lay rice fields, now stand apartment complexes. Malls, parking lots, take-out restaurants proliferate, and cities continue to sprawl; computerization dominates every phase of Japanese life, and the *jinrikisha* is a tourist attraction with pneumatic tires. Today, foreign students come regularly to Japan on study-abroad programs from high schools and colleges; tourists come with backpacks. No one packs a trunk; very few dress for dinner.

Yet Japan remains Japan. The respect for family and the elders, which has been the bane and blessing of Japan, continues to structure its society, and the shrines and temples are a formative part of Japan's daily life. When I went to *Atsuta* Shrine in Nagoya, a retired scientist and inventor walking the grounds on his daily visit, introduced me to the god of water and showed me His sacred dwelling. The shrines and temples dictate local festivals and national celebrations. In August, most of Japan celebrates *Obon* for three days. On these days, the spirits of the deceased return to be with their families. To honor their return, relatives living locally and those in far flung lands gather in a special part of the house before the *butsudan*, the shrine dedicated to family ancestors, to be with those who have passed. Graves are visited and tended, tombstones cleaned, and food offerings set out. So important are the days of *Obon* to Japan that, during that week, Tokyo is virtually an empty city with major corporations closed, its office workers and local residents off to be with their extended family in the family home site.

玄関の靴
GEN KAM NO KUTSU
Shoes at Entrance
Takamatsu 高松
April 2012

Oshōgatsu, which marks the beginning of the New Year, again brings families together. On the last day of the old year, Japan national television beams from all the great temples throughout Japan the 108 clangs of the bell which cleanse the listeners of the 108 worldly desires that would ensnare them. When New Year's Day arrives, in its earliest hours, families leave the temples and go to the shrines to pray for prosperity in the coming year. And throughout the months between *Oshōgatsu* and *Obon* and between *Obon* and *Oshōgatsu*, local and citywide festivals rooted in agricultural traditions and grand processions with *mikoshi*, the great carts in which the gods are enshrined, throng the streets. The returning Gambles would find Japan secure in its Kanji embrace, regularly cleaning and decorating its local shrines, enjoying its public baths, celebrating the cherry blossoms. Families honor their ancestors during *Obon*. Shoes are removed at the front door, the carp banners fly in May for Boys' Day, girls in kimonos celebrate *Hinamatsuri,* beauty is created in plates of food. And the rain still falls in buckets. ❏

京都の春
KYOTO NO HARU
Spring in Kyoto
April 2012

ENDNOTES

Japan 2012 (88). Clockwise: Greenhouse, Fujiya Hotel, Miyanoshita, Hakone; "Love Stone" sign, Jishu Shrine, Kiyomizudera, Kyoto; Carp Banners for May 5th, Tsuyama, Okayama; Daibutsu, Kōtoku'in, Kamakura; 25th of Month Bazaar, Kitano Tenmangū, Kyoto; Playground Duck, Kyoto; Wedded Rocks, Futami, Mie; Cow statue, Kitano Tenmangū, Kyoto.

[1] *Travelers Tales Japan: True Stories* (Palo Alto, California: Solas House, Inc., 2005) 310.

[2] *Choin'in, Kiyomizudera, Higashi Ōtani, Heian Jingū, Hōkoku Byō,* and *Nanzenji* are all in Kyoto.

[3] Annie Howe. *See* "p.xxv. Annie Lyon Howe" in Biographical Notes "Introduction" page 103.

BUDDHIST TEMPLE AT IKEGAMI
A Handbook for Travellers

APPENDICES

PROCESSION OF THE OIRAN

CLARENCE JAMES GAMBLE'S WRITING SCHEDULE

Two of Clarence's letters are shown below, the one on Kanaya Hotel stationery dated June 21, the other on Pacific Mail letterhead dated July 21. But the Gambles were in Miyajima on June 21 and did not reach Nikkō until July 11. Where did Clarence find Kanaya Hotel letterhead in Miyajima? And we know he was not on board a Pacific Mail ship on the day of July 21st.

So, as circumstances would seem to indicate, did he write of the family's adventures some time after the fact? Events of July 15 and later are written on letterhead of S.S. *Manchuria*, the ship that took them to China and returned them to San Francisco. Those of July 26 to July 31 are on letterhead reading "Vista del Arroyo, Pasadena, Cal." This could explain why we have photos of buildings and sites in Japan that are never mentioned in Clarence's Journal.

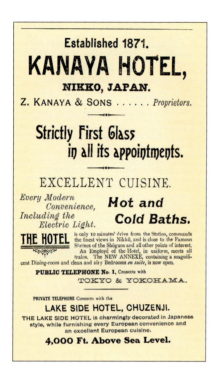

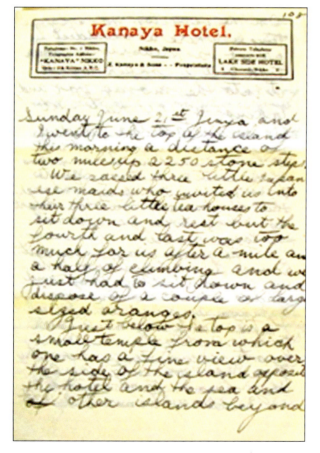

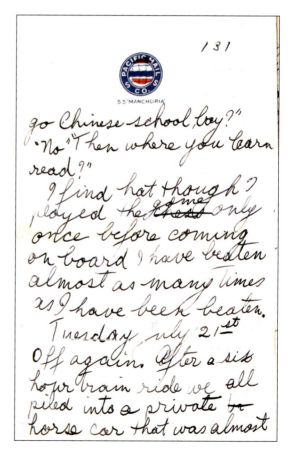

Between pages 6 and 7 of *A Handbook for Travellers in Japan* is found a chart, seen below right, of the annual rainfall in Japan. Clarence, too, takes note of the rain; his comments are less scientific but more heartfelt.

Sunday 4/12 "A rainy, foggy, and generally disagreeable day. We decided to go out nevertheless, so covered rickishas with rubber aprons took us to church."

Monday 4/13 "Still raining and foggy, but we decided to go to Tokyo for the day."

Wednesday 4/15 "We reached Nagoya at four in the pouring rain."

Wednesday 4/22 "Another procession comes off to-day, so, of course, the clouds are in evidence."

Thursday 4/23 "Still cloudy this morning with occasional shadows."

Monday 5/4 "Returning to the kindergarten, we saw the closing exercises. Umbrellas and the tall rainy day shoes were much in evidence, and they were needed, for it started to rain as the children left."

Tuesday 6/18 "Jinya met us in the pouring rain and accompanied us to the train. We reached Miyajima still in the pouring rain at about two."

Monday 6/22 "We packed all morning and left at two in the pouring rain."

Monday 6/29 "Regular Tokyo weather, or at least our idea of it. We drove in the pouring rain."

Wednesday 7/1 "Still we have Tokyo weather....It does seem as though it would never stop raining."

Thursday 7/2 "Still raining though not very hard."

Sunday 7/5 "We passed several fine waterfalls, which made us wish very much for a bright day and our cameras."

Tuesday 7/7 "After a short shower had passed, I started off again."

ANNUAL RAINFALL IN JAPAN

Saturday 7/11 "We arrived at Nikko in the pouring rain."

Sunday 7/12 "We ventured out to church in spite of the threatening skies."

Thursday 7/16 "Before today, the rainy season had been a succession of showers and cloudy days, but today it started in good earnest and kept it up steadily for over twelve hours."

Saturday 7/18 "Instead of sunshine, we had a thick mist to start out in and later pouring rain."

Sunday 7/19 "Raining all morning, so we didn't venture out."

Saturday 7/25 "Soon after we left the town, the fog in which we started changed to a heavy rain."

A Handbook for Travellers

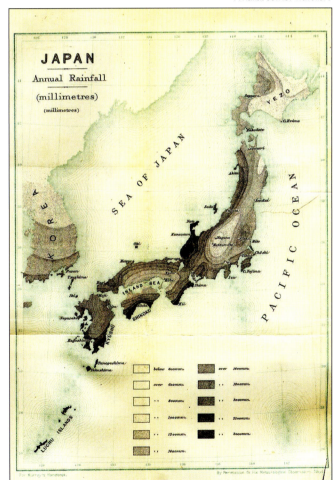

Japan 1908

BIOGRAPHICAL NOTES
"Introduction"

p. i. Clarence James Gamble (1894-1966) was the youngest son of David and Mary Gamble. He graduated from Princeton University and in 1922 was awarded his Harvard M.D. He planned on becoming a medical researcher, but meetings with Robert Dickinson and Margaret Sanger led him to join their search for a dependable contraceptive. With the help of a number of hard-working savy women as his co-workers, he funded the seeding of birth control clinics all over the world. His philanthropy supported extensive clinical studies in America, Japan, India, and Korea. These studies demonstrated the need for birth control and contributed to the development of The Pill. His marriage in 1924 to Sarah Bradley gave him a warm family life and descendants who individually and through Pathfinder International continue to make health care accessible to women.

p. i. David Berry Gamble (1847-1923) The seventh child and third son of James Gamble, co-founder of Procter & Gamble. In 1890, when P&G became a corporation, David Gamble became the first Secretary-Treasurer. In 1893, serious illness forced his retirement from daily office work. Once recovered, he continued to be involved in business and support of civic organizations in Cincinnati, and after The Gamble House was built in 1908, became as active in the Pasadena community. He died in Pasadena, much revered for his personal generosity, his philanthropy, and his many charitable community services.

p. i. Mary Huggins Gamble (1855-1929) was the daughter and step-daughter of Presbyterian ministers. She was a healthy little girl, but at the age of fourteen, she developed severe headaches, and her poor health interfered with her education. In 1877, she enjoyed one precious year at Smith College before marrying David Berry Gamble in 1882 at 27 years of age. She was devoted to supporting education for women and worked hand in hand with her husband in supporting Christian-based ministrations and educational institutions in Cincinnati, Pasadena, and Asia.

p. I. James Gamble (1803-1891) Irish by birth, soap maker by trade, in 1837 joined in business with his candle maker brother-in-law, William Procter. By building their trade on integrity and honest dealings, they prospered, and today Procter & Gamble is global in scope.

p. i. Sidney David Gamble (1890-1968) The second son of David and Mary Gamble, he devoted his life to the study of life in China between 1908 and 1932. The more than 5,000 black- and-white photos he took during those years are an irreplaceable record of early twentieth-century China, and his socioeconomic studies of northern China were pioneering works in the field of Sociology. His research and publications led to a new understanding of the society of China.

p. III. Margaret Sanger (1879-1966) In the face of brutal attacks, dedicated her life to giving to women their choice and fought unstintingly to make birth control legal. She founded what was to become Planned Parenthood and Planned Parenthood International.

p. iii. Yoshio Koya (1890-1974) Novelist, public health physician, and Director of Japan's National Institute of Public Health, who worked closely with Clarence Gamble..

p. v. Matthew C. Perry (1794-1858) Commodore of the U.S. Navy, with successful engagements in Mexican-American War (1846-1848), was influential in modernizing the Navy and called Father of the Steam Navy. On arriving at the Japan coast in 1853, he refused orders to leave and forced the Japanese to accept the letter from President Millard Fillmore that would ultimately initiate trade relations with Japan.

p. v. William Howard Taft (1857-1930) Secretary of War under Theodore Roosevelt, was the one-term twenty-seventh U.S. president, a trust buster, who promoted "Dollar Diplomacy" and saw passed the Sixteenth Amendment instituting federal income tax.

p. x. Theodore Roosevelt (1858-1919) Twenty-sixth U..S. president, vitalized the Conservation Movement, oversaw completion of the Panama Canal, promoted the U.S. as a forceful world power, and received the Nobel Peace Prize for his negotiations ending the Russo-Japanese War.

p. vi. Richard Henry Brunton (1841-1901) Scots civil engineer, who went to Japan in 1860 and spent seven and a half years there building twenty-eight lighthouses that would ensure safe shipping lanes. He greatly improved the infrastructure and design of Yokohama harbor and assisted in setting up Japan's first school of civil engineering.

p. vi. Edward Sylvestser Morse (1838-1925) American zoologist specializing in malacology (seashells), later lecturer at Harvard University. While in Japan as Professor of Zoology at Tokyo Imperial University, he discovered the Omori Shell Mound, leading to new archaeological findings. He was an expert on ceramics and Keeper of Pottery at Museum of Fine Arts, Boston, where one of his many collections is housed.

p. vi. Oscar Loew (1844-1941) Agricultural chemist born in Bavaria and educated at University of Munich, discovered the enzyme catalase and investigated the effects of calcium and magnesium on plant development.

p. vi. William Edward Ayrton (1847-1908) Physicist and electrical engineer was educated at University College, London. In India, he invented a method for detecting faults in lines, benefiting overland communication systems. In 1878, he introduced the electric arc light into Japan. He is credited with inventing a variety of electrical measuring instruments and with research on railway electrification.

p. vi. Charles Longfellow (1844-1893) son of the poet, was an avid yachtsman who spent his life travelling and had an especial interest in Japan, where he lived for two years.

p. vii. Rudyard Kipling (1865-1936) Popular English writer of poems, novels, and children's books, many set in India, and still popular. He was a major innovator of the short story. In 1907, he received the Nobel Prize in Literature.

p. viii. Bayard Taylor (1825-1878) World traveler, journalist, poet, and novelist, whose early published poetry brought him to the attention of Horace Greeley and publication in the New York *Tribune,* leading to a successful writing career.

p. viii. Horace Greeley (1811-1872) Founder and editor of the powerful and popular New York *Tribune*, ardent opponent of slavery, supporter of the common man, and vocal opponent of monopolies.

p. viii. Francis Hall (1859-1902) Bookseller and author, the New York *Tribune* correspondent, whose level-headed accounts of Japan in the 1860s are unparalleled, was also a business pioneer, whose firm became the leading American trading house in Japan.

p. viii. Isabella Bird (1831-1904) English travel journalist, intrepid explorer, whose successful travel writings allowed her the independent lifestyle unusual at that time for a woman. She describes her 1878 visit to the Kanaya Hotel in *Unbeaten Tracks in Japan* (1880).

p. viii. Iwakura Tomomi (1825-1883) Japanese statesman instrumental in the Meiji takeover and centralized government that followed. His Iwakura Mission, which travelled for two years throughout Europe and America studying the industrialization successes of the West, led to Japan's rapid modernization.

p. viii. Tsuda Umeko. See "A Daily Journal 1908" 64.

p. viii. Kaneko Kentarō (1873-1942) left the Iwakura Mission to study at Harvard. Returning to Japan, he held high-level government posts, always promoting close ties with America. He requested President Theodore Roosevelt to initiate negotiations ending the Russo-Japanese War.

p. ix. Charles Sumner Greene (1868-1957) and **Henry Mather Greene** (1870-1954) formed Greene & Greene, the influential California-based architectural firm whose large-scale homes, principally in Pasadena, are the finest examples of architecture in the American Arts and Crafts Movement.

p. ix. Frank Lloyd Wright (1867-1959) American architect extraordinaire and leader of Prairie School Movement built over 500 works, which were designed and constructed to be in harmony with their environmental settings.

p. x. Townsend Harris (1804-1878) A successful New York businessman and first United States Consul to Japan negotiated the Harris Treaty of 1856 that opened Japan to foreign trade after its 250 years of isolation.

p. xiii. Basil Hall Chamberlain. See "A Daily Journal" 1.

p. xiv. Cecil Huggins Gamble (1884-1956) First child of David and Mary Gamble graduated from Princeton University and was with Procter & Gamble from 1906 to 1917. When he moved to Pasadena, California, to reside in The Gamble House, he continued his extensive civil and philanthropic activities. Ultimately, he and his wife, Marguerite Louise Gibbons, whom he married in 1908, were responsible for ensuring that the design of The Gamble House remained unchanged throughout the years. In 1966, the heirs of Cecil and Louise Gamble presented The Gamble House to the City of Pasadena, which, in partnership with University of Southern California, make this architectural treasure available for educational and recreational purposes. In 1978, the United States Department of the Interior designated The Gamble House a National Historic Landmark.

p. xvii. Walter Frear (1863-1948) Lawyer, judge, and Third Territorial Governor of Hawaii (1907-1913). Frear Center at Hawaii Pacific University and Frear Hall at the University of Hawaii were built by a Frear trust.

p. xvii. Rt. Rev. Doremus Scudder (1858-1942) The Congregational minister, writer, and missionary was one of the third generation of the family of Scudders, whose progenitor had fourteen children, all of whom became missionaries. Doremus Scudder served in Japan from 1884 to 1889 and in Hawaii from 1902 to 1916.

p. xix. Mary Frances Smith (1834-1916) was one of the two graduates in 1854 of Milwaukee Female College, an early women's college launched by educator Catharine Beecher. Mary Smith taught and had her own art studio at Ingham University, New York, in the 1870s.

p. xxi. G. Sherwood Eddy (1871-1963) Highly popular evangelist and writer of thirty-seven books, he worked in India for the Y.M.C.A. Indian Student Volunteer Movement for fifteen years, then for the Y.M.C.A. International Committee for twenty years, without ever receiving salary.

p. xxi. John Mott (1865-1955) World-famous Methodist lay person, leader of the Y.M.C.A. and the World Student Christian Federation was heavily involved in the formation of the World Council of Churches in 1948 and recipient of the 1946 Nobel Peace Prize.

p. xxiv. Mutsuhito, Emperor Meiji (1824-1912) The hundred and twenty-second emperor of Japan, whose reign from 1867 to 1912 gave name to the Meiji Period.

p. xxv. Annie Lyon Howe (1852-1943) opened one of the first kindergartens in Chicago before going in 1887 to Kobe, Japan, where she remained for forty years. She was inspired by the ideas of Friedrich Fröbel, whose concepts led her to establish in Kobe her Glory Kindergarten; it became the model for kindergartens throughout Japan. Her ideas spread throughout all of Japan and, during her lifetime, she received many awards and honors in Japan for her farsighted approach to educating young children.

p. xxvii. Adolpho Farsari (1841-1898) Born in Italy, Farsari was an ardent abolitionist and emigrated to the United States to fight in the Civil war with a New York troop. After a failed marriage, he went to Yokohama and taught himself photography. He became an aggressive businessman, and his studio output was considered of such quality that he gained exclusive rights to photograph the Imperial Gardens.

p. xxx. John LaFarge (1835-1910) The erudite American painter, glass window-maker, muralist, writer, early student and pioneer of Japanese art, particularly known for his murals and stained glass works in Trinity Church in Boston, Massachusetts. He visited Japan in 1886 and his *An Artist's Letters from Japan* was published in 1897.

p. xxx. Mary Crawford Fraser (1851-1922) An American writer of memoirs and historical novels was married to British diplomat Hugh Fraser in 1874. In 1889, Hugh Fraser was posted to Japan, where he died suddenly in 1894. Mary Crawford Fraser continued to write as Mrs. Hugh Fraser.

LINE NOTES
"A Daily Journal 1908"

p. 2. Jinya Little is known about Jinya, but he was so well liked that when Mary Gamble and her sister Julia returned to Japan in 1924, Jinya was their guide. See photo p. 22.

p. 3. Gyōki (668-749) was a Buddhist monk whose sympathies for the commoners directed his life. At the age of thirty-six, he left his post as government priest to travel throughout the Kansai, preaching the spiritual precepts of Buddhism, but more importantly, teaching advanced farming and irrigation techniques and building at least forty-nine temples that served as hospitals and community centers for the poor. He was prosecuted by the government, but apparently his popularity encouraged the government to enlist him in their efforts. Ultimately, he played an important role in the building of Tōdai-ji in Nara, assisting Emperor Shōmu (701-756) in raising funds to erect the temple and was instrumental in the completion in 752 of the great bronze statue of Vairocana, known simply as the Daibutsu, and the largest bronze statue in the world.

p. 9. Katō Kiyomasa (1561-1611) Superior architect of fortified castles and brilliant, undefeated general under Hideyoshi; however, in the decisive Battle of Sekigahara, Kiyomasa fought for Tokugawa.

p. 21. Kanō Tan'yū (1602-1674) Official artist for the Tokugawa shogunate and famous for large scale works and paintings at the castles in Nijō, Osaka, and Nagoya.

p. 34. Sōami (1472-1575) Son and grandson of great painters who worked, as did Sōami, for the Ashikaga shogunate. A Zen Buddhist, he meant his works to bring spiritual enlightenment. Sōami was a landscape artist as well, credited with `the design of the garden at Ginkakuji and known to have designed the dry garden at Ryōan Temple in Kyoto. He was famous for his paintings on *fusuma-e* (sliding doors), and his large landscape paintings covered as many as twenty panels. He was also a poet, an art critic, and master of the tea ceremony, flower arranging, and incense ceremony.

p. 49. "quality has become of less value." At Morishima's in Kyoto, American visitor Seaman Knapp saw a "cake box 8 in. in diameter took 2 1/2 years to make. Lacquered 43 times....Go over black lacquer for best 23 times, then put on gold 5 to 10 times, dried each time 3 days in damp room. Best articles take from 3 to 5 years to make them."

p. 52. "Satsuma porcelain." Ivory-colored earthware pottery with cracked glaze and gold decorations, first produced in the late sixteenth century in Satsuma in southern Kiyūshi by skilled Korean potters, who were brought into the area to develop a pottery industry. It is popular today.

p. 58. Rev. Robert F. Fitch (1873-1954) was born in Shanghai of missionary parents. After graduation from Western Theological Seminary, he served in Hingpo and in 1906 was transferred to Hangchow Christian College, eventually becoming its president. He was an effective fundraiser and prolific writer, a photographer and a fellow of both the Asiatic Branch of the British Royal Geographic Society and of the Royal Geographic Society of Scotland. His guide book on Hangchow reached a fourth edition.

p. 58. Charles Husted Irvin (1869-1933) earned his M.D. at Ohio Medical University in 1893 and served from 1893 to 1910 as medical missionary based in Fusan, Korea.

p. 65. Elizabeth Patton Milliken (1860-1951) A member of the Presbyterian Church in the U.S.A. was appointed by the Board of Foreign Missions as a teacher and missionary to Japan in 1884. In Japan, she taughtp at Joshi Gakuin in Tokyo, a girls' school created by the merger of Dakurui Jo Gakeko, Tokyo, and Shinasakai School. Joshi Gakuin, a Christian high school for girls with a student body of no more than 250, was situated in one of the better residential areas of Tokyo, probably near the Botanical Gardens at Koishikawa, which now belong to Tokyo University.

On April 19, 1919, a *shaonkai*, or thanksgiving meeting, was held in honor of Miss Milliken, which applauded her thirty-five years of service at Joshi Gakuin. Some 500 attended, and Mrs. Sakurai, founder of the school, and Mrs. Uajima, former principal, along with others, spoke. Miss Milliken was presented with a check for 3,000 yen.

She was highly regarded because of her practice of visiting regularly in the homes of her students. Families invited her to weddings and spoke to her in time of trouble, both unusual to extend to a foreigner. She returned to the United States in 1924 to reside in Pennsylvania, where in died at the age of ninety.

p. 74. James Curtis Hepburn (1815-1911) An American Presbyterian medical missionary, who came to Japan in 1859, operated a clinic in Japan, founded what became Meiji Gakuin University in Yokohama, and compiled a Japanese-English dictionary. In the 1886 edition, he adopted a system for romanization of the Japanese language, and thus the system became known as the Hepburn romanization.

p. 74. Isabella Bird See page 103, "p, viii" in first column.

p. 74. Shinkō In 1902, the Great Flood washed away the original bridge constructed in 1638, and in 1907 the Sacred Red Bridge was still being rebuilt. Only the Emperor was permitted to walk on the Sacred Bridge, except twice a year when it was opened to pilgrims.

p. 75. "built originally as a Buddhist temple" Tōshōgū was built originally as a simple Shinto shrine honoring Tokugawa Ieyasu, who promised to become guardian of Japan after his death. Better to protect against the evil forces that flow from the north, his shrine was placed in Nikkō. Grandson Iemitsu grandly enlarged the simple shrine to create a complex that included highly decorated Buddhist temples and gates. Historically, Buddhist temples and Shinto shrines have stood side by side, the two religions melded into a specifically Japanese mode. But with the *Shinbutsu bunri*, the edict of the Meiji government in 1868 to separate Shinto and Buddhism, Tōshōgū became exclusively a Shinto shrine, until the relaxation of that policy around 1873. Subsequently, the historic melding of Shinto and Buddhism continues, usually with Shinto shrines the site of weddings and blessings for the newborn child, Buddhist temples the place for funeral ceremonies.

p. 80. "Priests...seem to be mixed" See **p. 75** *above*.

HISTORIC TIMELINE

This timeline recapitulates the historic events to which Clarence Gamble refers and to those mentioned in the editor's notes in "A Daily Journal 1908."

100	Nagoya: Atsuta Shrine in existence.		
500 *ca*.	Shimogamo Shrine founded.		
	Fushimi Inari Taisha founded.		
593	Osaka: Prince Shōtoku builds Shitennōji.		
	Miyajima: Itsukushima shrine begun.		
645	Tokyo: Asakusa Kannon Temple built.		
686	Nagoya: Atsuta Shrine built.		
692	First rebuilding of Ise Grand Shrine.		
710-74	Nara first capital of Japan.		
752	Nara: Tōdaiji built.		
766	Nikkō: Rinnōji established.		
767	Nikkō: Futuransan Shrine established.		
768	Nara: Kasuga Taisha established.		
778	Kyoto: Buddhist Enchin builds thatched hut and founds Kiyomizudera.		
784	Nikkō: Chūzenji established.		

794-1185 Heian Period

- **794** Kyoto (Heian) founded; Imperial Palace built; Emperor Kammu arrives at Shimogamo.
- **830 *ca*.** Miyajima: Misen Hondo built.
- **841** Ksuga Primeval Forest: Cutting forbidden.
- **947** Kyoto: Kitano Tenmangū built.
- **987** Kyoto: First Kitano *matsuri* celebrated.
- **1002** Murasaki Shikibu writes world's first novel, *Tale of Genji*.
- **1168** Miyajima Shrine enlarged.

1185-1333 Kamakura Period

- **1192** Kamakura Minamoto no Yuritomo sets up military government.
- **1202** Kyoto: Higashi Ōtani founded.
- **1227** Kyoto Imperial Palace destroyed.
- **1234** Kyoto: Chion'in original temple built.
- **1252 *ca*.** Kamakura Daibutsu completed.
- **1282** 5 May: Hōjō Tokimune defeats Mongols.
- **1291** Kyoto: Emperor Kameyama gives lower palace to Buddhist priest Fumon; Nanzenji founded.

1358-1408 Muromachi Period

- **1397** Kyoto: Ashikaga Yoshimitsu begins Kinkakuji.
- **1407** Miyajima: Toyotomi Hideyoshi commissions Senjōkaku Hall; Gojū no Tō built.
- **1479** Kyoto: Ashikaga Yoshimasa builds Ginkakuji.
- **1549** Nagasaki: Jesuits arrive in Kyūshū.
- **1586** Kyoto: Toyotomi Hideyoshi builds Hōkōkuji.
- **1596** Kyoto: Earthquake destroys Hōkōkuji.
- **1598** Kyoto: Hōkoku Byō built.
- **1600** Battle of Sekigahara gives victory to Tokugawa.
- **1601** Kyoto: Tokugawa Ieyasu plans Nijō Castle.
- **1602** Tokugawa Ieyasu splits Buddhist Jōdo Shinshū. into Higashi Honganji and Nishi Honganji.
- **1602** Kyoto: Nijō Castle construction begins.

1603-1867 Edo Period

- **1603** Tokugawa Ieyasu made shogun.
- **1610** Nagoya: Katō Kiyomasa commissions *Kinshachi*.
- **1612** Kyoto: Nagoya Castle completed.
- **1617** Nikkō: Tōshōgu completed.
- **1622** Ii Naotsugu completes building of Hikone Castle.
- **1626** Kyoto: Nijō Castle renovated for visit of Emperor Go-Mizunoo.
- **1633** Kyoto: Tokugawa Iemitsu rebuilds Kiyomizudera.
- **1633** Kyoto: Chion'in bell (74 tons) cast.
- **1638** Nikkō: Shinkyō (Sacred Red Bridge) constructed.
- **1659** Kyoto: Shūgakuin built for Emperor Go-Mizunoo.
- **1709**: Nara: Tōdaiji largest wooden building in the world.
- **1725** Nagoya: Dairyuji (500 *Rakan*) completed.
- **1831** Kyoto: Iida Shinkichi opens first Takashimaya.
- **1853** U.S. Commodore Matthew Perry reaches Japan.
- **1855** Kyōto Gosho Imperial City Palace built.
- **1865 *ca*.** Namikawa Yasusuki workshop active in Kyoto.
- **1866** Yokohama is a small fishing town.
- **1867** Fourteen-year-old Mutsuhito as 122nd emperor ascends Chrysanthemum Throne.

1868-1912 Meiji Era

- **1868** Fall of Edo; Imperial Restoration.
- **1869** Emperor moves to Tokyo.
- **1871** Fuke Zen Buddhism demise.
- **1871-73** Iwakura Mission tours the West.
- **1872** Tōkaidō Railway first stretch begun.
- **1875** Niisimi Jo founds Dōshisha University.
- **1878** Hakone: Yamaguchi S. opens Fujiya Hotel.
- **1883** Kyoto: Meiji alter Shūgakuin Villa.
- **1888** Yumoto Station, Odaware Horse-drawn Rwy.
- **1888** Mary Denton (Dōshisha) arrives in Japan.
- **1892** Yokohama: T. Enami opens Benten Dori studio.
- **1893** Nagoya: Atsuta Shrine restored.
- **1894** Kyoto: Namikawa Yasusuki Cloisonne factory.

1894-95 Sino-Japanese War

- **1895** Kyoto: Heian Jingū built.
- **1895** Kyoto: Higashi Honganji Miei-dō dedicated.
- **1896** Kyoto: Military Virtues Society founded.
- **1898** Kyoto: Hōkoku Byō built.
- **1899** Helen Hyde arrives in Japan.
- **1900** Tsuda Umeko founds Women's Institute.
- **1903** Women's Institute officially recognized.

1904-05 Russo-Japanese War

- **1906** Kyoto: Kinkakuji restored.
- **1906** Hakone: Fujiya Hotel builds Victorian-style wing.
- **1907** *A Handbook for Travellers*, 8th edition, published.
- **1907** Thomas O'Brien, U.S. Ambassador to Japan.
- **1908** Tokyo: Ōkura Kihachiro private art collection viewed by the Gambles.

SELECTED BIBLIOGRAPHY

Bayrd, Edwin. *Kyoto.* New York: *Newsweek,* 1974.

Benfey, Christopher. *The Great Wave: Gilded Age Misfits, Japanese Eccentrics, and The Opening of Old Japan.* New York: Random House, 2003; Paperback 2004.

Bennett, Ella M. *An English Girl in Japan.* London: Wells, Gardner, Dalton, 1906.

Bickersteth, M. *Japan as We Saw It.* London: S. Low, Marston, 1893.

Bird, Isabella L. *Unbeaten Tracks in Japan: An Account of Travels in the Interior including Visits to the Aborigines.* London: J. Murray, 1881.

Black, John R. *Young Japan: Yokohama and Yedo.* London: Trubner, 1880.

Brunton, Richard Henry. *Building Japan 1868-1876.* Kent, England: Japan Library, 1991.

Bosley, Edward R. *Greene & Greene.* London: Phaidon, 2003.

Carpenter, Frank D. *Japan and Korea.* Garden City, New York: Doubleday, Doran, 1925.

Chamberlain, Basil Hall. *Things Japanese: Being Notes on Various Subjects Connected with Japan; For the Use of Travellers and Others.* 5th ed. London: John Murray, 1905; Reprint Berkeley: Stonebridge Press, 2007.

Chamberlain, Basil Hall., and W.B. Mason. *A Handbook for Travellers in Japan including the Whole Empire from Saghalien to Formosa.* London: John Murray, 1907.

Clement, Ernest W. *Japan as It Was and Is: A Handbook of Old Japan.* Introduction by William Elliot Griffis. London: Kegan Paul, 1907.

Collcutt, Martin; Marius Jansen; and Isao Kumakura. *The Cultural Atlas of the World: Japan.* Alexandria, Virginia: Stonehenge. 1988.

Cook, M.B. *Japan: A Sailor's Visit to the Island Empire.* New York: John B. Alden, 1891.

Dobson, Sebastian; Anne Nishimura Morse; and Fredric A. Sharf. *Art & Artifice: Japanese Photographs of the Meiji Era.* Boston: MFA Publications, 2004.

Durston, Diane. *Kyoto: Seven Paths to the Heart of the City.* Japan: Mitsumura Suriko Shoin, 1987.

East, Alfred Edward. *A British Artist in Meiji Japan.* Reprinted Weatherhill, 1997.

Fields, Henry. *Nine Years in Nipon: Sketches of Japanese Life.* Mannows, 1895.

Fraser, Mary Crawford. *A Diplomat's Wife in Japan: Sketches at the Turn of the Century.* Edited by Hugh Cortazzi. New York and London: Weatherhill, 1982.

Griffis, William Elliot. *Japan in History, Folk Lore and Art.* Boston and New York: Houghton, Mifflin, 1894.

Griffis, William Elliot. *The Mikado's Empire.* 1887.

Guth, Christine M.E. *Longfellow's Tattoos: Tourism, Collecting, and Japan.* Seattle: University of Washington Press, 2004.

Hall, Francis. *Japan through American Eyes: The Journal of Francis Hall 1859-1866.* Edited by F.G. Notehelfer. Denver, Colorado: Westview Press, 2001.

Hall, John Whitney, and Takeshi Toyoda. *Japan in the Muromachi Age.* Berkeley: University of California Press, 1977.

Harris, Townsend. *The Complete Journal of Townsend Harris.* Introduction and Notes by Mario Emilio Cosenza. Garden City, New York: Doubleday, Doran, 1930.

Hearn, Lafcadio. *Glimpses of Unfamiliar Japan.* New York: Houghton Mifflin, 1910.

Heusken, Henry. *Japan Journal 1855-1861.* Translated and edited by Jeannette C. van der Corput and Robert A. Wilson. New Brunswick, New Jersey: Rutgers University Press, 1964.

Huffman, James L. *Japan in World History.* Oxford, UK: Oxford University Press, 2010.

Kipling, Rudyard. *From Sea to Sea: Letters of Travel and American Notes.* 1899.

Knapp, Seaman A. "Seaman A. Knapp's Journal." http://ereserves.mcneese.edu/depts/archive/FTBooks/knapp.htm.

LaFarge, John. *An Artist's Letters from Japan.* New York: The Century Co., 1897, Reprinted Nabu Public Domain Reprints.

Leonard, Jonathan Norton. *Early Japan.* New York: Time-Life Books, 1968.

Lloyd, Arthur. *Every-day Japan: Written after Twenty-Five Years Residence and Work in the Country.* London: Cassell, 1909.

Lowell, Percival. *The Soul of the Far East.* Boston and New York: Houghton Mifflin, 1888.

McClain, James L. *Japan: A Modern History.* New York: W.W. Norton, 2002.

Morse, Edward Sylvester. *Japan Day by Day: 1877, 1878-79, 1882-83.* Boston and New York: Houghton Mifflin, 1917.

Norgren, Tiana. *Abortion before Birth Control: The Politics of Reproduction in Postwar Japan.* Princeton and Oxford: Princeton University Press, 2001.

Scherer, James A.B. *Japan To-Day.* Philadelphia and London: J.P. Lippincott, 1905.

Seidmore, Eliza Ruhanah. *Jinrikisha Days in Japan.* 1891.

Sigur, Hannah. *The Influence of Japanese Art on Design.* Salt Lake City: Gibbs Smith, 2008.

Strong, Ruth Isabel. *Oriental Journal of a Flirt.* Cleveland, Ohio: Rowfant Club, 1997.

Towner, *Our County and Its People; A History of the Valley and County of Chemung. From the Closing Years of the Eighteenth Century.* Syracuse, New York: D. Mason, 1892.

Whitney, Clara A.N. *Clara's Diary. An American Girl in Meiji Japan.* Edited by William Seele and Tamiko Ichimata. Tokyo, New York, San Francisco: Kodansha International, 1978.

Wright, Edward Stager. *Westward 'round the World.* E.P. Dutton, 1908; Reprint Memphis: General Books, 2010.

SOURCES
"Introduction"

As explained above in Endnote 5 of the "Introduction," Clarence (*CJG*) made entries in a diary (*D*), a journal (*J*) and on various stationery (*S*), all manuscripts located in The Papers of Sarah Merry Bradley Gamble, MC368, Schlesinger Library, Radcliff Institute, Harvard University, Cambridge, Massachusetts, hereafter abbreviated as *SBG*.

Information in the "Introduction" and in the page notes in "A Daily Journal 1908" draw heavily on Basil Hall Chamberlain and W.B. Mason, *A Handbook for Travellers in Japan including the Whole Empire from Saghalien to Formosa* (London: John Murray, Albemarle Street, 1907), hereafter abbreviated as *BHC*.

The "Introduction" also quotes at length from Edward Stager Wright, *Westward 'round the World* (New York: E.P. Dutton, 1908; reprint, General Books, 2010), hereafter abbreviated as *ESW*.

 i "Later we went": *D* 4/17; "At the entrance": *D* 5/4.

 ii All quotes from *CJG* 1908 Diary, January 1 to March 29 and August 1 to 4 except "The goldfish are trained", which is from *J* 6/18.

 iii "Japanese children seemed": *D* 4/11.

 vii "wealthy authors": Rudyard Kipling, *From Sea to Sea: Letters of Travel* (1900); "brave women": Gertrude Adams Fisher, *A Woman Alone in the Heart of Japan* (Boston: L.C. Page & Company, 1906); "early feminists": Julia D. Carrothers, *The Sunrise Kingdom: or Life and Scenes in Japan, and Woman's Work for Woman There* (Philadelphia: Presbyterian Board of Publication, ca. 1879); "diplomat's wives": Mrs. Hugh Fraser, *A Diplomat's Wife in Japan* (London: Hutchinson and Co., 1898); "grandmothers": Mary Pruyn, *Grandmother's Letters from Japan* (Boston: J.H.Earle, 1877); "businessmen's daughters": Clara Whitney, *Clara's Diary: An American Girl in Meiji Japan* (1879); "a boy of eleven": Donald Gordon, "The Journal of Donald Gordon: 1889 Mar 1 [to] 1890 Dec 1": Thesis MS; "seamen": John Smith Sewall, *The Logbook of the Captain's Clerk: Adventures in the China Seas* (Bangor: Chas H. Glass, 1905); "scientists": Edward S. Morse, *Japan Day by Day 1877, 1878-89, 1882-83*, 2 vols. (New York: Houghton Mifflin, 1917); "Congregational Ministers": William Elliot Griffis, *The Mikado's Empire* (1876); "capitalists": Andrew Carnegie, *Round the World* (New York: Doubleday, Doran, 1884); "missionaries": Isaac William Wiley, *China and Japan: A Record of Observations Made during a Residence of Several Years* (Cincinnati: Hitchcock and Walden, 1879); "astronomers": Percival Lowell, *The Soul of the Far East* (1891); "artists": John LaFarge, *An Artist's Letters from Japan* (New York: The Century Co., 1903); "successful merchants": Arthur Collins Maclay, *A Budget of Letters from Japan: Reminiscences of Work and Travel in Japan* (New York: A.G. Armstrong, 1889); "wealthy tourists": *ESW* (1908).

 xii "The Jap, commercially": *ESW* 25; "Even the best": *ESW* 24.

 xiii "It is but fair": *BHC* 6.

 xiv "You will find": *ESW* 5; "Three cloth suits": *ESW* 3. "The great day": *D* 3/1.

 xvi "The first glimpse": *ESW* 7; "playing a game": *J* 3/14.

 xvii "Got a breadfruit": *D* 3/27.

 xviii "Our seats at": *D* 3/31.

 xix "The boat tipped": *D* 3/9.

 xxi "spread the Gospel": *BHC* 88.

 xxii "We went to": *D* 4/10; "From some of": *D* 4/11.

 xxiii "Great cotton mills": *ESW* 7; "These little carriages"...."The Chinese [tailors] are": *ESW* 9.

 xxiv "Prepare to bargain": *ESW* 3; "Tokyo is enormous"...."Before leaving Tokyo": *ESW* 12; "The little china": *D* 4/27; "The Japanese artist": *ESW* 17; "With the Japs": *D* 4/17.

 xxv "Three thousand girls": *D* 5/1; "Commercial interests is": *ESW* 10.

 xxvii "He, therefore, who": *BHC* 2.

 xxviii "conceited, insulting and": *ESW* 25; "extremely disgusting": Ruth Isabel Strong, *Oriental Journal of a Flirt* 27; "a strange and romantic people": Towner, *Our Country and Its People* 636; "slavish, humiliating customs":Clara Whitney, *Clara's Diary* 44; "sitting amid the terrible": James A.B. Scherer, *Japan Today* 50; "They have little music": Scherer, *Japan Today* 99; "dear little things": Strong, *Oriental Journal* 36.

CREDITS
Photographs
"Introduction"

 i "David Berry Gamble": *SBG* 23/414.

 ii "Mary Huggins Gamble": *SBG* 23/411.

 iii "Clarence & Sidney Gamble *circa* 1902": *SBG* 23/411.

 iv "Sidney David Gamble *circa* 1910": *SBG* 23/442.

 v "President Theodore Roosevelt": Mrs. John A. Logan, *Our National Government or Life and Scenes in Our National Capital* (H.L Baldwin Company, Minneapolis, Minn., 1908) 742.

 vi "Charles Longfellow": Google Images (http://news.harvard.edu/gazette/2004/02.26/11-japan.html). Retrieved 18 September 2011

 vii "Richards Merry and Amy Aldis Bradley": Personal Collection of Sarah Gamble Epstein.

 viii "Iwakura Mission": Wikimedia Commons (http://en.wikipedia.org/wiki/File:Iwakura_mission.jpg) Retrieved 18 September 2011.

 ix "The Gamble House": *SBG* 23/448.

 x "Farmer and his Wife": www.t-enami.org/services (a_ENAMI_-_ROSE_JPEG_FILES_002_5-1xx.150200939_std.jpg). Retrieved 18 September 2011.

 xi "Lacquer Album Cover": http://en.wikipedia.org/wiki/Adolfo_Farsari (Museum of Fine Arts, Boston, s.v. "Lacquer Album Cover" [Art & Artifice: Japanese Photographs of the Meiji Era – Selections from the Jean S. and Frederic A. Sharf Collection at the Museum of Fine Arts, Boston, with essays by Sebastian Dobson, Anne Nishimura Morse, and Frederic A. Sharf (Boston: MFA Publications, 2004], p. 12, bottom, p. 94). Retrieved 21 September 2011.

 xii "Winnowing Grain": www.t-enami.org/services (ENAMI_-_Winnowing_Grain-1.290231514_std.jpg). Retrieved 18 September 2011.

 xiii "Basil Hall Chamberlain": http://en.wikipedia.org/wiki/Basil_Hall_Chamberlain.Retrieved 20 September 2011.

xiv "Pacific Mail poster": http://en.wikipedia.org/wiki/Pacific_Mail_Steamship_Company (*The World Today Magazine* April 1906). Retrieved 16 September 2011.

xv "St. Francis Hotel": (http://en.wikipedia.org/wiki/File: St._Francis_Hotel_San_Francisco_1904.jpg [History Room of the Wells Fargo Bank, San Francisco]). Retrieved 18 September 2011.

xvi "Page 1 of 'A Daily Journal 1908'": *SBG* 17/349v.

xvii "Clarence James Gamble circa 1911": *SBG* 23/432.

xviii "S.S. *Mongolia*": Postcard 3.5 x 5.375 inches. Back: Edward H. Mitchell Publisher San Francisco; Front: Pacific Mail Steamship Company's Steamer "Mongolia" 27,000 Tons Operating on "The Sunshine Belt to the Orient" Between San Franciso, Honolulu, Japan, China and Manila."

xix "Avondale House": *SBG* 23/446.

xx "Mary Palmer Gorbold": Presbyterian Historical Society, Presbyterian Church (U.S.A.) (Philadelphia, PA).

xxi "Raymond Gorbold": Presbyterian Historical Society, Presbyterian Church (U.S.A.) (Philadelphia, PA).

xxii "Grand Hotel": Postcard 5.5 x 3.5 inches. Front: picture of Grand Hotel and printed line, "X38 4th JULY Yokohama (GRAND HOTEL)"; Back: "Union Postale Universelle CARTE POSTALE."

xxiii "Advertisement": *BCH*.

xxiv "The Hundred Steps": George Rose, H96 160/957, State Library of Victoria. Retrieved 18 September 2011.

xxv "Future Factory Workers": http://www.t-enami.org/services ENAMI_-_Close_Group_of_Country_Kids_02.44215514_std.jpg). Retrieved 7 February 2014.

xxvi "Daibutsu": http://commons.wikimedia.org/wiki/File:Farsari_Daibutsu.jpg Retrieved 18 September 2011.

xxvii "Old Woman Working a Mill Stone": http://www.t-enami.org/services (ENAMI_-_Old_Woman_Working_a_Mill_Stone_-_scan0703_2-2_d_WWW.50140352_std.jpg). Retrieved 18 September 2011.

xxviii "The Gamble Family in Asia": *SBG* 23/433.

xxix "Fuji from Lake Motosu": www.t-enami.org/services (ENAMI_-_ROSE_JPEG_FILES_022-2ab.272223533_std.jpg). Retrieved 18 September 2011.

**Art & Line Drawings
"The Gamble Family in Japan 1908"**

xxxi "Ame no Uzume Nomikoto": *BHC* 55.

xxxi "Amida Buddha": *BHC* 43.

xxxii "Yoroi no Tsuketa Bushi": Hand coloured photo by Felice Beato, 1860s. http://en.wikipedia.org/wiki/Samurai. Retrieved 18 August 2013.

xxxiii "Oda Nobunaga": A copy of a portrait of Oda Nobunaga painted by Italian Jesuit Giovanni Nicolao, probably commissioned by Oda himself. The portrait was introduced as authentic in Historia, History Channel. Date 1583. Source: http://www.shouzou.com/mag/p2.html. Wikipedia. Retrieved 7 March 2013.

xxxiii "Toyotomi Hideyoshi": http://www.google.com/imgres?imgurl=http://shogun2.heavengames.com Retrieved 39 January 2014.

xxxiii "Tokugawa Ieyasu": Wikipedia. http://en.wikipedia.org/wiki/File:Tokugawa_Ieyasu2.jpg. Retrieved 8 March 2013.

**Photographs
"A Daily Journal 1908"**

The 120 hand-tinted photographs of locations and people in Japan were taken by Clarence and Sidney Gamble and are found in a leather bound album, approximately 6 x 8 inches, in *SBG* 23/418v. The four photographs on page 58 of the individual Gambles are from *SBG* 23/417v, which is from the album of photographs taken by Clarence and Sidney Gamble in China. Additional photographs are from the following sources:

34 "Ashikaga Yoshimasa": Attributed to Tosa Mitsnobu. Portrait said to be of Ashikaga Yoshimasa. Latter half of 15th century. Colors on silk. Dimensions (detail) 44.2 x 56m (each). Current location Tokyo National Museum, Tokyo, Japan. Source/Photographer The Japanese book "Portrait paintings from the Muromachi period," Nara Prefectural Museum of Art, 2000. whttp://wikipedia.org/wiki/File: Ashikaga_Yokshimasa.jpg. Retrieved 24 June 2011.

64 "Tsuda Umeko": http://commons.wikimedia.org/wiki/File: Tsuda_Umeko.gif. Retrieved 24 June 2011.

65 "Helen Hyde": www.foundsf.org/idexphp?title=1894_Midwinter_Fair:_WOMEN_ARTISTS,_an_appreciation. Retrieved 25 June 2011; "Tokyo Home": http://www.p.cla.purdue.edu/waaw/jensen/hyde.html. Retrieved 25 June 2011.

73 "Mt. Fuji": Noah Porter (of Yale University), *Webster's Revised Unabridged Dictionary of the English Language* (Springfield, Mass: G & C Merriam Company, 1913).

76 "Kirifuri Waterfalls": Image by JVPD at http://Clipartof.com/1070790. Retrieved 17 August 2011.

76 "Honorable Mr. Cat": http://lccn.loc.gov/2003675444.Library of Congress Prints and Photographs Division, Washington, DC 20540 USA. Retrieved 25 June 2011.

82 "Daruma Dolls": *SBG* 23/433.

86 "Kamakara Buddha Daibutsu": Adolfo Farsari (Musée Nicéphore Niépce) http://commons.wikimedia.org/wiki/File:Farsari_Daibutsu.jpg. Retrieved 25 June 2011.

**Line Drawings & Maps
"A Daily Journal 1908"**

1, 53, 56 Yokohama, Osaka, Nagasaki maps, respectively. Courtesy of www.Japan-guide.com. Retrieved 28 June 2011.

2 "Yebitsu, or Ebisu, TheFisherman's Friend": "Collected Illustrations of Buddhist Images" (1690) www.onmarkproductions.com/html/ebisu.shtml (Page 5 of 6). Retrieved 24 June 2011.

5 "Tokyo": *BHC* Foldout after 136.

11 "Fox": *BHC* 47.

12 "Tokugawa mon": *BHC* 43.

26 "Kyoto": *BHC* Foldout after 318.

43 "Gekū Temple at Ise": *BHC* 304.

70 "Fuji and the Hakone District": *BHC* Foldout 146.

75 "The Three Wise Monkeys": http://etc.usf.edu/clipart/22000/22027/monkeys_22027.htm. Retrieved 25 June 2011.

79 "Jizo": *BHC* 47.

80 "Nikko": *BHC* Foldout 192.

81 "Ikao and Kusatsu": *BHC*, Foldout 180.
82 "God of Luck": *BHC* 53; "Daruma": *BHC* 71.82 "God of Luck": *BHC* 53; "Daruma": *BHC* 71.
83 "Torii": *BHC* 95.
86 "Yoritomo no Minamoto": http://upload.wikimedia.org/wikipedia/commons/3/3b/MinamotoYoritomo.jpg Retrieved 30 December 2013.
87 "Kannon" *BHC* 49.
98 "Buddhist Temple of Ikegami": *BHC* 43.
99 "Procession" Osaka *Asahi Shinbun* 1908 4/22.
101 "Distribution of Rainfall": *BHC* 22.

Advertisements
"A Daily Journal 1908"
All advertisements are from pages in *BHC* inserted between the end of the text proper and the back cover.

Photographs
"Afterword"
94 "Kyoto Hotel Okura": http://okura.kyotohotel.co.jp/english/about/; "Front Desk": courtesy of Nikkō Kanaya Hotel.
All other photos in "Afterword" taken by the editor.

SPECIAL CREDIT must be given to Rob Oechsle for the five T. Enami (*see brief bio page 2*) photographs that enrich our Introduction. Oechsle, a long-time resident of Okinawa, created and maintains the www.t-enami.org web site with its wealth of information. For the scholarship and generosity of Rob Oechsle, I am immensely grateful. Readers interested in knowing more about the nineteenth and early twentieth century of Japan are directed to t-enami,org for an extraordinary viewing of its history and culture.

A Handbook for Travellers

INDEX

A
Amaterasu Ōmikami xxxiii, xxxiv, 11, 43
ame 77
Amida Buddha xxxiii, 112; *art* xxxiii
Around the World in Eighty Days vi
anesama kaburi 83; *photo* 83
achery 67
armour 76
Artist's Letters from Japan, An 103, 106
Arts and Crafts Movement xix, 103
Asahi Shinbun 28; *art* 33
Asakusa Park xxxii, 66, 67
Asama xxvi, xxxii, 8, 83, 84
Ashikaga 86
Ashikaga Yoshimasa xxxiv, 34, 92, 105, 107; *art* 34
Ashikaga Yoshimitsu xxxiv, 34
Atsuta 7, xxv, xxxii, 10, 11, 28, 91, 96, 105; *photos* 10, 11
Avondale, Cincinnati xix, xxi, 107; *photo* xix
Ayrton, William Edward vi

B
bamboo xxvii, 74
basha 73
bazaar 34; *photo* 88
bean cakes 42
beech 47
beer 70, 86
beggar 24; *photo* 24
Beijing iv
bell 12, 22, 46, 47, 48, 50, 52, 53, 59, 75, 81, 97, 105
   bronze 52
   Chion'in 12
   tower 51
   small *see* kanetsukidō
Benten-dori 2, 7
bentō 8, 89
bettō 73
Big Hell 72
Binzuru *photo* 92
Bird, Isabella viii
Bluff 4, 6
Board of Missions xvii, xxi
Bodhidharma 81; *art* 81
bosatsu 79

Boston xxviii, 102, 103, 106, 109, 110
Boys' Day 55, 97
Bradley, Amy Aldis & Richards Merry *photo* vii
Bradley, Sarah vii
bronzes ix, xxvii, 16, 22
Brownie (camera) iv
Brunton, Richard Henry vi
Bryn Mawr College 64
Buddha xx, xxvii, xxxiii, 9, 12, 46, 47, 60, 79, 86, 87, 92, 107
   Dainichi 47
   Kamakura 86
   Vairocana 47
Buddhism xxxiii, 52
   Amida 12, 79
   Ch'an 82
   Fuke 13, 105
   Pure Land 12, 79
   Shakya Mune 47
   True Pure Land 12
   Tendai 15, 67
   Zen 13, 15, 21, 34, 82, 104, 105
bullomobiles 74, 78
Bund x, 4
Bunsui, Tsubame, Niigata 33
Butoku Kwai 34
butsudan 97

C
camphor 11
canal 17, 22, 37
carp *see* Tango no Sekku
carriage 64, 66, 67, 73
Cassatt, Mary 65
Castle & Cooke xvii, xxx
Castles, Hikone 37
   Nagoya 9
   Nijō 49
Catholicism 56
cedar *see* sugi
Centennial International Exposition ix
chair, four-man 72, 73
   traveling 75
   two-man 73
Chamberlain, Basil Hall xxi, xxx, xxx, xxxiii, 1, 2, 3, 4, 7, 8, 9, 16, 18, 20, 34, 42, 43, 49, 54, 69, 71, 73, 82, 83, 87, 98, 99, 101, 103, 106, 107, 108, 109
   life of xii–xiii; *photo* xiii

Chamorro 2
Chaplin, Charlie 69
cherry blossoms 30, 42
cherry dance 42
chess *see* **shogi**
chestnut jelly 34
Chicago ix, xv, 103
child labor xxv
Children's Day 55
chimaki 55
China i, iv, v, viii, xvi, xx, xxi, xxvi, 1, 20, 53, 57, 58, 68, 73, 100, 102, 106, 107
Chinese gamblers xv, xvi
Chinese tailors xxiii, 2
Chion'in xxxii, 12, 34, 92, 105; no Kane 12
chirashizushi 39
chō 71
chop-sticks 59
Christ Hospital xxx
Christian vi, xx, xxi, xxv, xxvii, xxx, xxxii, 86, 95, 96, 102, 103, 104
   college 54, 95
   kindergarten xxv, 30–31; *photos* 30, 31
   schools xx
   university 35
Christianity xxii, 35, 95
chrysanthemum 29, 42
Chuddasso 79
Chūzenji xxxii, 74, 105
Cincinnati i, ii, xix, xx, xxi, xxvi, xxx, 64, 84, 102, 106
Cincinnati Missionary Training School xx, xxx, 84
   University School ii
Civil War viii
cloisonné ix, xxvii, 8, 16, 20
coaling operations 56–57; *photos* 56, 57
Columbian Exhibition ix
coolies xxx
coppers 40, 66
Corea xxxvii, 64, 68
cotton mills xxiii, 52, 106
   spinning factory xxv, 53
cow, stone 41, 88
Crawford, Mary xxviii, 103, 106, 109
cream puffs 39
Cricket Ground 3
cryptomeria 46, 47, 74, 77, 80
curios xii, xxvii, 67, 68, 94
Cypress 74

D
daffodils 4
Daibutsu xxvii, xxxii, 47, 86, 92, 95, 98, 105, 107
   Kamakura *photos* 86, 88
Daibutsuden Hall 47
Daiganji 60
Daikoku 2
daimyō 33, 52, 62, 77
Dainichi 47
Dairyūji 9; *photo* 9
Daiyagawa 74
damascene xxvii, 12
danshi seito 38
Daruma xxxii, 82, 107, 108; *photo* 82
deer 22, 46, 47, 92
Denton, Mary Florence 7, 35, 95
devil's gate 26
Diamond Head xvii
Dickens, Charles xvii
Dime Shows 6
Diplomat's Wife in Japan, The xxviii
dog i, 54
Dole Food Company xxx
dolphins, golden 9
Dōshisha University 7, xxii, xxxii, 30, 35, 95, 105
Duke University iv
Dutch 56

E
Eastman, George iv, xi
East Sea Road 52
Eddy, G. Sherwood xxi, 103
Edo x
   Bay v
Elizabeth Gamble Deaconess Home Association xxx
emperor xii, xxxiv, 21, 25, 30, 66, 75, 79, 105
   Korean 75
Emperor's City Palace xxv, xxxii, 30
Enami Nobukuni 2; *photos* x, xii, xxvii
Enami, Tamotsu 2
Enchin 15, 105
Europe xiv, xvii, 9, 65, 103
Every-day Japan 48, 67, 110

F

factory, cotton spinning 53
Fannie, Aunt xvi
Farsari, Adolfo xxii, xxvii, 80, 86, 107, *photos* xi, xxii, 86, 07
fencing 34
ferry 59
firebombing 90
fires 69, 76
fish xvii, 8, 25, 39, 55, 60, 71, 85, 93
Fitch, Rev. Robert F. 58, 104
Foreign Settlement 4, 54
forts 55, 60
Frear, Governor Walter Francis xvii, 103
French xvii
Fugi *see* Mount Fuji 63
Fujiwara, Mr. 68
Fujiya Hotel xxvi, xxxii, 69, 71, 94, 98, 105; *art* 69, 88
Fusan, Korea 58, 104
Fushimi Inari Taisha 28
fusuma xxxiv, 21, 104
Futami, Mie 43
Futarasanjinja 80

G

ga gyu 40
gaikokujin vi, xxiii
Gales, Dr. 80
Gamble, Cecil Huggins xiv, 103
Gamble, Clarence James i–iii, 102, *passim*; Journal xv–xvi, xxx, 1, 86, 100; *photos* iii, xvii, xxviii, xxx, 21, 58, 62, 66
Gamble, David Berry i, 102; *photos* i, xxviii, 17, 36, 48, 58, 68
Gamble House, The ix, xix, 65, 102, 106; *photo* ix
Gamble, James i, xxx
Gamble, Mary Huggins 1, 102; *photos* ii, xxviii, 17, 36, 37, 48, 58,
Gamble, Sidney David iii–iv, 102; *photos* v, iv, xxviii, 8, 58
gas lamps 13
gate, largest wooden 12
Gautama *art* 47
Gekū shrine 43; *art* 43
German xvii
Gingko 11
ginkakuji xxxii, xxxiv, 34, 92, 104, 105
Gion-za Theatre 42
Glory Kindergarten xxvi, xxxii, 54, 95, 103
Gods of Happiness 82
Gojū no Tō 60
Golden Gate xv
Golden Pavilion *see* Kinkakuji
goldfish ii, xvii, 10, 34, 45, 59, 67, 71, 106
 Tea-house 71
gold lacquer work 49
Go-Mizunoo, Emperor 25, 49, 105
gongs 42
Gorbold, Raymond & Mary Palmer xxvi, xxxii, 38, 39, 40, 42, 46, 62, 82, 82, 85, 86, 107; *lives of* xx–xxii; *photos* xx, xxi
Gorintō 22; *photo* 22
Grand Hotel xxiii, xxxii, 90, 108
Great Britain vi
Greeley, Horace viii
Greene, Charles Sumner & Henry Mather ix, xix, xxx, 7, 109
Guam 2

H

habachi 6
Hachiman 80
hair ornaments 40, 42, 53, 59, 63
Hakodate x
Hakone xxvi, xxxii, 69, 72, 74, 105
 Lake xxvi, 72
Hall, Francis viii, x, xxviii, 103, 110
Hall of a Thousand Mats 60
Hall of Military Virtues Society 34
Hall of the Dragon 75
Hanami-kōji 42
Hanayashiki 67
Handbook for Travellers in Japan, A xiii, xxx, 1; *ads* xxiii, 2, 7, 12, 16, 20, 23, 37, 39, 47, 49, 52, 54, 63, 67, 69, 74, 79; *maps* 5, 26. 70, 80, 81, 101; *line drawings* 2, 11, 12, 43, 79, 82, 83, 87, 98, 99, 104, 108
hand-carved 77
Hangzhou xxvi, 58
 Presbyterian College 58
Harbor Point 59
Harris, Townsend x
Harris Treaty vi, x
Harvard Medical School iii
Hawaii xvii–xviii, xxx; Board of Missions xvii; Evangelical Association xvii
Hayakawa 71
Hearn, Lafcadio 50
Heian 7, xxxii, xxxiii, xxxiv, 21, 26, 30, 39, 92, 98, 105
Heian Jingū 21; *photo* 21
Higashi Honganji xxxii, 50, 51, 93, 105; *photos* 50, 51
Higashi Ōtani 15; *photo* 15
Higashiyama 15, 21, 22
Hikone xxxii, 7,.8. 36, 37, 80, 93, 105
 Castle 37
hinamatsuri 39, 97
hinaningyō 39
Hirohito 30
Hiroshima 59
hishi mochi 39
Hayashi. S 49
Hōjō xxxii, 21, 55, 105
Hōjō Garden 12
Hōjō Tokimune 55, 105
Hōkōji 22
Hōkōku Byō 22, 105; *photos* 32–33
Hokusai Katsushika 76
hollyhock 12, 75
honden 10
Hōnen 12
Honolulu xvii, xviii, xxx
"Honorable Mr. Cat" 76
Honshū 52, 84
horse xxiii, xxx, 73, 75, 76, 78, 81, 82, 89
 pack- 73
 sacred 75
horseback xvii, xxvi, 72, 76, 77, 78
horseracing 4
Hotei *art* 82
Hotel Ōkura Tokyo 68
hot springs xxvi, 69, 70, 72, 74, 78, 81, 82, 83
Howe, Annie xxvi, 95
Hozu 18–19; *photos* 18
Hundred Steps, The xxv, 4, 90; *photo* xxv
hyacinths 4
Hyde, Helen xxxii, 65, 74, 76, 77, 82, 105, 107; *photos* 65, 76
Hyde, Miss 65, 76, 77, 82
hydrogen sulfide gas 72

I

Ii Naomasa 37
Ii Naotsugu 37, 105
Ikaho xxxii, 81, 82
Imadegawa Street 30
Inari shrines 7, xxxii, 11, 28, 105
Inouye Makiko 94
International Student Volunteer Movement xxi
Iolani Palace xvii
iris xxxii, 3, 66; *photo* 66
Irwin, Mr. 58
Ise *see* Meoto Iwa 43, 105, 108; *photo* 43
 Ondo 43
Ishahara, Miss xxvi, 84
Ishidōrō 84
Island of Shrines 59
Itsukushima 59, 60
ivory 77
Ivory Soap 68
Iwakura Mission viii, ix, 64, 69, 103, 105, 106; *photo* viii
Iwakura,Tomomi viii, 103, *photo* viii
Iwazaru 75

J

Jakotsu-gawa 71
Jap i
Japan Craze viii
Japanese Cedar Tree 74
Japanese Imperial Court xxxv, 4, 39
 Crest 29
 Family 69
 Gardens xxiv, xxv
 Mint 48
 Navy 56
Japanese National Railways 74
 Treasure 12
japonismé 65
Jesuits 56, 105
Jimon School 15
Jingū Road 21
jinrikisha vii, xii, xxiii, xxv, 1, 5, 8, 18, 30, 36, 48, 89; *photo* 96; *art* 110
Jinya 2, 4, 6, 7, 8, 30, 36, 40, 42, 46, 50, 53, 55, 61, 66, 72, 73, 76, 78, 81, 82, 101, 104

Jishu Shrine 15
jiujitsu 34
Jizō-zazō 79
Jōdo 12, 50, 105
Jōdo Shinshū Buddhism 50
John Johns Hopkins 34, 35
Joshi Eigaku Juku 95
junrei 48; *photos* 2, 48, 62, 63, 71

K
kago 24, 73, 89
kakemonos 38, 42, 44, 45, 66, 67, 85
Kamakura 8, xx, xxvi, xxvii, xxxiv, 86, 92, 95, 98, 105
Kameoka 18, 19
Kameyama, Emperor 21, 105
kami xxxi, 43
kamishimo 29
Kammu, Emperor xxxiii, 21, 27, 105
Kamo Mioya Jinja 27
Kamo River 26, 27
Kanagawa Prefecture 70
Kanaya Hotel xxxii, 74, 94, 100
Kanaya Zenichi 94
Kaneko Kentarō viii
kanetsukidō 81; *photo* 81
Kanmangafuchi Abyss 79
Kannon, 67
Kannon Bosatsu 15
Kannon Temple 67, 105
Kanō 9, 21, 25, 49, 93, 104
Kanō Hidenobu 25, 93
Kanō Tan'yū 21
Kanto earthquake 90
Karuizawa 8, xxvi, 82, 83, 84, 85
Kashiwa Mochi 55
Kasuga Taisha xxxii, 47, 105; *photo* 46
Kasugayama 47
Katō Kiyomasa 9, 104, 105
Katsuden 9
Katsura River 19
Keiko, Emperor 7, 11
Keizai University 68
Kellar the Magician ii
Kidzu *see* Kizu Station
Kikazaru 75
Kikokutei 51
Kikuchi, Dairoku, 5
kimono xii, 20, 97
Kindergarten Hall xx, xxx, 84
  Training School 84

kinshachi 9
Kinkakuji xxxii, xxxiv, 34, 44, 45, 92, 93; *photo* 44
  Gardens 45; *photo* 45
Kipling, Rudyard vii
Kirifuri Falls 76
kisu 60
Kitano Tenmangū xxxii, 40, 41, 98, 105; *photos* 40, 41
kite 55
kitsune 11
Kiyomizudera xx, xxxii, 15, 92, 95, 98, 105
koans 21
Kizu Station 46
Kobe 8, x, xxv, 53, 54, 62, 63, 95, 103; beef 54
Kodak iv
Kodzu *see* Kōzu
Koinobori 55
Koi Nobori 55
Koishikawa 104
Kojimachi, Tokyo 64
Kōmei, Emperor 21
komusō xxix, 13
Korea i, xx, xxi, xxvi, 1, 58, 102, 109
Kōtoku'in 86, 98
Kōzu 73
kuro tamago 72
Kusanagi no Tsurugi 11
Kwannon *art* 87
Kyoto iii, xx, xxi, xxii, xxv, xxvi, xxxii, xxxiii, xxxiv, 3, 5, 10, 12, 15, 16, 17, 19, 20, 21, 22, 26, 27, 28, 29, 30, 33, 34, 37, 40, 41, 42, 43, 47, 50, 52, 53, 54, 61, 62, 63, 86, 89, 91, 92, 93, 94, 95, 98, 103, 104, 105, 107, 109
Kyōto Gosho 30
Kyoto Hotel 16; *photos* 17
Kyoto Imperial University 5
Kyūshū 41, 56, 105

L
lace xv, xxvii, 83
lacquer xi, 68, 75
LaFarge, John xxviii, 103, 106
Lake Ashi xxvi, 72
  Ashinoko 72;
  Biwa xxxii, 17, 22, 36, 37, 54, 80, 93
  Hakone xxxii, 72
lantern show xx
lanterns
  bronze 47, 75

magic xi
  stone 12, 23, 46, 47, 50, 60, 73, 75, 80; *photos* 46, 50
  paper 73
"Last Train to Takatsuki" 89
lava beds 84
lemonade 70
letterhead 100
lily roots 85
Lloyd, Arthur 48, 67, 110
Loew, Oscar vi
Longfellow, Charles vi, xi; *photo* vi
Longfellow, Henry Wadsworth vi
long-swordsmen v
Loomis, Mr. 2
lotus 45, 79
Love Stone 98

M
machinami 91
MacNair's xxvi, 84
Maeda 52
mameheitō 14
"Manchuria" *see* S.S. *Manchuria*
marble cake 35
Margaret Sanger iii
Mason, W.B. 1, 106, 109
matsuri 28-29; *photos* 28, 29
McClain, James L. 25
medicinal cow 41; *photos* 41, 88
Meiji vi, vii, xiii, xxiv, xxxv, 13, 20, 21, 25, 37, 56, 103, 105, 106, 107, 109, 110; Emperor *photo* xxiv
menukes 49
menuki xxvii
Meoto Iwa 43; *photos* 43, 88
Metropole 63
Miagina *see* Miyagino
Miei-dō 50
Mihashi 74
Mikado 24, 106, 109
mikoshi 28
Military Virtues Society 34
Milliken, Elizabeth Patton 64, 65
Minamoto xxvii
Minamoto Yoritomo xxxiv, 86, 105
Minister of Education 5
mino 66
Misen Hondō 61
Misenyama 59
Mishima Yukio 45

missionaries vi, vii, xi, xviii, xxi, xxvi, xxvii, xxx, 22, 35, 38, 53, 58, 83, 96, 103, 106
Congregational 35
missionary iv, xxi, xxv, xxvii, xxix, xxx, 83, 96, 103, 104
Mississippi Bay 4
Mitano, Miss 65
Mito 48
Mitsubishi 56, 90
Mitsukoshi 66
Miyagino xxxii, 71
Miyajima 8, iii, xxvi, xxxii, 59, 60, 61, 92, 100, 101, 105
  Ōtorii 59
Miyako Odori 42
miyamairi no haregi 15
Miyanoshita xxvi, 8, 69, 71, 72, 73, 94, 98
Mizaru 75
Modern History of Japan, A 25
Moji 57
Mongolia 8, xxvi, 54, 55, 63, 107
monk 63; *photo* 63
monkeys 75, 77, 108; *art* 75
Montgomery Ward xi
mon, Tokugawa 12; *art* 12
Morning Sun, Kyoto 28
Morse, Edward Sylvester vi
moss 75, 80
Motora Yūjirō 35
Mott, John xxi, 103
Mount Asama 83
  Fuji xxvi, xxix, xxxii, 8, 48, 63, 70, 71, 72, 73, 85, 86; *art* **73**, xxix
  Inari 28
  Kurokami 76
  Misen 61
  Tsukuba 48
moving picture shows 14
Mukan Fumon 21
Murata Shōhirō 65
Muromachi 86
Murray xiii, xxx, xxxvi, 1;
  your xii, xxx, xxxvi, 1;
  photo xxxvi
Murray of London xiii
musketeers v

N
Nagasaki 8, x, xxvi, xxx, 56, 57, 105, 107; *map* 56

Nagoya 7, 8, iii, xxiii, xxv, xxxii, 8, 9, 10, 11, 12, 28, 36, 43, 52, 90, 96, 101, 104, 105; Castle 7, xxv, xxxii, 9, 90, 105; *photo* 9
Naikū 43
Nakasendō, 85
Namikawa Cloisonem 20; *photo* 20
Namikawa Sosuke 20
Namikawa Yasuyuki 20
Nanakorobi Yaoki 82
nanohana 25, *photo* 25
Nanzenji xxxii, 21, 34, 92, 98, 105
Naples xvii
Nara 8, xxxiii, 46-47, 54, 74, 86, 92, 105, 107; Park 46; *photos* 46
natane abura 25; *photo* 25
National Historic Landmark xix, 102
National Institute of Public Health iii
Native Town xxxii, 4
navy vi, 60, 80
Neesima, Joseph Hardy 35
netsuke 3, 4, 7, 9
New Year's 12, 82, 97
nightingale floors 12
Nihon Teien 35
Niigata x, 33
Niijima Jō 35
Nijō Castle xxxii, 49, 105 station 18
Nikkō 8, xx, xxvi, 47, 65, 73, 74, 75, 77, 79, 80, 89, 92, 94, 96, 100, 105
 Electric Railroad Co. 74
 Prefectural Bazaar 75
Ninomaru Palace 49
Nishi Honganji 50, 105
Nobel Peace Prize xxi
Noh Theater 34

O

oak 47
obi x, 33
obon 7, 97
O'Brien, Thomas xxiv, 5, 105
Oda, Nobunaga xxxiv, xxxv, 11, 75, 107; *photo* xxxv
Odawara Horse-drawn Railway 69
Ohio i, xix, 76, 106
oil-paper 48
Oiran Dōchū xxxii, 32-33; *art* 104; *photos* 32-33
Ojigoku 72
Ōkura Kihachirō xxxii, 68, 94, 105
Ōkura Kishichirō 68
Ōkura Shōgyō Gakkō 68
Ōkura Shūkokan 68, 94
Old Curiosity Shop xvii
onsen 69, 70, 72
oranges 61
Order of the Sacred Treasure 35
Osaka 8, x, xxv, xxxiii, 25, 28, 52, 53, 89, 104, 105, 107; *map* 53
Oshōgatsu 97
Otabi-sho 28
Ōtorii 59
Ōwakudani 72
Owari Plain 11
o-yatoi-gai vi
Oyster Bay v
oyu 71

P

Pacific Mail Steamship Company xviii, xviii, 63
 poster xiv
 letterhead 106
pagoda 14, 52, 53, 60
Paixhans shell guns v
Palama Settlement xviii, xxx, 103
palanquin 73
Paris 65
Pasadena i, ii, ix, xv, xix, xx, 35, 100, 102, 103
Pathfinder Fund, The iii
Pathfinder International iii
peonies 3, 54
permits xi, xxiv, xxv, 4, 24, 61
Perry, Commodore Matthew C. v, vii, x
Philadelphia ix
Philippines vi
pickle shops 89
pickpockets 67
pigeons ii, iii, xx, 59
pilgrims *see junrei*
pine trees 71
pipe hoist 72
Planned Parenthood iii
pneumatic tires 96
porcelain i, ix, xxvii, 8, 14, 15, 16, 22, 33, 52; Satsuma 52
Portuguese 56
postals 68, 77
postcard 73, 77, 108
posters xxvii, 66
Presbyterian iv, xx, xxi, xxii, 58, 102, 104, 107
prime ministers 96
Princeton University iv, xx, 102, 110
 University Center iv
print maker 65
prints xxvii, 63, 65, 76
Procter & Gamble i, xxx
Progressive Era xviii
prostitutes 67
Pure Milk Depot xxx
Pusan xxvi
puzzles 21, 59
Pyongyang 58

R

rain v, xxiv, 5, 8, 48, 54, 59, 62, 64, 69, 73, 77, 79, 84, 97, 101
 buckets of v
rainfall, annual 101
rakan 9, 91
Rakushi-ken 25
rape seed 25; *photo* 25
red hat and bib 79
rice 8, 11, 28, 39, 43, 46, 55, 59, 60, 71, 85, 86, 96; cakes 39, 46, 55; paddle 60
rikisha xxiii, 3, 4, 5, 9, 12, 19, 30, 34, 36, 42, 53, 57, 69, 73, 76, 78, 81
Rinnōji xxxii, 74, 80, 105
Rinzai sect 21, 45
rōmon 41; *photo* 41
Roosevelt, Theodore v, ix, *photo* v
rope, human hair 50
Russo-Japanese War v, ix, xviii, 67, 102, 103
Ryōan Temple 104

S

S.S. Manchuria xviii, xxiii, xix, 1, 63, 80, 86, 100; *photo* xviii, 100
Sacred Red Bridge xxxii, 74, 79, 80, 105
 Treasures, Three 11
sailboats 60; *photos* 60, 61
sailing iv, vii, xix, 60, 72
sake xxiv, 3, 54
sampan 57
samurai iv; *art* xxxiv
San'en 75

San Francisco iv, xv, xvi, xxx, 1, 8, 63, 100, 106, 107, 110
Sanger, Margaret iii
Sanjō-dōri 20
Schlesinger Library i
Scudder, Rt.Rev, Doremus xvii, xxx, 103
Sears Roebuck xi, 2
seaweed soup 86
Seiryuro 211
Sekigahara, Battle of xxxv, 37, 104, 105
Sengenyama 71
Senjōkaku Hall 60
Seoul xxvi, 58, 80
shaden 21
shakuhachi 13
Shamoji 60
Shanghai xxvi, 20, 58, 63
shaonkai 104
Shaw, Alexander Croft 83
Shimabara 33
shimenawa 43; *photo* 43
Shimoda x
Shimogamo Jinja xxxii, 26-27, 92; *map* 26; *photos* 26, 27
Shimonoseki 8, xxvi, xxxii, 55, 58
Shimotsuke 76
Shinkyō xxxii, 74, 79, 80, 105
Shinsetsukyō Bridge 51
Shinto xxxiii, 11, 26, 27, 28, 43, 75, 80
shirozake 39
shirushibanten 85; *photo* 85
Shishinden Hall 30
Shitennōji 52
Shōdō Shōnin 80
shogi xvi, 7, 8, 80
shogun xxxiv, xxxv, 9, 22, 45, 75, 105
Shōseien Garden 51
Shōtoku, Prince xxxiii, 53, 105
shrine(s) ii, 11, 14, 15, 19, 21, 22, 26, 28, 40, 41, 43, 48, 59, 74, 75, 91, 97, 105, 112, 114
Shūgakuin 25
Siberia, S.S., xvi, xvii, xviii, 1, 4, 78; *photo* xviii
silk ix, xi, xiv, xv, xxiii, xxxiv, 22, 19, 32, 33, 63, 67, 107; factory 19
silver xxiv, xxvii, 9, 32, 33, 34, 66, 67, 77

Silver Pavilion *see* Ginkakuji
Singapore 20
Sino-Japanese War v
Sinology iv
skateboards 76
smoking 8, 10
smoothbores v
snow 2
Sōami 34
sōryo 42; *photo* 42
sōshiki 83; *photo* 83
spade 66
steam launch 1, 60
St. Elizabeth's School for Girls xxii
St. Francis Hotel xv; *photo* xv
St. Louis Exhibit xxx
stereopticon xi, 62
Stone, Mrs. xvii
straw, rice 71
    baskets 24, 56
    raincoat 66; *photo* 66
    sandals xxix, 48, 71
Stream of the Serpents' Bones 71
Suez Canal vi
Sugawara Michizane 41
sugi 47, 74
Sugi Namiki 77
suisha *photo* 77
Sumiyoshi Gukei 25
Sun Goddess xxxiii
sushi 29
sutras 60
swimming xvii, xxx, 73
switchplates 76
swords 68

T

T. Enami, *see* Enami Nobukuni
Tadasu no Mori 26
Taft, William Howard v, xviii, 102
Taipei, Taiwan 20
Taisha 7, xxxii, 28, 47, 105
Taiyūin Reibyō 74, 80
Tajima 54
Takasaki 82
Takashimaya 16, 20, 105; *ad* 16; *photo* 20
Takemikazuchi 47
Takaboko Island *photo* xxvi
Tametaka Kita 9
Temple, Ikegami *art* 98, 99
Tango no Sekku 25, 55, 97; *photos* 55, 88

Tartars 63
tatami mats 60
Taylor, Bayard viii
tea xxxiv, 61, 67, 68, 70, 71, 76, 78, 80, 82, 84, 93, 104
    ceremony xxxiv, 34, 104
    house(s) ix, 25, 43, 61, 78, 115
    room 34, 39
temple(s) i, iii, x, xx, xxvi, xxxiii, 5, 9, 10, 12, 14, 15, 17, 18, 19, 21, 22, 27, 28, 34, 40, 45, 46, 47, 50, 52, 53, 59, 60, 61, 67, 68, 74, 75, 80, 86, 92, 96, 97, 115
Temple of the Golden Pavilion *see* Kinkakuji
Tenmei eruption 84
tennis courts 83
Thatcher School, The iv, xxx
Thatcher, Sherman Day xxx
theatre xxxiv, 3, 14, 15, 42, 62
Theatre Street 42
The Shrine 11
Thieves Guild 67
Things Japanese 1, 109
Tibet 68
tiffin 2
Tiger and Bamboo 21
tigers 9, 49
Tōdaiji xxxii, 47, 86, 92, 105
Tōgō Heihachirō 67
Tōkaidō xxxii, 8, 52, 85, 105; Railway 52
tokonoma 55
Tokugawa xx, xxxv, 9, 11, 12, 13, 35, 37, 49, 50, 52, 74, 75, 77, 80, 104, 105, 107; *art* xxxv;
    mon 12
Tokugawa, Ieyasu xxxv, 9, 49, 50, 74, 77, 105, 107
Tokyo 8, v, viii, x, xii, xxii, xxiv, xxvi, xxxiii, 1, 3, 4, 5, 8, 17, 20, 30, 35, 52, 63, 64, 65, 66, 67, 68, 69, 70, 73, 81, 82, 83, 85, 86, 89, 90, 91, 94, 95, 97, 101, 102, 104, 105, 106, 107, 110
    Imperial University 1, 35
    Keizai University 68
    weather v, 64, 66, 101
Tomomi, Iwakura viii

Toppings, Mrs. xxvi, 84
torii 21, 23, 43, 59, 75; *photos* 26, 27, 43
torpedo boats 60
tortoise shell xxvi, xxvii, 33, 57; *photo* 57
Tōshōgū xxxii, 74, 75
Townsend Harris x
Toyotomi Hideyoshi xxxv, 11, 22, 60, 105, 107; *art* xxxv
Toyouke Daijingū 43
Toyouke Ōmikami 43
tramcar 81
Travelers Tales Japan: True Stories 98
Tree Tops 59
Treuda, Miss 64
Tribune, New York viii, x, xxviii, 103
Trinity Church xxviii, 103
T-shirts 76
Tsubame 33
Tsuda College viii, 64, 95
Tsuda Umeko viii, xxxii, 64, 95, 103, 105, 107
Tsuda Women's Institute xxii
Turk-fashion 73
turtles 46

U

Uda, Emperor 41
udon noodles 14
Ueno Park 5
Uji tea. 29
ukiyo-e 76
Umeko, Tsuda viii
Unbeaten Tracks in Japan viii
UNESCO World Heritage Site 15, 47
Unifiers xxxv, 23, 49, 75
University of Cambridge 5
Uzume xxxi; *art* xxxi

V

Vale, Miss 64
velvet picture 16, 19
Vermont, Brattleboro vii
Vern, Jules vi
Vienna ix
Visit to India, China and Japan, A viii

W

wages 53, 56
waraji 48: vendor; *photo* 71
Ward, Michael 89

waterfalls xxvi, 25, 70, 74, 76, 101
waterwheel *photo* 77
Wedded Rocks 43
Weltausstellung ix
Wesleyan College 64
West, Caleb xvii
Westward 'round the World see Wight, Edward Stager
Wherry, Mrs. xvi
William, Procter i
wistaria 3, 67
Women's Institute for English Studies 64
woodblock 65
World War II 7, 10, 11, 35, 64, 90, 91
Wright, Edward Stager ix, xii, xiii, xiv, xv, xvi, sviii, xxiii, xxiv, xxv, xxxix, xxx, 16, 69, 103, 106, 110
    Mrs. xiv, xv
Wright, Frank Lloyd ix, 69

Y

Yamada 42, 43, 46
Yamaguchi Sennosuke 69, 94
Yamanaka's xxxii, 22, 52; *ad* 23
Yebitsu 2, 107
Yellowstone 72
Y.M.C.A. iv, xxi, xxx, 58, 80, 103
    Hangzhou 58
    Shanghai 58
Yokohama 7, 8, vi, x, xi, xii, xviii, xxiv, xxv, xxvi, xxvii, xxx, xxxii, 1, 2, 3, 4, 6, 7, 52, 63, 70, 80, 85, 86, 90, 102, 105, 107, 108, 109; *map* 1
    Race Club 4
shashin x, xi, xii, xxvii, 80
Yoshio Koya iii
Yoshiwara 67
yu 71
Yumoto 8, xxxii, 69, 72, 73, 74, 78, 82, 105
Y.W.C.A. 64

Z

Zelkova 11

Photos of Clarence James and Sidney David Gamble by Category

Banners: Carp (Boys' Day) 55; Kimono advertisement 16
Boats 18, 60-61
Buildings 6, 20
    Bell tower 51, 81
    Shops 6. 7. 13, 14, 16, 42, 57,
Castle, Nagoya 9
Coaling operations 56, 57
Festivals and Processions 28-29, 32-33; Funeral procession 83
Flowers 3, 66
Gambles:
    Clarence 1, 21, 58, 66, 68
    David and Mary 17, 36, 37, 48, 58, 68
    Sidney 8, 58
Gardens 25, 35, 43, 44-45, 47, 51
Japanese people 13, 15, 19, 23, 24, 29, 31, 32, 33, 36, 48, 51, 53, 59, 60, 63, 68, 72, 77, 78, 83, 84, 85
    Children 3, 4, 15, 27, 30-31, 32, 38, 39, 72
    Monks and Pilgrims 48, 62, 63, 71
Lanterns 47, 50, 84
River 18
Seascapes 60-61
Shrines and Temples 9, 10-11, 15, 21, 22-23, 26-27, 40-41, 44-45, 46-37, 51
Torii 23, 26, 27
Waterwheel 77
Wedded Rocks 43

PHOTO RESTORATION

Cornelius Matteo (www.cmatteophotography.com) is responsible for the superb restoration of the photos, bringing details out of shadows and allowing us to see what the Gambles saw in 1908. The photos have not been altered in any way, but they have been cleaned and scratches removed. Hand-tinting, an art for which the Japanese were known, was a popular method for coloring photos in the years before color film became available and affordable. These photos bear the subtle stamp of the many individuals who colored them, for tone and color values differ among the various photos and the various sets of photos. Although the photos when discovered had been pasted into an album and stored out of the light, individual quality varied and many photos were badly faded. Fortunately, sufficient information was available so that the restoration seen here was possible

五月雨や大河を前に家二軒　松尾芭蕉

富士一つうづみ残して若葉かな　与謝蕪村

さまざまの事思出す桜かな　松尾芭蕉

Introduction Frontispiece: Haiku English Translations

*Remembering
so many things...
Cherry Blossoms.*

—Matsuo Bashou
(1644-1694)

*Spring leaves
will not bury
Fujisan.*

—Yosa Buson
(1716-1784)

*The long spring
rain,
And by the river
two houses.*

—Matsuo Bashou
(1644-1694)

ACKNOWLEDGEMENTS

Japan 1908: The Adventure of Fourteen-Year-Old Clarence James Gamble is dedicated to 濱田伝 Novick Hamada Tsutae. Her friendship and generosity introduced me to the beauty of a land and a culture that was quite unknown to me. Her keen focus located subtle errors and blatant wrongs and uncovered hidden riches in the details of photos and journal text. Her enthusiasm persuaded her community of friends in her home town of Takamatsushi to identify sites and items that would have been impossible for the non-native to discover.

In Takamatsushi, 中村進 Nakamura Susumu identified Heian Jingu; 薬師初夫 Yakushi Hatsuo recognized Hokokubyo; 濱田 三千夫 Hamada Michio identified Atsuta Shrine in Nagoya; 濱田重人 Hamada Shigeto matched past to current photos of Shimogamo and Kinkakuji Gardens; and 春木谷広義 Harukidani Hiroyoshi pointed out that the *shirushi banten* were being worn by workers from Yokohama..

Tsutae-san prevailed upon her old friend in Kyoto, 山村幸代 Yamamura Sachiyo, to research Japanese newspaper archives for mention of Oiran Dōchū and Fushimi Inari Taisha processions. For the contributions of the Takamatsushi community and of Yamamura Sachiyo, I am immeasurably grateful.

In Ashland, Oregon, Fujikawa Sachi graciously selected and loaned from her personal collection of books on Japan, for however long as I needed them, exactly the right combination of volumes to introduce and to provide an instant education and background on this subject of which I knew nothing. 智香子 Smith Chikako spent precious time thoughtfully and fully explaining the importance of Obon and current Obon customs and celebrations. Miyamoto Ron and Keiko listened patiently while I talked endlessly and then read thoroughly my entire manuscript; their proofreading was invaluable. Nelson Yumiko, 折原愛美 Orihara Manami, 白土希 Shirato Nozomi, 小田薫 Oda Kaoru, and 本田智也 Honda Tomoya graciously gave needed assistance despite heavy familial and academic demands. ジェンセン悦子 Jensen Etsuko was a gift from heaven with her humor and help. Thank you all for your time and aid.

I was most fortunate in having the long-suffering ear of Kendall Brown, Professor of Asian Art History, University of California at Long Beach, who came up with answers to the most impossible of questions and who furnished several elegant phrases that have been incorporated into the Introduction and elsewhere; 邦子 Brown Kuniko suffered my attempts at selecting Kanji and writing about this wonderful world of Japan and made innumerable corrections and suggestions. Professor Brown led me to Joe Capezzuto, an astute reader, whose prompt assistance and thorough examination of the Kanji was of inestimable value.

Nancy J. Taylor, Presbyterian Historical Society, Philadelphia, Pennsylvania, located the information on and donated the photographs of Elizabeth Patton Milliken and Raymond and Mary Gorbold, for which I am most grateful.

鷹屋八重子 Takaya Davis Yaeko, mother of my friend William Davis who kindly introduced us, shared her personal memories of being a student at Dōshisha

University and of visiting Miss Mary Florence Denton, still living on the Dōshisha campus, but under house arrest during World War II.

Ann Scheid, Greene & Greene Archivist, Huntington Library, San Marino, California, directed me to material on David and Mary Gamble. Edward Bosley, Executive Director, The Gamble House in Pasadena, California, gave most generously of his own time and offered feedback and encouraging ideas and suggestions. Anne Mallek was an interested listener. Diana Carey, Schlesinger Library, Radcliff Institute, Harvard University, continued to offer regular assistance. Rhonda Super responded to computer research questions in her after-hours.

In Ashland, Wallin Hiromi came to a last-minute Kanji rescue. Chis Harding identified the critical problem with layout. Much needed InDesign help was given by David Blatner, Katherine Kinney, and especially by Diane Burns, who repeatedly came to my rescue with her patience and expertise.

From Seattle, Professor Ken Tadashi Oshima, University of Washington, took his valuable time to give most welcome encouragement.

During our visit to Japan in April 2012, in Nikkō, Tsutae-san and I had an extraordinary meeting and gracious help from 秋山剛康 Akiyama Takayasu, Senior Advisor, Kanaya Hotel. Akiyama Takayasu shared with us much of the rich history of the Kanaya Hotel and continues to maintain interest in this book. At the Fujiya Hotel in Miyanoshita, Hakone, 葭田昌一 Yoshida Syouichi, General Manager, along with 折田道明 Orita Michiaki, Manager, spent much time with us and made us a copy of the 1908 signed registration of David Gamble. The staff at the Kyoto Hotel Ōkura in Kyoto answered our many questions, as did Tanaka Chisako, Curator, Ōkura Museum. Our contact with the Ōkura Museum was made possible by the diligent efforts of 渡辺雅子 Watanabe Masako of the New York Metropolitan Museum of Art. From Hikone, 山名弘祐 Yamana Kousuke kindly made a special trip to identify Nagoya Castle. 貫やよえ Nuki Yayoe and 松下勝代 Matsushita Katsuyo guided us through Shitennoji and—what was especially impressive—through 大阪駅 Ōsaka-eki, while also providing accommodations and good cheer.

中川真理 Nakagawa Mari at the Public Relations Office of Takashimaya Co. Ltd. most generously assisted us with information about Takashimaya and made available to us a visit to the exhibit "Art + Living: Takashimaya, The Department Store as a Culture Setter," shown at the Setagaya Art Museum in Tokyo in April 2013. For all the time and assistance extended to us by the many Japanese individuals in Japan, I am most grateful.

All of this was made possible by the inestimable Sarah Gamble Epstein, who has supported the long months and years of struggle and who has never lost her patience with the interminable process of piecing together this book, as it grew like Topsy, into the much more complicated, much more challenging, and much more comprehensive project than had ever originally been envisioned. Words are insufficient to express my gratitude to her.

CONTRIBUTORS

Clarence James Gamble (1892-1966) Princeton University B.S. 1914, M.S. 1916; Harvard Medical School M.D. 1920. International travel in 1902 and in Asia in 1908 and the example of his parents' life of service prepared the young Clarence for a life of service as well. Early in his career, he supported the maternal health clinics of Margaret Sanger and the legality of contraception. After World War II, at the Harvard School of Public Health, he pioneered family planning programs in India, beginning his international philanthropy. In the early 1950s, he was asked to assist the National Institute of Public Health of Japan, whose research he then supported for many years. In 1957, he founded Pathfinder International, a global non-profit organization, now active in more than twenty developing countries, offering education and services for family planning, adolescent sexuality, and HIV/AIDS care and prevention. Pathfinder International continues to fulfill the mission of its founder to support the right of all people to a healthy reproductive life.

Sidney David Gamble (1890-1968) Princeton University B.A. 1912, University of California, Berkeley M.A. 1916. Living and working in China during the years 1917-19, 1924-27, and 1931-33, Sidney Gamble produced scholarly works with imaginative insight that broke new ground and were unique to his profession as social scientist: *Peking: A Social Survey* (1921), *How Chinese Families Live in Peking* (1933), *Ting Hsien: A North China Rural Community* (1954), *North China Villlages* (1963). *North China Plays* was published posthumuously in 1970. His extraordinary photographs are in print in two published books and online at Duke University Digital Archives. Throughout his life, Sidney was actively involved in Christian social work, first with Princeton-in-Peking and the Peking Y.M.C.A., later with these organizations in the United States.

Frances Miriam Reed, UCLA Ph.D. 1980, editor, has written and performed solo play scripts, including "Margaret Sanger: Radiant Rebel"; written a biography, *Margaret Sanger: Her Life in Her Words* (Barricade Books 2003); created a DVD, "Clarence James Gamble: An Extraordinary Life" and a CD, "Hurrah for Woman Suffrage: Songs from the Women's Suffrage Movement 1848-1920"; and written a book on how to write: "The Sentence as Structure and The Structure of Content; or, How to Become a Great Writer (almost) Instantly"—all available on Amazon. Currently, she is writing "A Biography of Character," the lives of David and Mary Gamble. She lives in Ashland, Oregon, with her lively friend, Marnie, a Border Collie.

濱田伝 **Novick Hamada Tsutae** was born and raised in 高松 Takamatsu in southern Japan and came to America in 1987 and to Ashland in 1995. She is a ceramics sculptor and a student of the Ashland master, 杉山亘 Sugiyama Wataru. For six months of the year, she lives in her home in Japan. Tsutae met the editor at the One Dollar Store in Ashland, where, by chance, both were shopping. This meeting was the basis for many years of research in America and a trip to Japan, where additional research on *Japan 1908* was completed. See photo on page 90.

JAPAN 2012

EMAKAKE 絵馬掛け
絵馬 **EMA** *Prayers on boards hanging on an Emakake*
Kiyomizudera, Kyoto